CONTENTS

S. Hrg. 108–245

TERRORISM FINANCING: ORIGINATION, ORGANIZATION, AND PREVENTION

HEARING

BEFORE THE

COMMITTEE ON GOVERNMENTAL AFFAIRS UNITED STATES SENATE

ONE HUNDRED EIGHTH CONGRESS

FIRST SESSION

JULY 31, 2003

Printed for the use of the Committee on Governmental Affairs

U.S. GOVERNMENT PRINTING OFFICE

89–039 PDF WASHINGTON : 2004

For sale by the Superintendent of Documents, U.S. Government Printing Office
Internet: bookstore.gpo.gov Phone: toll free (866) 512–1800; DC area (202) 512–1800
Fax: (202) 512–2250 Mail: Stop SSOP, Washington, DC 20402–0001

COMMITTEE ON GOVERNMENTAL AFFAIRS

SUSAN M. COLLINS, Maine, *Chairman*

TED STEVENS, Alaska
GEORGE V. VOINOVICH, Ohio
NORM COLEMAN, Minnesota
ARLEN SPECTER, Pennsylvania
ROBERT F. BENNETT, Utah
PETER G. FITZGERALD, Illinois
JOHN E. SUNUNU, New Hampshire
RICHARD C. SHELBY, Alabama

JOSEPH I. LIEBERMAN, Connecticut
CARL LEVIN, Michigan
DANIEL K. AKAKA, Hawaii
RICHARD J. DURBIN, Illinois
THOMAS R. CARPER, Delaware
MARK DAYTON, Minnesota
FRANK LAUTENBERG, New Jersey
MARK PRYOR, Arkansas

MICHAEL D. BOPP, *Staff Director and Counsel*
DAVID A. KASS, *Chief Investigative Counsel*
MARK R. HEILBRUN, *General Counsel and National Security Advisor to Senator Arlen Specter*
JOYCE A. RECHTSCHAFFEN, *Minority Staff Director and Counsel*
DAVID BARTON, *Minority Professional Staff Member*
AMY B. NEWHOUSE, *Chief Clerk*

TERRORISM FINANCING: ORIGINATION, ORGANIZATION, AND PREVENTION

THURSDAY, JULY 31, 2003

U.S. SENATE,
COMMITTEE ON GOVERNMENTAL AFFAIRS,
Washington, DC.

The Committee met, pursuant to notice, at 10:16 a.m., in room SD–342, Dirksen Senate Office Building, Hon. Susan M. Collins, Chairman of the Committee, presiding.

Present: Senators Collins, Coleman, Specter, Levin, Akaka, Carper, Lautenberg, and Pryor.

OPENING STATEMENT OF CHAIRMAN COLLINS

Chairman COLLINS. The Committee will come to order.

Today, the Committee on Governmental Affairs is holding a hearing on the financing of terrorism. Terrorism costs money. From funds needed to buy explosives and airline tickets, to living expenses, to payoffs to the families of suicide bombers, terrorists must have constant and untraceable sources of money. Stopping the flow of these funds is a formidable task. Osama bin Laden is an experienced financier who once reportedly boasted that he and other al-Qaeda leaders know the cracks in the Western financial system like the lines on their own hands.

Immediately after the September 11 attacks, the President took strong action to close the gaps in our financial system by issuing Executive Order 13224 to block terrorist funds. Nevertheless, serious questions persist about whether we are doing enough. There are even more serious questions about whether some of our allies are doing enough.

Last year, the Council on Foreign Relations issued a report contending that U.S. efforts to curtail terrorism financing are impeded, "not only by a lack of institutional capacity abroad but by a lack of political will among American allies."

The report concludes that our government appears to have responded to this lack of will with a policy decision not to use the full power of our influence and legal authority to compel greater cooperation.

A key nation in the fight against terrorist financing is Saudi Arabia. It appears that from the joint inquiry by the House and Senate Intelligence Committees, which examined the kingdom's role in terrorist financing, that it is difficult to tell for sure exactly what the extent of the Saudi involvement is because almost an entire chapter regarding foreign support for the September 11 hijackers is classified. Even the parts that were published, however, raise serious concerns about Saudi Arabia's role in the September 11 attacks.

For example, the unclassified portion of the joint inquiry report describes the activities of Omar al-Bayoumi, a man who apparently provided extensive assistance to two of the September 11 hijackers. According to the report, a source told the FBI that he thought al-Bayoumi must have been a foreign intelligence officer for Saudi Arabia or another power. The report also finds that al-Bayoumi had access to "seemingly unlimited funding from Saudi Arabia." Al-Bayoumi is now reported to be living in Saudi Arabia.

Last month, the General Counsel of the Treasury Department testified before the Terrorism Subcommittee of the Judiciary Committee that in many cases Saudi Arabia is the "epicenter" of terrorist financing. The Council on Foreign Relations report found that for years individuals and charities based in Saudi Arabia have been the most important source of funds for al-Qaeda and that for years Saudi officials have turned a blind eye to this problem.

As our witnesses Ambassador Dore Gold and Steven Emerson will describe in some detail, there is evidence that enormous sums of money flow from Saudi individuals and charitable organizations to al-Qaeda, to Hamas, and other terrorist organizations. The key question now is whether the Saudi Government is doing enough to stop the flow of this money, and if not, what actions the U.S. Government should take to prompt the Saudis to take more effective action. The Saudi Government recently announced some changes in its banking system and charity laws, but it is not clear that these changes go far enough or will be truly effective.

We are fortunate to have with us today key counterterrorism officials from the FBI and the Department of Treasury. They will describe the administration's actions against terrorism financing, and they will help us better understand the level of cooperation our country is receiving from the Saudi and other governments. We also have three experts to discuss their views regarding the fight against terrorist financing generally and Saudi Arabia's role specifically.

As the discussion of the joint inquiry report has made clear, there are still many questions about Saudi Arabia's role, even if that role is inadvertent, in the September 11 attacks and about the extent of the Saudi Government's cooperation in the fight against terrorism. I hope today's hearing will help us get answers to some of these questions and will highlight areas in which our government needs to refocus its efforts in order to stop the flow of funds to terrorists.

I am very pleased today to pass the gavel to Senator Specter, who spearheaded this investigation and is one of the Senate's leaders in the war against terrorism. He has served as the Chairman of the Senate Intelligence Committee. He chaired a hearing about this very subject last November in the Judiciary Committee, and he has continued to investigate this matter as a Member not only of this Committee but the Judiciary Committee as well.

This hearing today is particularly timely given the release last week of the joint inquiry report on the September 11 attacks. I applaud Senator Specter for his leadership in this area, and I am pleased to join him in working on an issue and a challenge to our country that has profound impact on the safety of our Nation and all law-abiding nations.

Senator Specter.

OPENING STATEMENT OF SENATOR SPECTER

Senator SPECTER [presiding.] Thank you very much, Madam Chairman, Senator Collins. At the outset I compliment you on the outstanding job you are doing in chairing this very important Committee, a brief meteoric career so far in the U.S. Senate, and I thank you for your leadership on this important subject and for cooperating in this investigation and in this hearing and for handing me this mighty gavel. I appreciate it very much.

The issue of the financing of terrorists is one of enormous importance, and the Saudi role is especially important in the wake of the very extensive report published on September 11 with 26 missing pages identified as being Saudi involvement. There has been a decision by the Executive Branch not to release those pages, and I believe that puts a greater responsibility on Congress in oversight on hearings just like this.

The question of Saudi cooperation with the United States has been on my agenda for the better part of the last decade. When I chaired the Senate Intelligence Committee in the 104th Congress, I went to Khobar Towers, investigated the matter, and talked to the Crown Prince as part of a U.S. effort to get cooperation from the Saudis. And while they profess to be very cooperative, the fact was that they were very uncooperative. There had been a car bombing in Riyadh in 1995 where Americans were killed. Federal officials were not permitted to talk to the suspects. They were beheaded by the Saudi Government so that we never did find out what they had to say. And then on June 25, 1996, Khobar Towers was blown up, 19 airmen killed, 400 airmen wounded, and the issue has never yet been fully resolved.

A criminal indictment was returned naming Iran as a co-conspirator, and questions linger to this day as to whether some of those who were involved in Khobar Towers might have been involved in September 11. And our hearing today is going to probe this issue further to see if we can shed some light as to what the Saudi involvement is.

The business of the financing of terrorism has broader scope, which we have investigated on the Judiciary Committee, last year a hearing on the financing of Hizbollah. They go into a small town in North Carolina and reap millions of dollars on cigarette smuggling, which goes to show you the scope of the tentacles. Hamas is raising money in the United States, and we are pursuing an investigation to identify those who contribute to Hamas with a thought to hold them liable as accessories before the fact to murder.

When you contribute to a known terrorist organization and that terrorist organization then murders American citizens, those people who contribute knowingly could be indicted and prosecuted for being accessories before the fact to murder. And Saudi Arabia contributes reportedly about $4 billion a year to so-called charities which have dual purposes. And we really need to pull back the covers on this item, and this is a real challenge for the U.S. Government, and congressional oversight is a very important part.

We have some expert witnesses today from the Federal Bureau of Investigation and from the Treasury Department who will detail efforts to identify Saudi contributions, and we have experts who have been in government, former Ambassador to the UN, Dore Gold, and others on a second panel.

We are going to establish the time of 5 minutes for opening statements. Everything prepared in writing will be, as usual, made a part of the record, but that will leave us the maximum time for questions and answers.

Our first witness is John Pistole, Deputy Executive Assistant Director for Counterterrorism of the Federal Bureau of Investigation. Welcome, Mr. Pistole, and the floor is yours.

TESTIMONY OF JOHN S. PISTOLE,[1] ACTING ASSISTANT DIRECTOR FOR COUNTERTERRORISM, FEDERAL BUREAU OF INVESTIGATION

Mr. PISTOLE. Thank you, Senator Specter and Madam Chairman Collins. Thank you for the opportunity to be here today, and I will just take a couple of minutes, if I may, to make two points and then, as you mentioned, Senator Specter, to allow maximum time for questions.

The first point is the FBI's focus on terrorism financing and the radically changed organization that the FBI is today compared to prior to September 11, where today we have as our overriding emphasis the prevention of terrorist activity in the United States or against U.S. interests overseas. A key component of that is the identification of individuals involved in the financing of potential terrorist activity and trying to identify the full scope of the enterprise, the individuals associated with this group that is raising money that may be going to terrorist financing. And we see that as one of the key means of being able to disrupt and dismantle terrorist cells that may be operating here in the United States or overseas that may be targeting U.S. interests.

The second point that I would like to make is talking about the unprecedented cooperation that we have had with not only our law enforcement and intelligence community partners here in the United States since September 11 but also with foreign partners in both the law enforcement and intelligence communities in addressing terrorism matters overall. Terrorism financing remains one of those challenging issues that certain countries such as Saudi Arabia we believe can do more in, and we will address that shortly.

In terms of the FBI's response to September 11, I think the Committee is quite aware of the FBI's response in creating the Terrorist Financing Operations Section, or TFOS for short, which originally looked at the 19 hijackers and detailed every financial transaction that they conducted, overseas money coming in to them or while they were here in the United States. TFOS has evolved from that time into the central entity responsible for coordinating all terrorist financing investigations for the FBI and then working in concert with, again, our domestic law enforcement and intelligence community partners. And with me today is Dennis Lormel, the chief of the Terrorist Financing Operations Section, who has

[1] The prepared statement of Mr. Pistole appears in the Appendix on page 45.

been almost singularly responsible to develop and implement the TFOS strategy.

What TFOS has been doing is trying to follow the money, to identify those individuals who may be involved in terrorist financing and then to trace that money with law enforcement and intelligence aspects to ascertain where that money is going. And one of the key aspects of what the FBI is doing post-September 11 is addressing every terrorist investigation as an intelligence-driven investigation as opposed to strictly a law enforcement investigation.

The key here is to use all the tools available to us, whether it is the FISA court and the intercepts we are able to obtain through the FISA court, national security letters, any of the other tools available to us as a member of the intelligence community, and then to focus that investigation on the intelligence aspect, coupled with the law enforcement sanctions and tools that we have if we need to bring charges against individuals to take them off the street if they pose a threat or to elicit their cooperation.

Given that background and that new paradigm that the FBI has employed since September 11, TFOS has followed the terrorist trail in a number of situations, and rather than go into the detail that is enumerated in my statement, I will just touch briefly on a couple of the successes in general terms.

One of the key areas has been our outreach with and cooperation from the private sector. In that area, for example, we have developed the ability to conduct real-time monitoring of specifically identified financial activity, which has been invaluable not only to investigations here in the United States but to some of our foreign partners who have relied on that information, tracking money going from the U.S. overseas that may be used in terrorist activity and vice versa.

In support of a specific high-profile joint terrorist investigation on financing, a number of countries and agencies, such as United Kingdom, Switzerland, Canada, and Europol, have detailed their investigators to TFOS on a temporary-duty basis. We have engaged in extensive coordination with authorities of numerous foreign governments in terrorist financing matters, which has led to joint investigative efforts around the world, including identifying and exploiting the financing of several overseas al-Qaeda cells, including those in Indonesia, Malaysia, Singapore, Spain, and Italy.

There are a number of other relationships that have been established with central banks of foreign countries that have also enabled us to track terrorist funding in a way that we simply did not do prior to September 11.

The other aspect that is critical here is the information sharing where our greatest successes have come in the interagency forum, where we are part of the National Security Council's Policy Coordinating Committee on terrorist financing, which was created in March 2002. The information sharing we have found has simply been critical to any success we have had, and especially our relationship with the Central Intelligence Agency in some sensitive ongoing matters has allowed us to develop an expertise that simply the U.S. Government did not have prior to September 11.

Senator Specter, you mentioned the case in Charlotte, North Carolina, as one example. There are numbers of other examples which, again, I won't go into at this time. They are in my statement.

The other point that I want to touch on is the cooperation of the foreign governments, and specifically Saudi Arabia. As we all know, late on the evening of May 12 of this year, three large bombs were detonated in Western housing complexes of Riyadh, Saudi Arabia. The next day, I was on a flight to Riyadh to lead an assessment team of the FBI, working with the CIA, to assess what the Saudi Government, specifically the Mabahith, the Saudi counterpart of the FBI, would allow us to do in terms of bringing a team of investigators and experts in to go through the crime scenes, to talk to witnesses, and to assess who may be responsible for those acts.

As a result of the discussions, the Saudis allowed us to bring 75 FBI employees and an undisclosed number of agency people in to not only go through the crime scene, comb through it with shovels and screens, but also to analyze DNA from some of the human remains that were there, to do forensic tests on any and all evidence. They also gave us access to Saudi citizens who were witnesses to those three heinous acts.

To summarize, what they did after May 12, which I believe was a defining moment for the Saudis because al-Qaeda attacked Saudi interests in their homeland, what they allowed us to do was unprecedented. You mentioned the Khobar Towers and the OPM–SANG bombing prior to that where, frankly, we were frustrated beyond any recognition to accomplish what we were hoping to do, as you are well aware, Senator Specter.

What I would say is that post-May 12, the Saudis have had a wake-up call, and we have had unprecedented cooperation with them in virtually every area. To that end, the one key area and the focus of today's hearing is on terrorist financing. The Saudis last year made a number of representations and enacted a number of laws designed to identify and dismantle terrorist financing that may be emanating from Saudi. From our position, the jury is still out on the effectiveness of what they have done. We simply have not seen the results of those initiatives from a terrorism financing perspective. Since May 12, they have arrested hundreds of people, either detained or killed in an attempt to apprehend——

Senator SPECTER. Where do you say the jury is out? On what issue?

Mr. PISTOLE. On the terrorism financing issue as far as the effectiveness of the Saudi initiatives to stem the tide of financing through NGOs or charitable organizations.

Senator SPECTER. When the question and answer period comes, we are going to ask you when you think the jury will be in on that.

Mr. PISTOLE. OK.

Senator SPECTER. We would like to know. Could you sum up at this point?

Mr. PISTOLE. Yes. I would be glad to, Senator.

As a follow-up to a number of ongoing measures, there is a National Security Council team that is leaving Sunday to go to Riyadh, which I am participating in with State Department and Treasury Department senior officials, who are meeting with senior

Saudi officials to address a number of the issues that may arise in this hearing today.

That would conclude my opening statement.

Senator SPECTER. OK. Thank you very much, Mr. Pistole.

Our next witness is Rick Newcomb, who is the Treasury Office of Foreign Assets Control Director. Thank you for joining us, and we look forward to your testimony.

TESTIMONY OF R. RICHARD NEWCOMB,[1] DIRECTOR, OFFICE OF FOREIGN ASSETS CONTROL, U.S. DEPARTMENT OF THE TREASURY

Mr. NEWCOMB. Thank you, Senator Specter, Madam Chairman, Members of the Committee. I am pleased to have the opportunity to testify this morning about our efforts to combat terrorist support networks that threaten U.S. citizens and property worldwide.

The threat of terrorist support networks and financing is real. It has been our mission to help identify and disrupt these networks. There is much we know about how radical Islamic terrorist networks are established and still thrive. Wealthy individuals and influential individuals and families based in the Middle East have provided seed money and support to build a transnational support infrastructure that terrorists have used for their purposes. This network, fueled by deep-pocket donors and often controlled by terrorist organizations, their supporters, and those willing to look the other way, includes or implicates banks, businesses, NGOs, charities, social service organizations, schools, mosques, madrassas, and affiliated terrorist training camps and safe houses throughout the world.

The terrorist networks are well entrenched, self-sustaining, though vulnerable to the United States, allied, and international efforts applying all tools at our disposal. Today, I will explain our efforts being implemented in coordination with other Federal agencies, including the Departments of Defense, State, Justice, Homeland Security, the FBI, the intelligence community, and other agencies to choke off the key nodes in the transnational terrorist support infrastructure.

The primary mission of the Office of Foreign Assets Control of the Treasury Department is to administer and enforce economic sanctions against targeted foreign countries and foreign groups and individuals, such as terrorists, terrorist organizations, and narcotics traffickers, which pose a threat to the national security, foreign policy, or economy of the United States. We act under the general Presidential wartime and national emergency powers, as well as specific legislation, to prohibit transactions and block or freeze assets subject to U.S. jurisdiction. The origin of our involvement in the fight against terrorism stems from the initial conception of terrorism as being solely state-sponsored. Our mandate in the realm of terrorism was to compile available evidence establishing that certain foreign entities or individuals that were owned or controlled by, or acting for or on behalf of, a foreign government subject to an economic sanctions program. Such entities and individuals be-

[1] The prepared statement of Mr. Newcomb with attachments appears in the Appendix on page 54.

came known as SDNs and are subject to the same sanctions as the foreign government to which they are related.

The President harnessed these powers and authorities in launching the economic war against terrorism in response to the terrorist attack of September 11 and pursuant to the powers available to the President under the International Emergency Economic Powers Act. President Bush issued Executive Order 13224, entitled "Blocking Property and Prohibiting Transactions with Persons Who Commit, Threaten to Commit, or Support Terrorism," declaring that acts of grave terrorism and threats of terrorism committed by foreign terrorists pose an unusual and extraordinary threat to the national security, foreign policy, or economy of the United States. This order prohibits U.S. persons from transacting or dealing with individuals or entities owned or controlled, acting for or on behalf of, assisting or supporting, or otherwise associated with persons listed in the Executive Order and those designated under the Executive Order as specially designated global terrorists.

After the September 11 attacks, President Bush rallied the international community to unite in the economic war on terrorism. The U.S. Government has worked with the United Nations to pass resolutions that parallel U.S. authorities to designate entities supporting al-Qaeda. The international community, including our allies in the Persian Gulf, joined us and have committed to fully cooperating on all fronts against al-Qaeda and its supporters. On a regular basis, for example, the United States works cooperatively with Saudi authorities on issues relating to the war on terrorism. In some areas, cooperation is routine and systematic. In others, especially those touching aspects of terrorist financing and infrastructure, which touches all aspects of government, coordination is more complex.

We have acted with Saudi Arabia and other allies in targeting al-Qaeda and other terrorist infrastructure. These actions have included a number of multilateral efforts that many times resulted in notifying and listing at the United Nations under United Nations Security Council Resolutions 1267 and 1455.

Some of the terrorist supporters we targeted include financial networks, including the al-Barakaat network, a Somalia-based hawala operator that was active worldwide. And the Muslim Brotherhood-backed Nasreddin financial services network. Other efforts have targeted charitable fronts based in the United States, including the Benevolence International Foundation, Global Relief Foundation, and the Holy Land Foundation, and foreign-based charitable fronts including branch offices of the Revival of Islamic Heritage Society and the Afghan Support Committee. We also acted with our allies against major al-Qaeda-affiliated organizations such as Jemaa Islamiyah.

In the coming months, we are seeking to significantly expand these efforts and impact the implementation of the President's authorities under the Executive Order by adopting a more systematic approach to evaluating the activities of major terrorist organizations in various regions. This approach will focus on identifying key nodes that sustain the abilities of terrorist organizations to remain operational despite successful actions by the United States and its allies to capture and arrest terrorists, cell members, leaders, and operational planners.

In furtherance of this end, we have initiated a collaborative effort with the Department of Defense and other agencies to develop information and strategies against terrorist financing and infrastructure. Last fall, we began a pilot project with the U.S. Pacific Command and other DOD elements that identified terrorist support networks in Southeast Asia and selected key nodes or priority targets in these networks. The project focused special attention on al-Qaeda network affiliates in PACOM's AOR, including Jemaa Islamiyah, which subsequently carried out the Bali bombings, and the Abu Sayaff Group and others. This approach identified the key leaders, fundraisers, businessmen, recruiters, companies, charities, mosques, and schools that were part of its support network. Thus far, we have imposed sanctions against two of these key nodes and are coordinating actions against several others.

This process is the model that we are seeking to continue and expand in the collaborative efforts with DOD agencies and the combatant commands. We are working with USEUCOM headquarters. Meetings in the near future are planned to lay the groundwork for a continuing joint project. We also plan to begin projects with the Central Command Southern Command shortly thereafter. Working with these commands and other agencies provides us and DOD partners with, in effect, a force multiplier that brings together a variety of counterterrorism tools and resources to enhance opportunities for future efforts.

Taking a regional approach, following the various command's areas of responsibility, this effort will seek to identify and isolate the key nodes of the transnational terrorist support infrastructure in the respective AORs. This approach seeks to provide the opportunity to cripple an entire organization at one time through our implementation of the President's authority in coordination with possible actions in other departments and agencies and in cooperation with our allies at the UN.

We have already taken steps to implement this approach in some regions. For example, we are working with other DOD agencies, including the Office of Naval Intelligence, to fully identify the terrorism support infrastructure in the Horn of Africa. In this region, shipping and related drug-smuggling activities appear to be strengthening the terrorist networks in this area. Working with ONI provides us the opportunity to work with analysts who have unique experience in other areas less accessible to us.

I have today a few graphical representations of the key nodes approach that could be applicable to a terrorist support network in any region. It is related in Appendix 2 of my written testimony. Charts 1 and 2 are examples of the various steps of the funding process. Donors provide money to a variety of intermediaries often acting on behalf of charitable organizations to collect funds. The charitable organizations in turn use the funds both for legitimate humanitarian efforts but also, either wittingly or unwittingly, allow some funds to be siphoned off by facilitators who serve as the conduit to the extremist groups. Facilitators frequently are employees of the charitable organizations with close ties to the extremist groups or members of the extremist group with responsibility for liaising with charitable organizations.

Chart 2 is a theoretical model of how the key nodes of the terrorist support structure can be more systematically identified in their respective levels of participation in the funding network.

Chart 3 is a model of a terrorist support network with the key nodes highlighted that we believe economic sanctions could effectively impact. These include financial, leadership, and influence nodes, which are color-coded in red, blue, and green. Influence nodes can include individuals and institutions that provide spiritual or other guidance or serve as recruitment centers.

Chart 4 shows theoretically how designation and——

Senator SPECTER. Before you leave Chart 3, what does Chart 3 show?

Mr. NEWCOMB. Chart 3 shows in green the financial targets, in red the leadership targets, in purple the influence targets. And by using an effects-based targeting approach, we are able on an interagency basis to identify who the key leaders of these various participating entities are so that when taking them out, we can result in Chart 4, which shows theoretically how designation will isolate the key nodes of Chart 3 and sever the critical ties within the overall network and thereby disrupt its overall functioning. By removing these key nodes of the support structure, the leadership, the influence, the financial, the terrorist group is unable to mobilize people and resources in support of terrorists, thus rendering it ineffective.

The funds necessary for a terrorist organization to carry——

Senator SPECTER. Mr. Newcomb, you are double time now plus. Would you sum up? And we will go to Q and A.

Mr. NEWCOMB. I have perhaps another minute.

Senator SPECTER. OK.

Mr. NEWCOMB. The funds necessary for a terrorist organization to carry out an attack often are minimal, but the support infrastructure critical for indoctrination, recruitment, training, logistical support, the dissemination of propaganda, and other material requires substantial funding. The President's power under Executive Order 13224, as well as other legislation, provide the United States with authorities that are critical to attacking this threat posed by these terrorist organizations. Our effectiveness in implementing these authorities requires strong coordination with other U.S. departments and agencies and support from U.S. allies under United Nations Security Council Resolutions 1267 and 1455.

Terrorist organizations including al-Qaeda, the Egyptian Islamic Jihad, Jemaa Islamiyah, Al-Ittihad Al-Islamiyya, Hamas, Hizbollah, and others rely on their infrastructure for support and to shield their activities from scrutiny. The secretive nature of their activities and their frequent reliance on charitable, humanitarian, educational, and religious cover are vulnerabilities we can exploit by making designations under the Executive Order. Decisive action against high-impact targets deters others, forcing key nodes of financial support to choose between public exposure of support for terrorist activities or tarnishing their reputation, to the detriment of their business and commercial interest.

Thank you, Senator.

Senator SPECTER. We will now proceed with questioning, 5-minute rounds, and the Chairman has deferred to me for the first round.

Mr. Newcomb, in interviews by staff preparatory to your coming here, you advised that a good many of your recommendations for sanctions were rejected. Would you amplify what has happened on that?

Mr. NEWCOMB. Yes, Senator. In identifying key nodes, our responsibility is to identify how these terrorist organizations fit their activities together.

Senator SPECTER. Well, after you have identified them and made the recommendation—I only have 5 minutes. I want to focus very sharply on the rejections on the recommendations which involve Saudi sources. Precisely what has happened on that?

Mr. NEWCOMB. Well, the designation, as we indicated in our discussions, is not the only possible action. There is also law enforcement, intelligence, diplomatic, and military——

Senator SPECTER. Well, let's focus on economic sanctions, which is my question, before we go into other possible actions. I want to know about the recommendations on economic sanctions as to Saudis which have been turned down.

Mr. NEWCOMB. Senator Specter, we have made numerous recommendations, including relating to Saudi Arabia and other terrorist support organizations and groups. This goes through a Policy Coordinating, PCC process, where all the equities of the government come to the table, including——

Senator SPECTER. Well, my question focuses on recommendations which you have made for sanctions as to Saudi organizations which have been rejected.

Mr. NEWCOMB. Well, first let me say it is not—it is the policy not to comment on internal policy deliberations within the government. I can tell you these issues have been discussed with all the key players at the table, and when there is another possible action that can be taken, we have achieved our goal by teeing issues up.

Senator SPECTER. I am not asking about internal deliberations. I am asking you—and let me be specific with some organizations which have been discussed with you by staff prior to your coming here.

Were there recommendations as to the National Commercial Bank of Saudi Arabia for economic sanctions which were rejected?

Mr. NEWCOMB. No, Senator Specter, there was not.

Senator SPECTER. Were there recommendations for sanctions against the World Assembly of Muslim Youth?

Mr. NEWCOMB. There, as in others, these are issues that we looked at and examined very carefully. There was no recommendation out of our office on either of those.

Senator SPECTER. Well, what conclusions did you come to on the World Assembly of Muslim Youth?

Mr. NEWCOMB. That along with the whole variety of charitable organizations operating head offices in Saudi are organizations that we are looking at, as well as the whole range of several hundred or so possible organizations that may be funding terrorist activities. Rising to the level of a recommendation is a complicated policy——

Senator SPECTER. Well, I am not concerned about several hundred others. I would like to know, what about the World Assembly of Muslim Youth? Were they funding terrorist organizations, subject to economic sanctions, without any action being taken?

Mr. NEWCOMB. I can not conclude that in this hearing today. It is an organization that we——

Senator SPECTER. You can or you can not conclude——

Mr. NEWCOMB. Cannot.

Senator SPECTER. At this hearing today?

Mr. NEWCOMB. Well, we did not conclude that in our deliberations, so I can not say that was a recommendation of our office.

Senator SPECTER. How about the International Islamic Relief Organization? Were there recommendations for sanctions there which were rejected by higher officials in the Treasury Department?

Mr. NEWCOMB. This is an issue that we looked at, and, again, your question relates to policy deliberations within the administration which I can not comment on. I can tell you we did look at that organization.

Senator SPECTER. I am not interested in your policy deliberations. What I am interested in is your conclusions. Were there economic sanctions taken against the International Islamic Relief Organization?

Mr. NEWCOMB. To date, there have not been as of this date.

Senator SPECTER. Do you think there should be?

Mr. NEWCOMB. It is something that we would look at very carefully along with the others participating in the policy process.

Senator SPECTER. Well, when you look at it very carefully, how long have you been looking at it up until now?

Mr. NEWCOMB. Certainly since immediately in the aftermath of September 11.

Senator SPECTER. Well, that is almost 2 years. How long will it take you to come to a conclusion?

Mr. NEWCOMB. We can recommend and we can designate, but there is a policy process which takes into account all the variety of——

Senator SPECTER. I have got 16 seconds left. Have you recommended as to any of the organizations I have mentioned to you some tough economic sanctions which were turned down by higher officials, implicitly because they were Saudi organizations?

Mr. NEWCOMB. I can not say it is because they were Saudi organizations.

Senator SPECTER. Well, could you say whether they were turned down?

Mr. NEWCOMB. I can say that there have been some charities and other organizations that we have considered, we have had at the table, and that have been deferred for other actions which I would deem as appropriate.

Senator SPECTER. Well, my red light went on in the middle of your last answer, but I will be back.

Mr. NEWCOMB. OK.

Senator SPECTER. Senator Akaka.

OPENING STATEMENT OF SENATOR AKAKA

Senator AKAKA. Thank you very much, Mr. Chairman, for holding this hearing on terrorism financing.

I agree with my colleagues Senator Shelby and Senator Graham, who say that we need to make public much of the information from a congressional report on intelligence and the activities surrounding the terrorist attacks of September 11, 2001. There needs to be a full and open debate on these issues. And this is an effort partly today at this hearing.

I am also concerned about terrorism in Africa, and I think that we should put an end to the illicit trade in so-called blood diamond funds, which funds activities of Liberian President Charles Taylor, and also supports conflicts in Angola and the Congo.

I am equally concerned about terrorism in Asia. We must stop the activities of terrorists in Bali and the laundered money there that financed the bombing in Bali. These confront us as we look into Saudi Arabia and our tracking and coordinating intelligence with them and the lack of some of this information from them.

What we are learning is that there is a lesson that we cannot afford to ignore, and this Committee is certainly moving out on this.

Mr. Pistole, the House-Senate September 11 Commission report states that intelligence resources to fight terrorism are stretched thin. Do you believe that the FBI has adequate resources, people, and funding for training in place to combat terrorism?

Mr. PISTOLE. Senator, you have identified some critical issues for the FBI in terms of ensuring adequate training. To answer your question, I believe we have sufficient personnel, nearly 29,000 employees right now, over 11,000 of whom are special agents, to address the counterterrorism issue facing the United States domestically. But it is through the enhancement or augmentation through the Joint Terrorism Task Forces where we have over 2,000 FBI and other agency, law enforcement, and intelligence community personnel dedicated to 84 JTTFs around the country that we're able to leverage our limited resources in an effective means of being the arms and the operational node of the U.S. Government in fighting terrorism in the United States

Senator AKAKA. Mr. Pistole and Mr. Newcomb, we know there are frustrations, as you mentioned, Mr. Pistole, about what we are doing about tracking and coordination. My question to each of you is: What more needs to be done to improve tracking and coordination of terrorist funding intelligence?

Mr. PISTOLE. I think one of the keys is to achieve the cooperation of foreign governments such as Saudi Arabia where the assessment is much of the funding stems from, and as I mentioned earlier, I am leaving Sunday to go to Jiddah. I hope to achieve some success in that arena with my colleagues from Treasury and from State and from the National Security Council.

There are a number of issues on the table that will be discussed, and I would be willing to give the Committee a follow-up briefing after that trip, if they so desired.

Senator AKAKA. Mr. Newcomb.

Mr. NEWCOMB. Thank you, Senator. I share my colleague's point of view that we need to continue doing the work that we are doing, working within the administration and other government agencies but also with foreign counterparts, to have a unified front utilizing authorities under the United Nations to take joint action, coordinating fully with local law enforcement authorities, but continuing our current efforts.

Senator AKAKA. My time is up, Mr. Newcomb, but I noted that your written statement discusses a terrorist supporter identification program that has been developed with the Pacific Command. Given that Hawaii is the gateway to and from the Pacific, this is of interest, of course, to me, and I certainly want to hear more about that.

My time is up, but I wish to learn more about that project.

Mr. NEWCOMB. Fine, Senator. I would be happy——

Senator SPECTER. Thank you, Senator Akaka. Chairman Collins.

Chairman COLLINS. Thank you very much, Senator Specter.

Mr. Newcomb, I want to make sure that the Committee understands how you compile the list of suspected terrorist financers. First of all, it is my understanding that the Office of Foreign Assets Control has the power to recommend that individuals and entities that are involved in financing acts of terrorism can be placed on a government list, and the listing of that individual or entity is critical to depriving them of the ability to provide funds for terrorists. Is that accurate?

Mr. NEWCOMB. That is accurate. I would also point out and add that we also are the implementing and enforcement agency as well. So it is those two nodes, a recommending function and an implementation function.

Chairman COLLINS. And after your office recommends an entity for listing, that recommendation is then reviewed by an Interagency Policy Coordinating Committee that you referred to in your discussions with Senator Specter. Is that correct?

Mr. NEWCOMB. That is correct, Madam Chair.

Chairman COLLINS. Have you ever recommended that an entity be listed and had that recommendation rejected by this Interagency Policy Committee?

Mr. NEWCOMB. We have made numerous recommendations on a variety of different targets, as is our responsibility. And it goes to the Policy Coordinating Council which has a multitude of different points of view—State Department, the Justice Department, the FBI, the CIA, and others. So long as there is a responsible action to be taken, designation per se is not the only possible tool within the President's ambit of foreign policy——

Chairman COLLINS. And I understand that, that there may be other ways to approach the problem. But I assume that when you recommend the listing of an entity, that is based on an investigation that you have conducted and that there is a sound factual record for the listing of the entity, that is why you brought that recommendation forward. Is that correct?

Mr. NEWCOMB. That is correct. When we have a target we wish to designate, we develop evidence so that, should a designation happen, we are able to sustain a challenge to that in Federal court. So we do develop evidentiary packages as the basis for recommendations.

Chairman COLLINS. And it is correct—and I understand there may be other action taken, but it is correct that your recommendations are sometimes turned down by this interagency committee, correct?

Mr. NEWCOMB. The issue I think we are having somewhat of a debate about is the characterization of "turned down." Turned down——

Chairman COLLINS. For listing on the terrorist financers list.

Mr. NEWCOMB. Oftentimes they are not adopted for purposes of listing at this time.

Chairman COLLINS. That is the same as being turned down, not adopted, not—entities that you recommend be listed are not always listed as a result of the committee, the interagency committee, not accepting your recommendation that they be listed. Is that correct?

Mr. NEWCOMB. That is correct, but I have to add the caveat that because there are other agencies—for example, the FBI may say we have law enforcement equities in that particular target at this time. If you move forward now, you will disrupt those equities. That is, in my opinion, and in the opinion of the PCC, a very responsible way to proceed. Let us not interfere with your case. We will stand down until an appropriate time. And there have been examples when that objection has been removed.

Chairman COLLINS. What percentage of your recommendations to list Saudi entities or individuals have been rejected?

Mr. NEWCOMB. Madam Chairman, I don't have the answer to that information. You sent that to——

Chairman COLLINS. We have asked for that, as you know.

Mr. NEWCOMB. You have asked for it, and we will get it to you for the record.

Chairman COLLINS. Would you say that more than 50 percent of the recommendations that you have made to list Saudi entities or individuals have not been accepted by the committee?

Mr. NEWCOMB. I am going to have to get that information for you for the record. I don't have it at this time.

Chairman COLLINS. In conversations with staff, you were asked whether it might be as high as 95 percent. Do you recall telling the staff that you did not believe it was quite that high?

Mr. NEWCOMB. Yes, I certainly did say it wasn't that high. I don't have the exact figure. Let me also explain to you, there are a range of specific areas where we have been looking where there are considerable other equities at stake. I think the point that has to be made is that there are a whole range of targets that we are prepared to move forward on, can move forward on, have developed evidentiary packages on, and other equities come into play that are responsible equities.

I don't know if the number in every one of these categories is that high, but we do a thorough examination of potential targeting.

Chairman COLLINS. One final question on this area, since my time has expired. On this interagency committee, as you point out, there are representatives from various departments and agencies like the FBI, departments like the State Department and Justice. Which agency is responsible for most of the rejections of your recommendations to list Saudi entities and individuals?

Mr. NEWCOMB. I would say it is a combination of deferring action based on recommendations from the State Department, the FBI, the Justice Department, and the intelligence community based on a variety of equities that they have involved—diplomatic, law enforcement, intelligence, and others.

Chairman COLLINS. So no one agency or department on the committee is responsible for rejecting your recommendations more than any other agency or department?

Mr. NEWCOMB. I think in all conversations relating to foreign policy and foreign relations, we look very strongly to the State Department, and the State Department is always a very active player in these. So they do have a view, as well as the other agencies. But I think it is a combination of all of those.

Chairman COLLINS. Thank you.

Senator SPECTER. Thank you very much, Senator Collins. Senator Lautenberg.

OPENING STATEMENT OF SENATOR LAUTENBERG

Senator LAUTENBERG. Thank you, Mr. Chairman.

There are things that concern me—and I want to examine the specifics. Unfortunately, we are pushed for time, and I look at the clock and realize that you have another panel, Madam Chairman, and we have to get on with it. But I do want to say I have an active interest in the relationship with Saudi Arabia. In 1991, immediately after the first Gulf War, I went to Saudi Arabia, and I was outraged at diplomats, Senators, and Congressmen with an Israeli stamp on their passports were prohibited entry. And I got the Saudis to change that in a hurry, and it is no longer a restriction, that is, for officials of the U.S. Government. But I think if you are an ordinary citizen of this great country, you are prohibited entry if you have had an Israeli stamp in your passport.

It is outrageous. When they dial 911, we answered the phone immediately, sent over 500,000 people to the area to try and provide a rescue operation and the resuscitation effort, because that is what I specifically want to call it. All was lost there, Kuwait, Saudi Arabia, and then the ingratitude of the Government of Saudi Arabia not to present a witness here, not to present someone to offer testimony. Very frankly, it is compounded even to a more aggravating degree when the President has refused to permit the full record established in the 900-page report to be out there when the Saudis themselves say they would like to clear the record. Or are we looking at a sleight of hand, forgive the suspicion, that a routine was set up that said, well, OK, we in the Saudi Government will say make it public, and, Mr. President, we would thank someone in the administration if they would simply say that it is being withheld for methods, etc. It is pitiful.

I am using this time knowledgeably, Mr. Chairman, and I would like to ask Mr. Pistole for a short view on the Saudi Government's willingness to cooperate in investigations subsequent to terrorist attacks on the embassies in Africa and the *USS Cole*?

Mr. PISTOLE. Subsequent to those two incidents, Senator, as I think you are aware, there was very limited cooperation from the Saudi Government. As I mentioned in my opening statement, I believe May 12 was the defining moment for the Saudis in that the fact that they were attacked, that Saudi citizens were killed in the attacks, and that al-Qaeda seemed to be thumbing their noses at the royal family to say we will conduct attacks in the homeland here and you can not stop us. The cooperation since May 12 on the Riyadh bombings, as I mentioned, has been unprecedented in all areas but for the financing issue, which is still ongoing, and there are a number of issues on the table for that.

Senator LAUTENBERG. So there is still a reluctance to open up the relationship and to say, "America, you are without a doubt our best and most needed friend." I find that more than just a curious response to this kind of symbiotic relationship that we have had for a long time.

I yield back the time here.

Senator SPECTER. Thank you very much, Senator Lautenberg. Senator Coleman.

OPENING STATEMENT OF SENATOR COLEMAN

Senator COLEMAN. Thank you, Mr. Chairman.

Following up on the questions from my distinguished colleague from New Jersey on the level of cooperation, first let me backtrack a little bit. I believe in the written testimony of Mr. Winer, one of the subsequent panelists, he noted that, "Saudi Arabia has been the most significant source of terrorist funds for al-Qaeda."

Mr. Pistole, would you agree or disagree with that assertion?

Mr. PISTOLE. I would at this point say the FBI does not have enough intelligence or law enforcement information to agree or disagree with that. There is obviously a tremendous amount of money that has flown through NGOs and charitable organizations. As Mr. Newcomb mentioned, the question is how much of that has gone specifically for terrorist activity. And in limited situations, we can document that, and I can tell you affirmatively, yes, that this money has gone for this act. But to trace it from the government to a particular terrorist, I can not sit here and tell you that has been done.

Senator COLEMAN. Mr. Newcomb, could you respond to that?

Mr. NEWCOMB. I agree with my colleague from the Bureau. We are aware of large amounts of money going to charitable organizations. They are dual purpose in the fact that some of the otherwise legitimate activities are subverted. The extent to which that takes place is not completely clear, but I would characterize it as considerable.

Senator COLEMAN. Mr. Pistole, on the issue of financing, you indicated at least in the willingness to cooperate there has been substantial improvements in some areas but still work to be done on the financing side. Can you identify two or three things that need to be done that aren't being done today?

Mr. PISTOLE. Yes, Senator, several areas. One is the Saudi Government payment of defense counsel, for example, here in the United States of Saudi citizens who have been charged with crimes. That is an issue that we have raised with the Saudi Government and pursuing next week in follow-up meetings. To us, that is tantamount to buying off a witness, if you will, and so that gives us concern if the government is supplying money for defense counsel.

Other areas that we are addressing is the specific funding through whether it is NGOs or charitable organization, that they know or should know is going to specific terrorist organizations or individuals associated with terrorism.

Senator COLEMAN. Again, short questioning periods. I am going to switch gears for a second, and I apologize I wasn't here for your oral testimony, but I read your written testimony. You give a very spirited defense of the PATRIOT Act, which has certainly been the source of a lot of discussion.

Can you help me connect the dots? Is there something in the PATRIOT Act that you didn't have before that specifically allows you to break an organization that was doing something it shouldn't be doing?

Mr. PISTOLE. Absolutely, Senator. The most compelling part of the PATRIOT Act has been the elimination of what we refer to as "the wall" between law enforcement and intelligence collection activities. For example, if Mr. Newcomb was an FBI agent sitting in New York working a criminal investigation on Osama bin Laden, and I was an intelligence agent, because of prohibitions under "the wall," we would not be allowed to share that information. With the passage of the PATRIOT Act, we are now able to share that information and "connect the dots." That is the most compelling part of the PATRIOT Act.

Senator COLEMAN. Does that break in the wall also go down to the level of local sheriffs, local law enforcement? And let me explain why I ask. There has been concern raised about crop dusters and the ability to spread, for instance, something like anthrax. And I know the FBI often has been notified about that, but I wonder if our local sheriffs—they know where the grass fields are. They know where the crop dusters are.

Mr. PISTOLE. Absolutely, and this week, in fact, with tomorrow's deadline, our Joint Terrorism Task Forces are going back and recontacting all those individuals we contacted after September 11 to see if there has been any suspicious activity.

To answer specifically your question about sharing with local and State law enforcement agencies, that is done primarily through the Joint Terrorism Task Forces, and obviously it is a matter of, if there is classified information, whether they have the appropriate clearances. We still pass the information of the threat related but just may not identify the source or method of acquiring that information, for example, overseas.

Senator COLEMAN. Thank you. Thank you, Mr. Chairman.

Senator SPECTER. Thank you, Senator Coleman. Senator Levin.

OPENING STATEMENT OF SENATOR LEVIN

Senator LEVIN. Thank you, Mr. Chairman. Just very briefly a few comments, and then my questions.

Saudi behavior towards terrorism, particularly towards terrorism aimed at the United States, has been very lax and very disturbing for many years. The reference has already been made to the attack on Khobar Towers in Saudi Arabia in 1996 where we lost 19 American servicemen, after which the FBI complained that Saudi officials failed to cooperate with the United States probe and denied requests to question key Saudi officials.

During the 1990's, the Saudi Government became one of the few governments in the world that supported the Taliban, despite the Taliban's link to terrorists.

At the same time the Saudi Government was taking steps to strengthen its relations with the United States, it is said, it was funding extreme Muslim clerics in educational schools, the madrassas, that routinely called for attacks on the United States and hatred of all things American. And those madrassas in Pakistan, funded mainly by Saudi money, have provided recruits for the Taliban.

Anti-American statements became standard fare in Saudi-supported newspapers and publications. In 2001, after the September 11 attack killed 3,000 people in the United States, we found out that 15 of the 19 hijackers were Saudi nationals.

The recently released report by the joint inquiry on the September 11 attack states in the unclassified section that a Saudi citizen employed by the Saudi Civil Aviation Agency paid many of the expenses of two of the hijackers and "had access to seemingly unlimited funding from Saudi Arabia."

Until recently, Saudi Government officials and prominent Saudi citizens routinely contributed huge sums to Muslim charities which supported terrorism, including support for families of terrorists. The United States finally shut down several of those charities which were operating in the United States.

The question that the President asked not too long ago—"Are you with us or against us in the war on terrorism?"—in the case of the Saudis has got to be answered, "Yes." Both. The rhetoric is that they are with us, but the actions too often have been that, in fact, they have been against us. And, of course, there is now a new issue with U.S.-Saudi relations, and that is that 28-page piece of the September 11 joint inquiry report which has been redacted, blanked out. These deletions have been described by the former chairman of the Intelligence Committee, Senator Shelby, as being related to embarrassing information and not to information which should be properly classified. And it seems to me that there just has to be declassification of all or almost all of that material if we are going to make public what is in there which is so critically important.

[The prepared opening statement of Senator Levin follows:]

PREPARED OPENING STATEMENT OF SENATOR LEVIN

Terrorists need money to carry out acts of terrorism. They need money for explosives, for communications, for travel, and for all the other details involved in carrying out plans for mass murder and mayhem. Global terrorist organizations need global financing. They need to be able to transfer funds across international lines, move money quickly, and minimize inquiries into their finances, their activities, and their supporters.

Since the 9-11 attack, stopping terrorist financing has become a U.S. priority. This Committee has contributed in a significant way to that priority through a 3-year anti-money laundering investigation conducted by our Permanent Subcommittee on Investigations. This investigation, which produced extensive hearings and reports, not only documented little known methods for transferring illegal funds into the United States, but also provided important recommendations for strengthening U.S. laws to detect, prevent, and halt terrorist financing. These recommendations were included in S. 1371, a bipartisan bill I introduced in early 2001; they were picked up by the Senate Banking Committee which improved and expanded them; and they were then included in Title III of the USA Patriot Act, which was enacted into law in October 2001, six weeks after the 9-11 attack.

The new anti-money laundering provisions in Title III of the Patriot Act boosted U.S. efforts to stop terrorist financing. For example, Title III tightened the rules for money transfers by completely barring foreign shell banks from opening U.S. financial accounts, making it harder for offshore banks to arrange transfers of money into the United States, and requiring U.S. banks and securities firms to exercise more care before opening accounts for foreign persons and financial institutions. Title III also targeted informal money transfer systems, called "hawalas," which are often used in the Middle East to transfer funds outside normal banking channels without paperwork or regulatory oversight. The new law essentially requires these operations to register with the U.S. Government or risk shutdown and criminal prosecution.

Title III also made it easier to prosecute money laundering offenses involving foreign offenders by making it easier to freeze and seize foreign funds, obtain information from foreign jurisdictions, and prosecute foreign individuals and companies. The new law also required more U.S. financial institutions to establish ant-money laundering programs, verify customer information, and report suspicious financial transactions. Title III also modernized U.S. anti-terrorism criminal statutes by making it a crime to bring into the United States or take out of the United States large amounts of cash without disclosing the action and, if asked, providing an explanation for the funds, and by making it clear that anti-money laundering prohibitions apply to funds obtained legally if intended for use in planning, committing or concealing a terrorist act. The new law has enabled U.S. prosecutors to apply anti-terrorism prohibitions to funds legally collected by a charity if that charity intends to use the funds to support terrorism.

The U.S. Government has started to make good use of these new anti-money laundering provisions to intensify the fight against terrorist financing, but it would be incorrect to say that the United States has yet won this fight. We will hear testimony today about the difficulties of shutting down terrorist financing when some foreign governments are reluctant to take the necessary steps and may even, directly or indirectly, support persons or entities facilitating the movement of terrorist funds.

The example the Committee has chosen to highlight today is Saudi Arabia. For years, there has been disturbing Saudi behavior regarding terrorism. In 1996, for example, after bombs killed 19 U.S. servicemen at Khobar Towers in Saudi Arabia, the FBI complained that Saudi officials failed to cooperate with the U.S. probe and denied requests to question key Saudi suspects. Also during the 1990's, the Saudi government became one of the few governments in the world to support the Taliban in Afghanistan, despite its links to terrorists. The Saudi government also funded some extreme Muslim clerics and schools known as madrassas that routinely called for attacks on the United States and hatred of all things American. Madrasses in Pakistan, funded mainly by Saudi money, provided recruits for the Taliban.

Anti-American statements became standard fare in some Saudi-supported newspapers and publications. In 2001, after the 9-11 attack killed more than 3,000 people in the United States, it was determined that 15 of the 19 hijackers were Saudi nationals. The recently released report by the Joint Inquiry into the 9-11 attack states in an unclassified section that a Saudi citizen employed by the Saudi civil aviation agency paid many of the expenses of two of the hijackers, and "had access to seemingly unlimited funding from Saudi Arabia."

Saudi government officials and prominent Saudi citizens have routinely contributed millions of dollars to Muslim charities which support terrorism, including supporting families of terrorists killed in bombings or other terrorist attacks. The United States finally shut down several such charities that were operating in the United States. The United States also decided earlier this year to vacate its military posts in Saudi Arabia at least in part due to discontent within the country at having a U.S. presence and continuing attacks on the United States by some Saudi clerics and in some Saudi publications.

There are some recent actions taken by the Saudi government to stop terrorism. Saudi officials have openly identified their country as a strong U.S. ally and a foe of anti-American terrorism. In May of this year, after terrorist suicide bombings in Saudi Arabia killed 35 people, the Saudi government began a series of raids to arrest terrorists within its borders. One such raid in July reportedly resulted in the arrest of 16 persons linked to al Quaeda and the dismantling of a weapons arsenal with 20 tons of bomb-making chemicals, detonators, rocket-propelled grenades, and rifles. Saudi officials also allegedly used information uncovered in this raid to halt several terrorist plots. We will also hear testimony today that the Saudi government has taken steps to strengthen cooperation in terrorist financing cases and other anti-terrorism efforts.

Today, there is a new irritant in U.S.-Saudi relations. It arises from the 28-page gap and other blanked out information in the 9-11 Joint Inquiry report. These deletions have been described as based less on protecting U.S. national security than on protecting Saudi Arabia from embarrassment. The former head of the Senate Intelligence Committee, Senator Richard Shelby, recently said, for example, that he had closely reviewed the deleted information and "90 to 95 percent" involved simply "embarrassing" information that should be declassified and disclosed. Recently, the Saudi government itself called for declassifying the information. Disclosure is the right course to set the record straight.

The evidence of the past few years indicates that Saudi Arabia has a mixed record when it comes to stopping terrorism aimed at the United States. Some of the madrassas and some of the government-controlled press continue to teach hatred of Americans and the United States. Some Saudi nationals, including Osama bin Laden, have led terrorist organizations focused on U.S. destruction. Some Saudi-supported charities collect money that supports anti-U.S. terrorism. Some Saudi-supported clerics continue to praise suicide bombings that kill Americans.

The overly simplistic question of President Bush—"Are you with us or against us in the war on terrorism?"—is seemingly answered "yes" in the case of Saudi Arabia. The disturbing question remains: Is Saudi Arabia, in too many cases, failing to take the actions needed to cut off terrorist funding and failing to encourage tolerance and moderation rather than the hatred and extremism that breeds new terrorists.

Senator LEVIN. My question of you, Mr. Newcomb, is the following: You have indicated that the recommendations that your Department has made relative to listing of entities that have contributed or have links to terrorist organizations in a number of cases were not accepted. And you have declined to identify the organizations, those charities and other entities that you recommended. On what basis do you decline to share with us those recommendations? Are you asserting Executive privilege here this morning?

Mr. NEWCOMB. No, Senator, I am not.

Senator LEVIN. Then what is the basis for your refusal to share with this Committee the names of those entities that you have recommended?

Mr. NEWCOMB. Let me be real clear about what it is we have done. We have looked at evidence or information we believe was credible, and we have surfaced the target to a Policy Coordinating Committee chaired by the Treasury Department to determine what action is appropriate, whether it be designation, law enforcement, intelligence, or diplomatic. A number of agencies have come forward in a variety of different contexts and recommended that action be deferred.

As to the specific names, it is matters that are sensitive because of law enforcement or other equities that are at stake. If you wish to have a briefing in a classified session, that would be more appropriate. But today, in a public hearing, it is not appropriate to mention actions that we may be taking to subvert the element of surprise or to in any way interfere with ongoing diplomatic, law enforcement, or other actions.

Senator LEVIN. Is that information classified?

Mr. NEWCOMB. Oftentimes——

Senator LEVIN. No, not oftentimes. Specifically, are the names of the entities that you have recommended for listing classified?

Mr. NEWCOMB. The evidentiary packages we prepare in most instances are.

Senator LEVIN. Now let me ask my question again. My time is up? I will still ask it one more time, if I may, Mr. Chairman. I know the Chairman tried very hard and others have tried very hard to get this information, so let me try again.

Are the names of those entities classified? The names classified that you have recommended for listing. It is a yes or no question.

Mr. NEWCOMB. The names themselves are not classified.

Senator LEVIN. Then I think you ought to present them to us today.

Mr. NEWCOMB. I don't have them with me, Senator.

Senator LEVIN. I think you ought to present them to the Committee within the next 24 hours if they are not classified, unless you are asserting Executive privilege that the President only can assert.

Thank you.

Senator SPECTER. Thank you, Senator Levin. When I passed you the note that the time was up, I was enjoying your questioning, not so much the answers but the questioning. But we have got a lot of Senators here and another panel.

Senator LEVIN. I appreciate that.

Senator SPECTER. Thank you. Senator Pryor.

OPENING STATEMENT OF SENATOR PRYOR

Senator PRYOR. Thank you, Mr. Chairman.

I have a question first for Mr. Pistole, and that is, have you found Saudi Arabia in general to be cooperative with your agency?

Mr. PISTOLE. There is a clear delineation between prior to May 12 and the bombings in Riyadh and after May 12. Prior to May 12, there was a lot of frustration. Several Senators have mentioned Khobar Towers, tremendous frustration with that. Since the May 12 bombings where Saudi citizens were killed, and U.S. citizens were killed, there has been, as I described it, unprecedented cooperation.

Senator PRYOR. When you say unprecedented, do you feel like it is totally transparent cooperation, or do you feel like they are still holding some things back?

Mr. PISTOLE. Oh, clearly, I believe they are holding some things back, just as I think we would in any investigation if we have the Mabahith come here to conduct an investigation because Saudi citizens were killed. We would not share everything with them because of national security concerns. So I don't for a minute doubt that they are withholding some information, what they perceive as in their national security interest. But the level of cooperation that we have had is such that, for example, having direct access to interview Saudi citizens who were eyewitnesses, direct access to the evidence, to bring back to the FBI laboratory if we so desired to do any type of analysis we wanted, that is what I describe as unprecedented.

Senator PRYOR. Mr. Newcomb, I would ask you the same question, and that is, the level of cooperation from Saudi Arabia to your agency.

Mr. NEWCOMB. Yes, we have achieved a number of successes. One was the joint designation of two branches of the Al-Haramain charitable organization in Bosnia and Somalia, as well as an individual that was affiliated with one of the charities, Mr. Julaidan. At meetings that we participated bilaterally with the Saudis, they announced to us and then subsequently announced in a press release the creation of a ministry specifically for the oversight of charities. In discussions we had with the Jeddah Chamber of Commerce, they implemented a code of conduct relating to standards for charitable giving. And we have had dialogues with a variety of deep-pocket Saudi individuals going through the responsibilities that we believed they were presented in the sanctions initiative and the United Nations resolutions.

We have had meetings in Saudi and here, people soliciting us and us soliciting them. So those are things I would point to of things we have been able to do together, Senator.

Senator PRYOR. Thank you. I would also join with Senator Levin, Mr. Newcomb, that if the names are not classified, I think you should provide those to the Committee, hopefully within the next 24 hours.

The last thing I wanted to ask—this is a general question probably for both of you, and that is, as I understand Saudi Arabia, there are a lot of internal pressures relating to terrorist activity, and perhaps the government does not either have the will or in the final analysis maybe the total control over some terrorist activities that may be going on within its borders. And as I understand it, the royal family there has been subject to acts of terrorism and near acts of terrorism on a number of occasions.

Has that changed since—you were talking about May 11? I have forgotten the date.

Mr. PISTOLE. May 12.

Senator PRYOR. Has that changed since May 12?

Mr. PISTOLE. I believe so because I think that the royal family in particular sees themselves as being vulnerable to al-Qaeda efforts in the kingdom and that no longer is this simply an entity that is focusing on Western interests but has now turned on the kingdom and the royal family that represents the kingdom. So, yes, I think they see themselves in a struggle for survival at this point.

Senator PRYOR. Mr. Newcomb, do you have any comments on that?

Mr. NEWCOMB. I don't. I have not had discussions since that date so I could base any summary or conclusions, so I cannot add to that.

Senator PRYOR. Thank you. That is all, Senator Specter. Thank you.

Senator SPECTER. Thank you very much, Senator Pryor.

Mr. Pistole and Mr. Newcomb, there are obviously many more questions to be asked, but we have another panel. What we would request that you do is stay in the hearing room because something may arise in the course of the testimony from the next panel which would lead us to want to ask you some follow-up questions, if that should arise.

We will now turn to Dore Gold, former Israeli Ambassador——

Senator CARPER. Mr. Chairman, could I ask one quick question of these panelists before they leave?

Senator SPECTER. One quick question?

Senator CARPER. Yes.

Senator SPECTER. With an answer?

Senator CARPER. Hopefully.

Senator SPECTER. OK.

Mr. Pistole, we have had a late arrival here. Senator Carper has arrived and has one quick question.

OPENING STATEMENT OF SENATOR CARPER

Senator CARPER. Gentlemen, and Mr. Chairman, thank you for your consideration.

Gentlemen, the report issued last year on terrorist financing by the independent task force sponsored by the Council on Foreign Relations States, "It is true that Saudi Arabia has taken two or three important steps to improve its capability to cooperate on these matters with the United States, for which it should be commended. A hundred more steps, and Saudi Arabia may be where it needs to be."

That is the quote, and that sounds like Saudi Arabia is about 1 percent of the way where it needs to be. Is that a fair characterization?

Mr. NEWCOMB. Senator, I would respond by saying at least from where we sit, Saudi has taken some important first steps, steps I have mentioned in answer to Senator Pryor's questions. I think then the question becomes follow-up, how are they implementing, what are the oversight of charities that this new ministry is doing, what future joint designations are we going to make, and how are they going to be implementing the regulation of charities and other such activities. So I think it is an ongoing process and one that we need to continue.

Senator SPECTER. Senator Carper, you have a second quick question?

Senator CARPER. Thank you, Mr. Chairman.

In terms of getting the other 99 percent of the way, what do we need to be doing at our end, the legislative end, to encourage that along?

Mr. NEWCOMB. I think we need to be doing more of what we are doing, what we are doing except more of it, and I think we need to continue dialogues where we are able to focus on the issues that are relevant to the relationship.

Senator CARPER. Mr. Pistole, do you want to add any comments on this?

Mr. PISTOLE. My only insight on that, Senator, is that it is such a broad issue for the U.S. Government as a whole with so many equities represented that, from an FBI perspective, we are having some significant successes that we are trying to build upon and that anything that we would do would need to be done in concert with the National Security Council, with all the other equities represented. So we are building on the successes. We are trying to get into things that we have never been allowed to before, and we have had some incremental successes.

Senator CARPER. All right. Thanks very much.

Senator SPECTER. Thank you very much, Senator Carper.

We will now proceed to the second panel. The first witness is former Ambassador Dore Gold, Israeli Ambassador to the United Nations, a recognized expert on Middle Eastern strategic affairs, author of "Hatred's Kingdom: How Saudi Arabia Supports the New Global Terrorism." Ambassador Gold, we are very tight on time, and we will set the clock at 5 minutes, and we look forward to your testimony.

TESTIMONY OF DORE GOLD,[1] FORMER ISRAELI AMBASSADOR TO THE UNITED NATIONS, AND PRESIDENT, JERUSALEM CENTER FOR PUBLIC AFFAIRS

Mr. GOLD. Thank you very much, Madam Chairman and Senator Specter and the Senators who are Members of this Committee, for inviting me to this panel. I should start by saying my testimony here, I am speaking on my own behalf. I don't represent the Government of Israel or any other institution. I think, however, that there are three dimensions of what Israel has experienced over the last number of years that will be of interest to the Committee and to the American people at large because of the concern about Saudi Arabia's role in support, both ideological and financial, of the new terrorism that we are facing.

I believe some of the lessons and some of the experiences that we are having have direct connections and implications for the issues that are of concern to you.

Let me begin with a little bit about how we have gotten into this subject, and I am going to basically restrict my presentation to just a number of issues that are in a PowerPoint presentation. You have my written testimony, if you want to go into further detail on historical elements as well.

If today, for example, a young Palestinian wishes to see what are the ideological sources on what basis he should commit a suicide bombing attack against Israelis, and he goes to the website of the Hamas organization, what you will find here—and you see it here on the PowerPoint. This is directly from a Hamas website. Of, let's say, the number of clerics that are mentioned here who justify suicide attacks, the use of suicide bombing, and the fact that the person is regarded as a martyr in Islam, the largest national grouping of clerics that support these positions are Saudis.

This immediately opened up the question of the Saudi relationship to the wave of suicide bombing that Israel is facing. But the problem of ideological support that we are seeing for these kinds of suicide attacks is not just confined to the area of Israel.

If we go on to the next presentation, right after the September 11 attack a book was published on a Saudi website which was rather alarming since it basically—it is called "The Foundations of the Legality of the Destruction That Befell America." This basically justifies the attacks on the United States.

Now, when you find a book like this on a Saudi website—and what was interesting, of course, is one of the men who is one of the authors of this book is mentioned on the Hamas website—you have to ask: Are we dealing with a Saudi extremist, someone who is on the periphery of society, somebody who is maybe the equivalent of a Timothy McVeigh in the Saudi system?

Well, we did biographical research on these individuals, particularly the two that wrote the introduction to the book. One of them

[1] The prepared statement of Mr. Gold with attachments appears in the Appendix on page 77.

is Sheikh al-Shuaibi, who recently died last year, in 2002, and he, of course, is one of the ideological sources on the Hamas site as well. He happens to be an individual who grew up in the Saudi system, who studied under the Grand Mufti of Saudi Arabia when King Faisal was in power. His students look like a "Who's Who" of Saudi Arabia, including the former Minister of Islamic Affairs of Saudi Arabia and the current Grand Mufti. And, therefore, when someone like this puts his name on a book justifying the attacks on September 11 and we find that that individual has a leading role in the education of elements of the Saudi establishment, that is a source of very serious concern about what is going on in Saudi Arabia in terms of religious support for the new wave of attacks that we are facing.

It also has a relationship to the financial side as well, because if leading clerics are taking position of this radical nature, what does that suggest to members of society who are thinking about what to do about charitable contributions, and even if an organization is considered tainted because of terrorist connections? Therefore, looking into the ideological support structure of the new terrorism becomes very important.

Just to give you a sense of where things can possibly lead, once you can justify attacks on the United States of September 11, it doesn't become surprising that we have now a new fatwa that was released in May 2003 which justifies the use of weapons of mass destruction against the United States, including the killing of 10 million Americans or other infidels.

Now, the author of this particular fatwa—his name is Nasser al-Fahad—happens to have been imprisoned by Saudi Arabia recently, which is a positive development because I know many of the Senators are following the post-May 12 developments. But, nonetheless, that these ideas are out there, that these ideas influence young people, are of tremendous concern. And, of course, we have also seen in the past in the 1990's where extremist clerics were put in prison by Saudi Arabia were subsequently let out. So this is an issue that you should be looking at.

Let me move now into the issue of the terrorist financing with direct implications for your Committee and for your concerns. This may be difficult for you to read, but this particular element of the powerpoint presentation outlines the three largest Saudi charities that have been suspected of being involved in terrorist financing: IIRO, WAMY—that is the World Assembly of Muslim Youth—and al-Haramain. I think the important element in this particular slide that you should pay attention to is many times you hear in a lot of these hearings Saudi NGOs, non-governmental organizations. And you would think from that, therefore, that the government responsibility in Riyadh is somewhat minimal when you see connections between Saudi charities and particular terrorist organizations.

But someone doing the most minimal declassified work possible, going to the websites of each of these organizations, in Arabic, you would find—when you try to see who is at the head of these organizations, what you will find is that these are not NGOs. These are GOs. These are government organizations, and let me be very specific.

When you look to see who is the head of the IIRO, which is a branch or a subset of the Muslim World League, you find that the chairman of the Constituent Council of the World Muslim League, the Muslim World League, is no less than the Grand Mufti of Saudi Arabia, who is, by the way, a member of the Saudi cabinet. If you look both at WAMY and al-Haramain—I understand you should have before you also these papers so that you can see them more clearly—you will see that at the head of both WAMY and al-Haramain, the chairman of these organizations, the chairman of the WAMY Secretariat and the chairman of the al-Haramain Administrative Council, is the Minister of Islamic Affairs of Saudi Arabia, who is also a Saudi cabinet member. So that the ultimate corporate responsibility in each of these organizations is in the hands of a member of the Saudi Government.

Now, in following how these organizations have been active, probably one of the earliest sources of evidence of some problem in the way that these organizations function comes from documents that were found in Bosnia in the late 1980's. One of these documents is on the stationery of the International Islamic Relief Organization, and it summarizes a meeting between bin Laden representatives and the Secretary General of the Muslim World League. This document is, of course, not an Israeli document. It wasn't found by Israeli sources, but it is certainly well known among those who are following this issue in the intelligence community.

But I think what directly relates to Israel is the following document. In Operation Defensive Shield in the West Bank, when Israel went into Palestinian headquarters, a number of Saudi documents were found, not just Palestinian documents, on the pattern of terrorist funding. This document is on stationery of the International Islamic Relief Organization, and it summarizes the disbursement of $280,000 to 14 Hamas front organizations. So here we have IIRO——

Senator SPECTER. Do you have a date on that document?

Mr. GOLD. I can get the date for you, but this document was undated. We can probably approximate it in the year 2000.

Now, what is very important, I think, for your study of this situation of Saudi financing of terrorism is to look at the statements that Saudi officials are making about issues which we can document. For example, Adel Jubeir, who frequently appears on American television—he is the foreign policy adviser of Crown Prince Abdullah—stated on August 16, 2002, on "Crossfire," "We do not allow funding to go from Saudi Arabia to Hamas." And he has made repeated references of this sort. On the other side, in the Foreign Ministry of Saudi Arabia, the Foreign Minister, Prince Saud al-Faisal told Arab News, an English newspaper of Saudi Arabia, the following on June 23, 2003. He was asked if the kingdom had ever financed Islamic movements in Palestine, meaning Hamas and Islamic Jihad, whether directly or indirectly. And Prince Saud said that since the establishment of the Palestine Liberation Organization as the sole legitimate representative of the Palestinian people, the Saudi Kingdom has been sending the remittances through the PLO. So, again, we have another firm denial of any Saudi Arabian support for Hamas.

Senator SPECTER. Ambassador Gold, you are now double time, so could you sum up?

Mr. GOLD. Yes. I will wrap up with one more document.

One of the strongest sources of evidence showing Saudi Arabian support for Hamas, a recognized international terrorist organization, is actually a letter written by Mahmud Abbas, also known as Abu Mazen, the Prime Minister of the Palestinian Authority today. This letter was written in December 2000. It was a fax that was sent to Prince Salman, governor of Riyadh and a full brother of King Fahd. In this letter, Abu Mazen specifically requests that the Saudis stop funding al-Jamiya al-Islamiya, which is a Hamas front in the Gaza Strip.

I would just end by showing you the kind of activities that this organization does, because many people say, oh, well, they are involved in civilian activity. This is a graduation of 1,650 kindergarten students in the Gaza Strip in 2001 in which the children are in uniforms. They are re-enacting terrorist attacks. For example, here is a young girl re-enacting the lynching of Israeli soldiers. Many of them are also wearing suicide belts as well. So this is the kind of education which Saudi Arabia has been funding and the kind of education which Abu Mazen has sought that the Saudis stop.

One last element, because terrorist financing is—and this will be my final slide. This is a check, a corporate check from the Chase Manhattan Bank in New York. The corporate check belongs to Al-Rajhi Banking and Investment Company, which has long been suspected of being a conduit for terrorist financing by many authorities. In this case, we actually found a check from 1999 showing how an American account could be used for funding Hamas. The organization the check is written to is Lajna Sakat Tulkarm, which means the Tulkarm Charity Board, which is an unquestionable Hamas front.

I will stop here, and we can go into further elements of my presentation.

Senator SPECTER. Thank you, Ambassador Gold.

The Committee had invited Adel al-Jubeir, foreign policy spokesman for the Kingdom of Saudi Arabia, to appear and he declined. I want that to be known publicly.

Our next witness is Jonathan Winer, formerly Deputy Assistant Secretary of State for International Law Enforcement, and now an attorney with the firm of Alston and Bird. Thank you very much for joining us, Mr. Winer, and we look forward to your testimony.

TESTIMONY OF JONATHAN M. WINER,[1] ALSTON AND BIRD

Mr. WINER. Thank you, Mr. Chairman. Before the team goes off to Saudi Arabia to try and work these issues out, it may be useful to recollect what has happened in past missions.

Back in 1998, 5 years ago, right after the bombs went off in Dar es Salaam and Nairobi, the Executive Branch convened an interagency meeting on the International Emergency Economic Powers Act to determine whether there should be designations in connection with those bombings in relationship to terrorist finance. We

[1] The prepared statement of Mr. Winer appears in the Appendix on page 110.

tried to assess as a government then what the basis was for al-Qaeda to carry out its activities around the world, and we had two false conclusions we were basing our assessment on at the time. The first is it doesn't take a lot of money to be a terrorist, and the second is bin Laden is wealthy and doesn't need money from anybody else. It was an incomplete theory of the case, an inadequate theory of the case, and ultimately a wrong theory of the case.

The actual case was it cost a lot of money to create al-Qaeda. It was a constant fundraising operation. And it took us some months until late 1998 to figure that out. We now had a theory. The question was what to do about it.

What we sought to do then was to map the network with fragmented information, identify the key nodes, and then try to disrupt those nodes. We also had as a government the enormous power of the International Emergency Economic Powers Act to freeze assets of foreign entities—banks, businesses, charities, whatever. And we recognized that this important power was not recognized or understood by many countries, including countries where we saw terrorist finance to be a problem.

We came to the conclusion that we should do an International Emergency Economic Powers Act designation against the Taliban as one way of taking action against al-Qaeda, as a means of putting pressure not only on the Taliban but their supporters, as well as other governments in the region. We wanted to increase the leverage that we had.

We had had sporadic contacts at that point with embassies in the region, including with the Saudis. These were not particularly focused, and they weren't particularly high level. We recognized in late 1998, early 1999 as a government that the only way you can really deal with the Saudi Government is from the top down. There were communications between the Vice President's office and Crown Prince Abdullah which took place in which the United States said we want to send a team over that is very high level to discuss something that is very important in connection with our embassies having been attacked.

In May or June 1999, these meetings took place in Saudi Arabia. They were interagency meetings, very similar to the interagency meetings that are about to take place once again in Saudi Arabia that have been discussed earlier today in these hearings.

We had said we didn't want one-on-one's, this agency meeting with that agency on either side, because when you have one-on-one's agency after agency, you can get the runaround: We would love to help you, but you have to go talk to someone else. We wanted a unified, integrated approach government to government. That is my understanding of what took place. I was not directly part of that mission. I received reports when it came back.

The delegation talked about IEEPA to the Saudi Government. They talked about how the use of IEEPA could hurt U.S.-Saudi financial and economic relationships and even result in substantial freezes of Saudi funds and freezes of funds of high-level individuals in Saudi Arabia with international prominence. These meetings took place 4 years ago, prior to the September 11 attacks.

We advised them that we would be shutting down Ariana Airlines, the Taliban's airline, and that any airports that continued to permit Ariana flights to take place, they could potentially get shut down. At that point, the Moscow airport and the Saudi airport were two of the airports that Ariana was using, given cover in part by the Russians. The Saudi ability—Ariana Airlines' ability to use Saudi Arabia was stopped at that time, and that provided the first use of IEEPA in that area relevant to the terrorist area.

We hoped that this would start a new relationship on the subject of terrorist finance. I left the government in late 1999. I was told that there was a second meeting in early 2000. Another U.S. interagency delegation went to Saudi Arabia. The readout that I hear on an unclassified basis very generally is that there was only marginal benefit from the second meeting, that the desert sands of Saudi Arabia had ground down this initiative like so many before it. Again, 3½ to 4 years ago, prior to September 11.

One problem we ran into was that the Saudis had very little centralized integration and their government agencies didn't talk to one another, didn't trust one another, didn't work together, didn't communicate with one another. And that had an impact on the political will of the Saudi Government.

Now, I was asked also to talk briefly about the designation process. I participated in IEEPA designation processes on various issues when I was in the Clinton Administration, and I can tell you that, yes, sometimes it was the State Department who said no, we don't want to get our foreign partners upset—not my part of the State Department but other parts of the State Department. And, of course, geographics trump functionals most of the time at the State Department. State relationships are more important. Sometimes it was the FBI. Quite often it was the FBI because they didn't want to have criminal cases interfered with. Sometimes it was the Justice Department backing up the FBI.

In my experience, it was never the CIA or the intelligence agency. It may have happened in other cases, but not in any case that I participated in. And very rarely—rarely—it was the White House or the Treasury, but very rarely. Usually State or FBI in my experience.

Now, did we shoot down designations that Treasury had the ability to put together and, in fact, recommended? We absolutely did. It did not happen to be in the terrorist area during my time. It was in other areas. But it certainly happened, in which foreign policy or other considerations trumped decisions or recommendations made by OFAC. I can say that as a general matter.

A couple of final points before I run out of time. It has been my experience that collective leadership is not usually a mechanism to forceful action. In the Clinton Administration, through much of the time a fellow named Dick Clark pushed counterterrorism in a central way, including terrorist finance. I am sure there is someone doing this in the administration today. I just don't happen to know who it is. I am concerned that there isn't somebody in the White House with that job. I think there should be.

Finally, with regard to the Saudis and this latest mission, coming 4 years after the first mission on exactly this topic, denial is not just a river in Egypt, and those who forget the past are condemned to repeat it.

Thank you, Mr. Chairman.

Senator SPECTER. Thank you very much, Mr. Winer.

Our next witness is Steve Emerson, an expert on terrorism and terrorist financing, the author of "American Jihad: The Terrorists Living Among Us." Mr. Emerson is currently NBC's terrorism analyst and a special investigative correspondent for CNN.

Thank you for joining us, Mr. Emerson, and we look forward to your testimony.

TESTIMONY OF STEVEN EMERSON,[1] EXECUTIVE DIRECTOR, THE INVESTIGATIVE PROJECT

Mr. EMERSON. Let me clarify that I was formerly a correspondent for CNN. Thank you to the Committee for holding this hearing this morning. I think that shining a light on the whole issue of the very intricate web of connections between the Saudi Government and the funding of terrorism is absolutely pivotal to preventing another September 11.

Just recently, in the last month, Adel al-Jubeir, foreign affairs adviser to the Crown Prince Abdullah, denied that Saudi Arabia was funding terrorism, and when asked about whether Saudi charities had complied with the new regulations, he said he hoped so. He also stated, "If the UN is headquartered in New York, is America responsible for everything the UN does?"

Now, I think it is very important to bear out in the very beginning here that the analogy that Mr. Jubeir has referred to is not correct. The fact of the matter is that major Saudi NGOs, non-governmental organizations, as they have been designated legally, either in Saudi Arabia or in conjunction with the United Nations, have been tied for years directly and indirectly to the support for al-Qaeda, Hamas, Islamic Jihad, and other terrorist groups. Often, it must be stated, the connections are not neatly compartmentalized, largely because of the very complex ways in which terrorist funding has been laundered to terrorist groups. Still at other times, the evidence shows that NGOs carry out activities that are "totally legitimate and legal." Indeed, it is the very external legitimacy of these groups that provides the perfect cover to siphon off, divert, or launder financial support or to provide cover for terrorist cells. There is also a problem sometimes in determining whether an affiliate group makes the entire organization corrupt or whether, in fact, there is just one bad rogue chapter in that organization.

Let me just briefly go over some of these things that I have presented in the written testimony to give an indication of why the problem is not just limited to either select chapters and why it is connected to the Saudi regime itself.

For example, we have collected several textbooks used and distributed in the United States, distributed by the Saudi Embassy in Washington, D.C. They have the full imprimatur of the Kingdom of Saudi Arabia on the textbooks. In the testimony, I refer to the curricular used in grades 4 through 11, but let me just cite a quote from the 7th grade class Book 5. The book says, "'What is learned from the Hadith?'. and teaches, 'The curse of Allah be upon the Jews and the Christians.'" Grades 8 through 11 continue to emphasize the notion and piousness of the jihad, and in grade 11 it warns

[1] The prepared statement of Mr. Emerson appears in the Appendix on page 131.

against taking the Jews and Christians as friends or protectors of Muslims.

I think this, unfortunately, helps develop a whole generational mind-set that leads to terrorism, noting that terrorism is really the culmination of indoctrination and recruitment. Much of that indoctrination is entirely legal, with terrorism being the violent, illegal expression ultimately and representing the culmination of the indoctrination and recruitment.

The Muslim World League, as has been referred to previously, is a group that was established in 1962 by the Saudi Arabian regime. It has continued to fund major Islamic movements around the world, often defending itself by claiming it is only involved in promoting education or repelling hatred against Islam.

However, it is absolutely clear that U.S. investigators, law enforcement for the FBI and intelligence investigators at the CIA, have collected abundant material showing MWL connections to al-Qaeda and to Hamas during the past 20 years—15 years in Hamas, to be specific, and in the case of al-Qaeda going back to the late 1980's. Similarly, other groups in Saudi Arabia, NGOs such as the International Islamic Relief Organization, established in 1978 as an arm of the MWL. Let me just briefly point out that in 1994, Muhammad Jamal Khalifa, Osama bin Laden's 37-year-old brother-in-law, was arrested in California coming from the Philippines. In his possession were documents connecting Islamic terrorist manuals to the International Islamic Relief Organization, the group that he had headed in the Philippines. In addition, the Canadian Government has stated in testimony in Canadian courts in the last 2 years that the IIRO secretly funded terrorism.

I think it is also important to note that Fayez Ahmed Alshehri, one of the September 11 airline hijackers, told his father before he set out for the hijacking conspiracy that he was going to work for the IIRO.

There is another group that is also involved and controlled by the Saudi Government and also has been cited in terms of its ties to Bosnian terrorists and to al-Jemaa Islamiyah. This group is al-Haramain.

Last, I would like to point out that the group called WAMY, the World Assembly of Muslim Youth, is an organization that, even though Saudi officials claim have no official connection, is largely funded by Saudi officials and by senior Saudi philanthropists. This organization has been tied to the 1993 World Trade Center bombing and has been repeatedly tied to al-Qaeda in numerous activities around the world. Most of that material I submit for the record in the testimony.

Thank you very much.

Senator SPECTER. Thank you, Mr. Emerson.

I had asked FBI Official Pistole to stay, and I have one question for you at this point as a follow-up to Mr. Winer. Is Mr. Pistole present?

Mr. LORMEL. I am Dennis Lormel, sir. Mr. Pistole had to go back to the office. I stayed behind. I am chief of the Terrorist Financing Operations Section.

Senator SPECTER. Well, when we ask witnesses to come, we request that they stay for the full hearing because in the course of the hearing other issues arise where we would like to have them here.

Mr. LORMEL. Sir, that is why I stayed. If I could answer the question, I would be happy to.

Senator SPECTER. Well, when the Committee asked Mr. Pistole to stay, he ought to stay. In his absence, I will ask you the question.

It has been reported that the FBI will not pursue a criminal investigation where probable cause exists for the investigation if there is an objection from the State Department. Is there any validity to that report?

Mr. LORMEL. No, sir, I don't believe so. Maybe if you could explain a little more, I could better understand the context.

Senator SPECTER. Well, the report is that where there is probable cause to pursue an investigation under the criminal laws of the United States, the State Department can interpose an objection and prevent that investigation from going forward. And that is a very relevant point of inquiry at this particular hearing. It is a point that I have inquired about before.

Would you do two things? Would you identify yourself for the record? Do that now.

Mr. LORMEL. Dennis Lormel, and I am the chief of the Terrorist Financing Operations Section in the Counterterrorism Division of the FBI.

Senator SPECTER. OK. And would you relay that question to higher authorities in the Federal Bureau of Investigation and respond to this Committee?

Mr. LORMEL. Yes, sir, I will.

Senator SPECTER. Thank you.

Mr. LORMEL. And to my knowledge, I am not aware of any such cases. I can specifically speak to terrorist financing, and in our investigations there has been no such interaction with the State Department requesting that we stand down on criminal cases.

Senator SPECTER. Well, take the question up with higher authorities in the FBI, and while you are doing that, tell them that when the Committee asks a witness to appear, we like to have them here for the entire hearing, like the Senators are here for the entire hearing.

Mr. LORMEL. Yes, Senator.

Senator SPECTER. Mr. Winer, you very delicately stated that the State Department doesn't want to get our foreign partners upset. That is a magnificent understatement. Have you ever heard of a report that the FBI would not pursue an investigation, a criminal investigation, where probable cause existed if the State Department raised an objection at the highest levels?

Mr. WINER. I have not heard such reports, sir. In the time that I was at the State Department as the senior person for international law enforcement, I was aware of no such request from the State Department to the Bureau. Certainly I made none or would have encouraged or permitted the making of none.

However—and it is an important caveat—when requests of that nature are made, they are not written down and they are not done within the system, and they are done at a high level. I don't mean this specific request because I don't know of such a request. But if a foreign government wished to be protected from a particular action by the U.S. Government and a Secretary of State so chose to do it, they do have the capacity and, in my experience, take advantage of that capacity to go around the system on any number of highly sensitive matters to arrange to have things done.

I think it is very undesirable because I believe every decision made should be on the record. I believe it is critical for the integrity of the system not to have decisions taken off the record. But it did take place during my time in government, not in connection with the FBI, not in connection with a criminal justice matter.

Senator SPECTER. Well, what was it in connection with and what was it?

Mr. WINER. Inquiries that other people were making other than the FBI. Matters were essentially calmed, quieted, stopped as a result of very high-level interventions, but not criminal justice pertaining to terrorism, not law enforcement per se. Regulatory.

Senator SPECTER. Can you be a little more specific in 12 seconds?

Mr. WINER. I can not, not because I am trying to protect any information from the Committee but because while I recollect it happening more than once, the exact circumstances are not at my fingertips, unfortunately. The memory of it is absolutely precise, but the substance, unfortunately, is not, sir.

I will say last, if I may, that in the regulatory review process, the fact that there is no process for integrating the equities into a solution is a huge problem when it comes to IEEPA. And, generally speaking, the way in which the Bureau deals with the State Department is that simply the Bureau does its thing, the State Department does its thing, and never the twain shall meet. So the problem is, when you get into everyone asserting their equities within the interagency process for an IEEPA designation, if one component objects, often that terminates, shuts down the whole thing, and that is not a good outcome.

Thank you, sir.

Senator SPECTER. Well, there is considerable concern by many in the Congress about Saudi Arabia being shielded for foreign policy reasons.

Mr. WINER. I have that concern, sir.

Senator SPECTER. That has been broadly expressed here today and in virtually every quarter. And one of the inquiries which has to be pursued is to what extent that is done and what are the policy ramifications, and it may be appropriate on public policy lines. But when you have a criminal investigation, an investigation into the U.S. Criminal Code, and there is probable cause to proceed, and it does not proceed because of foreign policy considerations, that is a matter which should attract the attention of the Congress at the highest levels. And that is an issue which is being pursued. It is not an easy issue to get answered.

Chairman Collins.

Chairman COLLINS. Thank you very much, Senator Specter.

Ambassador Gold, your exhibits are extremely persuasive and convincing in casting much doubt on the repeated claims by the Saudi Government that it is not funneling money to terrorist groups such as Hamas. Our previous FBI witness believes that there has finally been a sea change in the commitment of the Saudis since the bombing in May in Riyadh.

I want to ask you two questions. First, what is your general assessment of the commitment by the Saudis in the wake of the May bombing? Do you believe there really is an attitude change and a commitment now? And, second, have you seen any evidence that the May 12 bombings have caused the Saudis to cut back on their financial and other support for Hamas?

Mr. GOLD. Let me answer your question, Madam Chairman. I think one has to draw a fundamental distinction between what is going on domestically in Saudi Arabia and what might be going on globally. Certainly that is the evidence that I have at this point.

I think it is clear, anybody just perusing newspapers since May 12, that Saudi Arabia is taking a large number of counterterrorist actions at home in terms of unveiling different units of al-Qaeda or—and, by the way, in geographically different parts of the kingdom—or trying to find weapons caches. That seems to be what is going on there. Counterterrorism activity at home seems to be considerable in comparison to what existed before.

However, I can report to you with, let's say, full authority and perhaps even encapsulating the national intelligence assessment of Israel that at present, as we speak, approximately 50 to 70 percent of the Hamas budget comes from Saudi Arabia. And I would say that portion, the Saudi portion of Hamas funding, is growing rather than declining.

Now, that is all I can say about the particular case of Saudi Arabia and Hamas. I think it would be interesting to compare what is going on globally in the Philippines, in Russia, in East Africa, and with respect to al-Qaeda as well outside of Saudi Arabia to see whether their action is only aimed at protecting themselves domestically, but it is basically the same old business overseas.

Chairman COLLINS. Thank you.

Mr. Emerson, you raised a very good point in your statement that it is not only a matter of Saudi support, financial support for terrorist organizations but, rather, the curriculum, the schools, what Saudi children and Saudi-supported schools elsewhere are teaching young people and whether or not they are instilling a hatred of Christians and Jews. And to me that is equally disturbing because it helps raise a whole new generation of people who are going to be susceptible to terrorists, to involvement with terrorist groups.

Have you seen any change in Saudi schools since the events of September 11 or more recently since the bombing in Riyadh?

Mr. EMERSON. Since September 11, I can tell you Saudi officials have declared that they have reined in some of the clergy and they fired or, "re-educated more than a thousand clerics."

On the other hand, the fact of the matter is if one looks at the FBIS reports, the Foreign Broadcast Information Service reports, plus the Saudi media and Saudi television, which is openly available on satellite television, one can see routine demagoguery leveled against the United States, against Christians and Jews routinely. Saudi websites features are the demonization of Jews and Christians as well as moderate Muslims. And I think you should be aware of something else, very disturbing. This incitement is not necessarily illegal. It is considered free speech, and particularly in the United States. The problem is: How does one combat incitement within the context of an open society?

It is my feeling that incitement needs to have the sunshine to expose the whole virus of extremism, and those groups, entities, individuals that are propagating the incitement need to be delegitimized, or invited to the United States, or embraced. And I think that goes to the heart of getting Saudi Arabia to understand and recognize that it must rein in the extremists that in turn breed the terrorists that carried out September 11.

Chairman COLLINS. Thank you. May I do just one quick question for Mr. Winer?

Senator SPECTER. Absolutely.

Chairman COLLINS. Thank you.

Mr. Winer, you have experience in a previous administration, and I am trying to better understand why the U.S. Government has not been tougher with the Saudis. Do you believe that one factor, aside, perhaps, from our bases or oil, but I have heard that the U.S. Government has been hesitant to go after some suspected financers of terrorist groups because they are prominent Saudi business people. Do you think that is accurate?

Mr. WINER. Yes.

Chairman COLLINS. Could you expand further on why you think the Federal Government under both the previous administration and perhaps this administration as well has been somewhat reluctant to fully confront the Saudi Government in the wake of all of this compelling evidence?

Mr. WINER. I think a number of the factors are institutional and bureaucratic before you get to the additional factors pertaining to Saudi Arabia itself.

First, institutionally and bureaucratically, the only businessmen really that the U.S. Government went after prior to September 11 were Colombian businessmen who were also major cocaine traffickers. Prior to that, we used the International Emergency Economic Powers Act against countries or against military leaders, that kind of thing. These were businessmen. We were able to go after them because we found a computer in Colombia from the Cali cartel that listed all the businesses owned by these people who we had chapter and verse as drug traffickers. Easy case to make. Justice led making that case. Treasury, Mr. Newcomb strongly supported doing that because he felt all the facts were there, and it wasn't going to put IEEPA powers at risk, because what the U.S. Government is worried about, if we reach too far and somebody who is well funded goes after us and says you don't have the authority to do that, you don't have the public evidence to do that, we might lose some of that power. So there is an institutional concern. Don't overreach and then lose some of the power you have. Those are institutional and bureaucratic but very important constraints.

In the area of Saudi businessmen, you have got the problem of the fragmentary nature of the information, the fact that money is fungible, and just because a businessman funded a huge charity and that charity engaged in terrorist logistical support and recruitment in the Philippines and in the Middle East and in Chechnya and Bosnia and wherever, while also doing lots of wonderful other things, how do you know that that businessman when he gave that money intended the bad things as well as the good things? A difficult case to make.

So prior to September 11, you are having tremendous tensions over what is the right thing to do in light of those institutional issues, legal issues, practical issues, even before you get to the sensitivity of the Saudi relationship itself. The facts about terrorist finance, while voluminous, are also often rather murky and difficult to fully decipher. Our intelligence was poorly arrayed prior to September 11 to gather all the information we needed. The interagency process didn't work as well as it should have, although Dick Clark tried valiantly to put it together and did, I think, a remarkable job. We didn't have as many facts as we should have. But we went to the Saudis as a government, shared with them what we had, asked them for more information, warned them of what might take place, and ultimately nothing happened. I think those are all facts that are undisputable. The why's and the wherefore's and the what should's are really up to you all to determine next.

Thank you very much, Madam Chairman.

Chairman COLLINS. Thank you, Senator Specter.

Senator SPECTER. Thank you, Chairman Collins. Senator Pryor.

Senator PRYOR. Thank you.

Mr. Winer, if you can educate this Committee just very briefly, as I understand Saudi Arabia—tell me if this is true or not. But as I understand Saudi Arabia, the economic power and the political power really are merged into one in the sense of there are families and it is pretty much one and the same.

Mr. WINER. I know of no facts to dispute that assessment. I think that is right.

Senator PRYOR. OK. So sometimes when we talk about individuals doing something versus the government doing something, a lot of times it is a matter of an individual maybe in their personal capacity versus in some other official capacity, right? It is all a hodgepodge. It is all mixed up. Is that fair to say?

Mr. WINER. Yes, sir.

Senator PRYOR. One thing that we are sensitive to obviously here in this country is al-Qaeda as a terrorist organization. I know that Ambassador Gold has mentioned a few times, Hamas. In this country, we are not quite as tuned into that. But, Ambassador Gold, what other terrorist organizations in your personal view have ties to Saudi Arabia besides al-Qaeda and Hamas?

Mr. GOLD. Well, many of these organizations are part of all the same network. In fact, al-Qaeda should probably be seen as a consortium of terrorist organizations where they use the assets, sometimes manpower assets, sometimes financial, conduit assets, sometimes expertise in explosives, and share them around the world. Some of those assets are in the Philippines. Some of those assets are in Indonesia. Some of those assets are in Chechnya and Dagestan in Russia. Some of those assets are in Egypt. And Hamas, by the way, is part of that network to a large extent.

I think you can find the fingers of Saudi financial involvement through these charities with most of the countries that I mentioned.

Let me just add one other point to my presentation at this time. Many times you are going to see Saudi denials, very firm denials, that they have cleaned up their act, that these charitable contacts around the world no longer are with suspected groups. For example, there was a press release put out on October 18, 2002, by the Saudi Embassy in Washington, and in it the Saudis asserted that, since September 11, all charitable groups have been audited to ensure that there are no links to suspected groups.

Now, I don't know what a suspected group is and they don't clarify it, but you would think that a suspected group would be groups that are on the State Department list of terrorist organizations. Well, the very same month that in Washington the Saudis were putting this out as a press release to the Washington Press Corps, you had another little event going on in Riyadh, Saudi Arabia. You had a WAMY conference. And that photograph of Khaled Mashal, one of the highest leaders in the Hamas organization, was taken by Reuters at a WAMY conference in October 2002, the very same month. So, in Washington, they are saying that they are cutting off their contacts, the contacts of the charities, with suspected groups, yet in Riyadh you have the Saudis inviting one of the leaders of Hamas to a WAMY conference in Saudi Arabia.

By the way, the Hamas actually prepared a record of Khaled Mashal's meetings in Riyadh, and it was found by Israeli forces the following month in the Gaza Strip. And according to that record, Khaled Mashal was not just a peripheral guest of a peripheral organization, WAMY. He actually had a for-eyes meeting with Crown Prince Abdullah, who actually chaired that WAMY conference.

Senator PRYOR. Mr. Winer, if I may ask you, with the increased financial security on terrorist organizations around the world, do you see some new tactics out there that they are trying to do to get around some of our efforts? And what are those tactics, and what do we need to be looking for?

Mr. WINER. Yes, sir. One quick observation. I am not aware of any individual or entity that has been arrested for terrorist finance in Saudi Arabia to date. If there have been any such arrests, none of them have been publicly announced.

As to new techniques, gold markets and precious metals generally, commodities, diamonds, as Senator Akaka raised before, remain essentially unregulated globally. Regulation of charities globally still is extremely poor, and charities remain a tremendous opportunity well outside Saudi Arabia for moving terrorist funds.

The underground alternative remittance systems are still, by and large, extremely poorly regulated. In every country, we are beginning a crackdown. Here we have required them to register in theory. I am not sure whether that is as effective as it should be. Certainly registration of hawalas in the Middle East remains relatively minimalist in practice, and those networks are very substantial. Money continues to move back and forth in terms of currency from Yemen to Saudi Arabia and into and out of UAE. So our ability to track all of that, particularly in connection with remittances, some of which involve legitimate remittances and some of which don't, is poor. And the religious schools around the world generally have no oversight in terms of movements of money.

In the United States, if you go to the IRS filings for religious groups, mosques, synagogues, or churches—it doesn't matter what religion—all you have to do is say, "I am a mosque," "I am a church." That is all you have to report to the IRS. There is no further detail in the public filings beyond that. That is in the United States, which is presumably one of the better regulated countries. So I think that is still a potentially significant problem.

That said, formal financial institutions cannot risk being associated with terrorist finance. If the U.S. Government were to go after any major financial institution anywhere in the world with a terrorist finance designation, it would create such a chilling impact that one would imagine further due diligence, regulatory efforts be put into place by financial institutions all over the world to ensure that didn't happen to them and to protect shareholder interests and equities.

Thank you.

Senator PRYOR. Thank you for that answer, and I want to thank the panel for being here.

Senator SPECTER. Thank you, Senator Pryor.

The Committee intends to pursue the question as to whether economic sanctions are being imposed, and there are very substantial indicators that they are not. When Saudi Arabia is involved, we are soft on economic sanctions. But there is a broader picture which is emerging, and that is the potential for criminal sanctions.

We have held in the Judiciary Committee hearings several years ago on the focus on U.S. citizens being murdered in Israel by terrorist organizations. And we are pursuing the question of bringing those terrorists to the United States for trial.

In 1986, we passed the Terrorist Prosecution Act, which gives extraterritorial jurisdiction to the United States to bring terrorists into our courts and to impose the death penalty. And there are two cases which we are currently focusing on with Israeli Attorney General Rubenstein and U.S. Attorney General John Ashcroft. One involves an individual who is in the United States where requests have been made to get witnesses to testify about his conduct involved in terrorism and murder of American citizens, and that evidence has to be provided by Israel. And contacts have been made at the very highest level with the Israeli Government, and some assurances have been received that there will be cooperation.

There is another individual who confessed on television, with no question about the voluntariness of the confession. And the issue is getting that individual extradited to the United States, which is complicated because, as is well known, Israel does not have the death penalty. But there are exceptions under Israeli law where national security is involved. And when we go through the very impressive chart, Ambassador Gold, that you put up about Saudi national charities and the financing of international terrorism, and they are not non-governmental organization, they are governmental organizations, those individuals who finance Hamas are potentially liable for prosecution in the United States criminal courts because Hamas takes credit for the killings. The murders at Hebrew University were American. U.S. citizens were murdered.

So this is a matter that we need to pursue further on the hard evidentiary line. But I think that economic sanctions are fine. I would like to see them imposed, but there is a lot more that can be done.

Let me yield at this point to Senator Collins, and I will come back to questioning.

Chairman COLLINS. I just want to thank you, Senator, for spearheading this investigation. It is important, and the evidence we have heard in the statements this morning from the experts are compelling in painting a picture of the Saudi Government's many links to these charitable organizations and those organizations linked to terrorist groups. So I applaud your initiating this investigation, and I look forward to continuing to work with you.

Senator SPECTER. Well, thank you. Thank you, Senator Collins.

Senator Pryor, do you have any further questions?

Senator PRYOR. No.

Senator SPECTER. Then let me proceed just a bit further.

Ambassador Gold, you have testified about the document which was signed by the current Palestinian Prime Minister requesting that Saudi official stop financing Hamas. Would you go through that again and elaborate on precisely what it says?

Mr. GOLD. Well, we actually have an English translation.

Senator SPECTER. That is from Abu Mazen?

Mr. GOLD. Abu Mazen, yes. Also known as Mahmud Abbas.

Senator SPECTER. Who is the Palestinian Prime Minister.

Mr. GOLD. He is the Palestinian Prime Minister, and he wrote in his own handwriting a fax that was sent to Prince Salman, the governor of Riyadh and full brother of King Fahd, probably the fourth most powerful man in Saudi Arabia. And I can just read this paragraph to you that I have on the screen, which is an exact translation of the relevant material.

Senator SPECTER. Please do.

Mr. GOLD. "I hereby wish to inform you that he"—meaning Yasser Arafat—"has spoken with me on the telephone and asked me to transmit to you his request that you mediate and interfere and express his view concerning the ongoing situation in our homeland. The Saudi committee responsible for transferring the donations to beneficiaries has been sending large amounts to radical committees and associations, among which the Islamic Society"—that is a translation of al-Jamiya al-Islamiyah—"which belongs to Hamas, the al-Islah Association"—an association known to be a Hamas institution in Gaza—"and to the brethren who engage in jihad in all regions. This fact badly influences the internal situation. It also results in strengthening these brethren and has, therefore, a negative impact on all sides. Moreover, the Committee does not send any money or assistance to members of Fatah."

So this is, again, written not by an Israeli but by perhaps the No. 2 man in the Palestinian Authority today——

Senator SPECTER. Perhaps the No. 1 man.

Mr. GOLD. Well, a lot of people are hoping to make him the No. 1, Prime Minister Mahmud Abbas. It is in his own handwriting, and it was written in December 2002.

Senator SPECTER. I will come to you in a minute, Mr. Winer.

And it is directed to whom, again?

Mr. GOLD. Prince Salman is the governor of Riyadh, and it is directed to him. He is a full Sudairi brother of King Fahd, and I would say about the fourth most powerful man in Saudi Arabia.

Senator SPECTER. Do you have a judgment as to why the letter was written to him?

Mr. GOLD. Well, apparently they had sent messages to others as well, such as Prince Naif. But Salman has always been a kind of critical figure in many of the charitable enterprises, and perhaps that was why he was chosen.

Senator SPECTER. And when the last line says that no contributions were given to Fatah, what do you make of that?

Mr. GOLD. Well, I think here there is a desire, clearly, to make sure that all resources coming from Saudi Arabia go through the Fatah organization, which is the largest national component inside the Palestinian Authority. They want the money in their hands and not going to Hamas.

I think the importance of this document is that it clearly indicates that Saudi Arabia was funding Hamas in the year 2000, and we would say, as I said earlier, that funding is continuing to this day, in fact, becoming more significant as we speak.

Senator SPECTER. Mr. Winer, you had your hand up indicating a wish to say something?

Mr. WINER. It relates to this topic. Last year, FBIS reported that President Musharraf in Pakistan sent a similar communication to senior Saudi officials asking the Saudi Government to stop funding or Saudi Arabia to stop funding radical militants in madrassas in Pakistan who were creating problems of Islamic militancy within Pakistan for President Musharraf.

Senator SPECTER. What do you think we ought to do about that, Mr. Winer? You are a former State Department official.

Mr. WINER. I think that the Congress and the White House still speak with the bully pulpit, that they are communicating, as you are doing today, is important. Beyond that, I think sanctions have to be taken against particular entities, when we have sufficient evidence to determine that an entity, regardless of who——

Senator SPECTER. How about sanctions against the Saudi Arabian Government?

Mr. WINER. I think the first thing to do is sanctions against economic entities that are substantial where we have definitive information that those entities have been used to fund terrorism. That is what our law permits. That is what we have warned Saudi Arabia, among others, we could do. To the extent that we have the ability to do that and the evidentiary packages are sufficient, I think we should do it. That is my opinion.

Senator SPECTER. Ambassador Gold, to what extent, as you produce documents and show charts, is there an evidentiary chain which would go to these officials of the Saudi Government who are chairmen of these organizations, IIRO, WAMY, al-Haramain, to show the connection between those individuals and their direction of funds through these specific organizations to Hamas, which then results in the murders of U.S. citizens?

Mr. GOLD. I cannot supply the evidence to show that the heads, the chairmen of these organizations know where every dollar is going in these particular allocations to Hamas. But, again, the material showing that the organizations are allocating to Hamas is clear-cut.

I would say there is one other aspect here, I think, that should be taken into account. I cannot speak about how the U.S. Government should respond. I am an Israeli citizen. But we are now——

Senator SPECTER. We are going to reserve those questions for State Department officials. We are not going to ask an Israeli former Ambassador to tell us what to do.

Mr. GOLD. But I will comment on one aspect affecting policy today because the United States is now leading the way to implement what is called the road map, a performance-based road map to a permanent two-state solution. And in phase one of the road map—this is from the Department of State website—you can see that Arab States are expected to cut off public and private funding and all other forms of support for groups supporting and engaging in violence and terror. Therefore, I would say the crown jewels of U.S. Middle East policy, that is, the road map, specifically refers to cases like Saudi Arabia. In short, Saudi Arabia ought to go under the road map.

I would also add that at the Sharm El-Sheikh Summit on June 3, 2003, President Bush made a declaration in which he said he had the assurances of all those present that there would be no more terrorist funding, and here is the actual phrase that he used at the summit: "The leaders here today have declared their firm rejection of terror regardless of its justifications. They have also committed to practical actions to use all means to cut off assistance, including arms and financing, to any terror group."

So what you have is clear-cut U.S. policy to make sure that Saudi Arabia doesn't continue funding Hamas. I would say from the testimony you have heard today, the same networks that are working with Hamas are also working with al-Qaeda. If you make sure that the funding to Hamas stops, you will also, to a large extent, improve the national security of the United States by cutting off the funding routes to al-Qaeda as well.

Senator SPECTER. Ambassador Gold, when you say you can not say that these officials in these organizations, these governmental officials knew where every dollar went, I can understand that. But if they know that there are some dollars going to Hamas and they know Hamas is engaged in terrorism, and that terrorism results in murders of U.S. citizens, that is—you don't have to find where every dollar goes. You just have to be able to prove that they know that some dollars are going to terrorists.

Mr. GOLD. I would suggest they have a kind of corporate responsibility standing at the head, at the apex of these organizations to know about it.

Senator SPECTER. You can not establish criminal liability as the head of a corporation. You have got to prove that they knew what was going on, knowledge, participation, and acquiescence.

Mr. GOLD. The documents that I can supply can show the organizations' links to Hamas. I can also show you how the organization is structured. But you would have to go probably to U.S. agencies to find out whether any other information is available linking these individuals to Hamas funding.

Senator SPECTER. And when you have the connection to al-Qaeda, it is a much broader criminal responsibility. There you have the murders of 3,000 American citizens.

Mr. GOLD. That is absolutely true. But, again, I will only make statements here about things that I can document. What I have stated in this Committee hearing I can document.

Senator SPECTER. Well, the statement by the President that you have got on the board is about as good as you can get for him to extract those promises from the leaders of Saudi Arabia and other countries. And now the issue is pursuit to see to it that they live up to what they have said.

One other subject before adjourning. Mr. Emerson, your comment, I think, about the 7th graders who were having hate materials in their educational portfolios, that has been a problem ongoing for quite a long time. We have seen in the Palestinian Authority materials in grade schools, and part of the funding of the Palestinian Authority after Oslo, before we stopped the funding, was conditioned on changing, taking those materials out of the textbooks.

You have had considerable experience in this field. What recommendations would you have as to how to deal with the problem of this hate literature going to the next generation?

Mr. EMERSON. I think it is probably the most frustrating problem to deal with insofar as asking Saudi Arabia to stop the incitement within its own borders is basically asking it to essentially renounce its own Wahhabist ideology. There is a fundamental contradiction here.

On the other hand, as a result of the Riyadh attacks, I think more members of the family realize that the tiger is now coming to bite it and it cannot afford to keep paying off cooptation money overseas or even trying to essentially incite its citizens against Christians or Jews or Israelis or Americans in an effort to dissuade them from being frustrated with the regime itself.

But there is a fundamental contradiction here. My belief is that Saudi Arabia, as you have noted here, should be subject to the sanctions that were empowered by the PATRIOT Act because of the fact that foreign national central monetary institutions are allowed to be subject to sanctions if their funding mechanisms do not stop or are aware of terrorist financing. And I think the body of evidence of terrorist ties going back for the last 15 years on WAMY, IIRO, al-Haramain, and several other Saudi, "NGOs are so demonstrably present that it would be reckless disregard for anyone to say that they were unaware of those ties, let alone not taking responsibility."

At this point, I can tell you based on the information we have collected that there are direct ties between Saudi Government officials, the members of the family—not all, but some—and all of those NGOs in terms of the financial support and the largesse they receive.

One other point I would just like to add, because you have been very good in terms of pressing the government to make sure that it does not succumb to any political pressure. I can tell you based on discussions that I have had with law enforcement officials and prosecutors that while no one has said to me that they received a red light from the State Department, they have repeatedly expressed their frustration at the resistance within the government decisionmaking process to fully give them the green light to go after and conduct criminal investigations against Saudi entities and individuals. Part of the frustration is because Saudi Arabia has provided diplomatic immunity or actually pulled back some of the key witnesses, material witnesses that were being held here or subject to investigation and not made them available to the U.S. Government.

In other cases, it is the fear of antagonizing the Saudi regime that has basically put a red light to some of the key law enforcement prosecutions that are being considered at this point as we speak.

Senator SPECTER. Well, first you say there is no red light, and then you say there is not a green light. And we are not looking for amber in between. And then you just concluded by saying that there was a red light on criminal investigations. Could you amplify that a bit?

Mr. EMERSON. The red light insofar as a document that says we will not support a criminal investigation because of fear of engendering antagonism of the Saudi regime, I know of no such document that would ever be produced.

Senator SPECTER. Well, you wouldn't necessarily expect to have a document under seal, notarized. You might have a conversation. Who would want to put that in writing? Some congressional committee might get a hold of it.

Mr. EMERSON. Right, but you might not even have the conversation. It might just die, on the wane. In other words, it might not be acted upon.

Senator SPECTER. Well, there would be a reason for why it wasn't acted upon.

Mr. EMERSON. Well, there would be some type of bureaucratic reasons. Look, I can tell you documents we received under FOIA going back to 1996, 1997, and 1998, show that certain radical Islamic charities were being categorized as terrorist conduits back in those years—and yet they weren't frozen or had any sanctions against them until 2001. So something intervened to stop that designation and stop the asset forfeiture.

Now, I can not tell you what stopped it because I haven't received the documents—and I deal only with empirical evidence. But I know something stopped it, and I can only imagine that it was diplomatic pressure.

Senator SPECTER. Well, those are subjects we are going to pursue. One final comment. When you talk about Saudi textbooks responding to Wahhabi philosophy, there is a limit to how far you can go, even under those circumstances, as far as inciting murder. That crosses international lines, and it is an international crime. And we have got to look at the toughest lines, economic sanctions, criminal sanctions, whatever it takes.

Well, thank you very much, gentlemen. I think this has been informative, and stay tuned.

[Whereupon, at 12:41 p.m., the Committee was adjourned.]

APPENDIX

Senate Committee on Governmental Affairs
John S. Pistole
Deputy Assistant Director
Counterterrorism Division
Federal Bureau of Investigation

July 31, 2003

"Terrorism Financing: Origination, Organization, and Prevention"

Good morning Madam Chair Collins, Senator Lieberman, and other distinguished members of the committee. It is an honor to testify before this committee regarding the FBI's efforts in identifying, tracking and dismantling the financial structure supporting terrorist groups.

Prior to the events of September 11, 2001 (9/11), the FBI had no mechanism to provide a comprehensive, centralized, focused and pro-active approach to terrorist financial matters. While the FBI examined financial records at the time of previous terrorist attacks, as part of the investigation into each of the attacks, the events of 9/11 identified a critical need for a more comprehensive, centralized approach to financial matters. The Terrorist Financing Operations Section (TFOS) of the FBI's Counterterrorism Division was formed, after 9/11, in response to this critical need. The mission of the TFOS has since evolved into a broader strategy to identify, investigate, prosecute, disrupt and dismantle incrementally, all terrorist related financial and fund-raising activities.

Identifying, tracking and dismantling the financial structure supporting terrorist groups is critical to successfully dismantling the organizations and preventing future terrorist attacks. As is the case in most investigations, locating and "following the money" plays a critical role in identifying those involved in the criminal activity, establishing links among them, and developing evidence of their involvement in the activity.

Terrorists, their networks and support structures, require funding in some form to exist and operate. Whether the funding and financial support is minimal or substantial, it usually leaves a financial trail that can be traced, tracked, and exploited for pro-active and reactive purposes. Being able to identify and track financial transactions and links after a terrorist act has occurred or terrorist activity has been identified, represents only a small portion of the mission; the key lies in exploiting financial information in efforts to identify previously unknown terrorist cells, recognize potential terrorist activity/planning, and predict and prevent potential terrorist acts.

In forming the TFOS, the FBI built upon its traditional expertise in conducting complex criminal financial investigations and long established relationships with the financial services communities in the United States and abroad. Integrating these skills and resources with the Counterterrorism Division, allows the FBI to bring its full assets to bear in the financial war on terrorism.

The TFOS is both an operational and coordinating entity with pro-active and reactive responsibilities. As a coordinating entity, the TFOS is responsible for ensuring that a unified approach is pursued in investigating terrorist financing networks. The TFOS achieves this directive by: 1) coordinating the financial aspects of FBI Field Office and Legat terrorism investigations; 2) establishing overall initiatives, policy and guidance on terrorist financing matters; 3) participating in the National Security Council's Policy Coordinating Committee (PCC) on Terrorist Financing; 4) coordinating national liaison with the financial services sector; 5) cooperating in and coordinating criminal terrorist financing investigations with the Department of Justice; and 5) providing support and training to Field Offices to include the designated Terrorism Financing Coordinator (TFC) .

It is critical that the financial aspects of terrorism investigations be adequately addressed and that a concerted, coordinated effort is made to investigate terrorist finance issues by experienced financial investigators. Rarely will a terrorist financing investigation be confined to the territory of one field office, rather they normally span not only multiple field office jurisdictions, but the globe; i.e., these types of investigations will frequently be linked to investigations and/or issues in other jurisdictions and other countries. It is imperative that these investigative efforts be effectively coordinated, placed into perspective with other counterterrorism efforts, prioritized in accordance with national and global strategies, and addressed in concert rather than in a disjointed, inefficient manner. Prior to the establishment of the TFOS, there did not exist within the FBI a mechanism to ensure appropriate focus on terrorist finance issues and provide the necessary expertise and overall coordination to comprehensively address these matters.

So how far have we come in the war on terrorist financing since 9/11? There currently exists a much better understanding of terrorist financing methods. More sophisticated and effective processes and mechanisms to address and target terrorist financing continue to develop and evolve. Pro-active approaches are increasingly being utilized. The awareness around the world on the part of law enforcement, government agencies, regulators and policy makers, and the private sector of terrorist financing methods, suspicious financial activity and vulnerabilities is much higher since 9/11. International cooperation has reached unparalleled levels. Outreach with, and cooperation from, the private sector has been outstanding and continues to develop, particularly the level of two-way interaction between law enforcement and the private sector. The ability to access and obtain this type of information immediately has significantly enhanced the FBI's ability to identify, investigate, and resolve immediate threat situations involving potential terrorist activity. For example, the ability to conduct real-time monitoring of specifically identified financial activity has been invaluable to not only investigations ongoing in the US, but to foreign law enforcement and intelligence agencies in related investigations. Another example of not only more pro-active measures but also of increased cooperation and coordination with the international community.

Extensive training and support of international investigations by TFOS has led to Agent visits/exchanges and training programs involving a variety of countries from Europe, Southeast Asia, the Middle East, South America, etc. In support of specific high profile joint terrorist financial investigative matters, a number of countries and agencies, including the United Kingdom, Switzerland, Canada and Europol, have detailed investigators to TFOS on a TDY basis. TFOS has engaged in extensive coordination with authorities of numerous foreign governments in terrorist financing matters, leading to joint investigative efforts throughout the world. These joint investigations have successfully targeted the financing of several overseas al-Qa'ida cells, including those located in Indonesia, Malaysia, Singapore, Spain, and Italy. Furthermore, with the assistance of relationships established with the central banks of several strategic countries, successful disruptions of al-Qa'ida financing have been accomplished in counties such as the UAE, Pakistan, Afghanistan, and Indonesia.

TFOS has developed a specific terrorist financing/money laundering crimes curriculum for international training which includes topics such as: acquiring and handling evidence in document intensive financial investigations, major case management techniques, forensic examination tools, and methods of terrorist financing. At the request of the US Department of State, TFOS has led an interagency team to provide this curriculum to a number of countries (and is scheduled to provide to approximately 38 countries) identified as needing law enforcement training on conducting terrorist financing investigations.

TFOS has cultivated and maintains a contact database of private industry and government sources/persons who can provide financial data, including real-time monitoring of financial transactions. Many of these contacts can be reached or accessed on 24 hour/7 days a week emergency allowing TFOS to respond rapidly to critical incidents.

Through these contacts the TFOS has access to data and information from a variety of entities including: Banking, Credit/Debit Card Sector, Money Services Businesses, Securities/Brokerages Sector, Insurance, Travel, Internet Service Providers, Telecommunications Industry, Law Enforcement, State/Federal Regulatory Agencies, Public and Open Source Data Providers, the Intelligence Community, and International Law Enforcement and Intelligence Contacts. The timeliness and accessibility of the data is contingent on a variety of factors including whether the acquisition of the information requires legal process, the search capabilities of the data provider, and the size and depth of the data request. The ability to access and obtain this type of information in a time sensitive and urgent manner has significantly enhanced the FBI's ability to identify, investigate and resolve immediate threat situations involving potential terrorist activity. For example, the ability to conduct real-time monitoring of specifically identified financial activity has been invaluable to not only investigations ongoing in the US, but to foreign law enforcement and intelligence agencies in related investigations.

Being able to identify and track financial transactions and links after a terrorist act has occurred or terrorist activity has been identified represents only a small portion of the mission; the key lies in exploiting financial information in efforts to identify previously unknown terrorist cells, recognize potential terrorist activity/planning, and predict and prevent potential terrorist acts. Prior to 9/11, there was not enough emphasis placed on addressing the mechanisms and systems associated with terrorist financing and disrupting them before they could be utilized to further terrorist activities. Since September 11, TFOS, together with the Counter-Terrorism Section (CTS), Criminal Division of the Department of Justice (DOJ), have begun a number of pro-active link analysis initiatives to identify potential terrorists and terrorist related financing activities.

The overriding goal of these projects is to pro-actively identify potential terrorists and terrorist related individuals/entities, mechanisms or schemes through the digital exploitation of data. To accomplish this, TFOS seeks to 1) identify potential electronic data sources within domestic and foreign government and private industry providers; 2) create pathways and protocols to acquire and analyze the data; and 3) provide both reactive and proactive operational, predictive and educational support to investigators and prosecutors.

Information sharing is critical to all of our efforts. The intelligence community, including the FBI, produces and obtains tremendous amounts of classified intelligence information. While much of the information can be of significant value in terrorist finance investigations, the value will not be realized nor maximized absent the ability to filter the information, analyze it, and disseminate it in an appropriate manner to those who can make the best use of the information. Toward this end, the TFOS participates in joint endeavors involving the CIA, FBI, Treasury Department, Department of Justice, and the Department of Homeland Security involving potential terrorist related financial transactions, in addition to other joint participation between TFOS and the intelligence agencies. TFOS has personnel detailed to the CIA/CTC/FINO and personnel from there work directly with TFOS on financial intelligence matters.

The National Security Council formalized the Policy Coordinating Committee (PCC) on Terrorist Financing at the end of 2001. Treasury chairs the PCC and representatives from the Central Intelligence Agency, the Department of Defense, the Department of Justice, the Federal Bureau of Investigation, the Department of Homeland Security, the National Security Council and the State Department attend meetings.

The PCC generally meets at least once a month to coordinate the United States government's campaign against terrorist financing. The meeting generally focuses on ensuring that all relevant components of the federal government are acting in a coordinated and effective manner to combat terrorist financing.

Terrorist Financing Successes

In addition, the FBI, working in coordination with other entities of the US government, has participated in the following successes:

- An FBI Joint Terrorism Task Force in Charlotte used racketeering statutes to obtain convictions which disrupted and dismantled a Hizballah procurement and fund-raising cell. Twenty-six individuals were arrested for crimes including immigration fraud, visa fraud, cigarette smuggling, interstate transportation of stolen property, fraud, bank fraud, bribery, money laundering, racketeering, and providing material support to a terrorist organization.

- The FBI coordinated with the Office of Foreign Asset Control (OFAC) to justify the blocking of Holy Land Foundation for Relief and Development (HLF) assets and the closing of its US offices, shutting down HAMAS' largest fund-raising entity in the US. The HLF had been linked to the funding of HAMAS terrorist activities, and in 2000, HLF raised $13 million.

- Offices of the Benevolence International Foundation (BIF), a US based charity, were shut down and its assets and records blocked following an OFAC and FBI investigation which determined that the charity was being used to funnel money to Al Qa'ida. In February 2003, Enaam Arnaout, the head of BIF, pled guilty to racketeering conspiracy, admitting he fraudulently obtained charitable donations in order to provide financial assistance to persons engaged in violent activities overseas.

- As a result of information developed by the FBI, a foreign security service, in conjunction with US Intelligence Community agencies, apprehended one of the most significant money launderers associated with Usama Bin Laden, for funneling $67 million through international accounts to al-Qa'ida and the Taliban.

- A criminal case against Sami Al Arian, the alleged US leader of the Palestinian Islamic Jihad (PIJ), and the World Islamic Studies Enterprise has forced the closure of several front companies suspected of funneling money to support PIJ operations against Israel. In August 2002, the investigation led to the deportation of Mazen Al-Najjar, the brother-in-law of Sami Al Arian and a known PIJ member. In February, following a 50-count indictment for RICO and Material Support of terrorism violations, the FBI arrested Al-Arian and three other U.S.-based members of the Palestinian Islamic Jihad, including Sameeh Hammoudeh, Hatim Naji Fariz, and Ghassan Ballout. The FBI also executed seven search warrants associated with this action.

- TFOS has provided operational support to FBI Field Divisions across the United States to enhance the intelligence/criminal investigations of individuals and groups, associated with or providing material support to, terrorist organizations and activities. This assistance is provided in the form of conducting intelligence/criminal financial investigations, financial analytical support, major case management, financial link analysis, and the deployment of teams of experts to develop investigative plans to analyze large volumes of documents and data. TFOS has provided this operational support in the Al Qa'ida sleeper cell cases in Buffalo and Portland, as well as in the Richard Reid, John Walker Lindh, Jose Padilla, Al Haramain, PIJ, and Mohamed Almoayad cases, among many others. This type of operational support has also been provided to Divisions investigating NGOs, such as the Holy Land Foundation for Relief and Development, Benevolence International Foundation and the Global Relief Foundation.

- TFOS has engaged in extensive coordination with authorities of numerous foreign governments in terrorist financing matters, leading to joint investigative efforts throughout the world. These joint investigations have successfully targeted the financing of several overseas Al Qa'ida cells, including those located in Indonesia, Malaysia, Singapore, Spain, and Italy. Furthermore, with the assistance of relationships established with the central banks of several strategic countries, successful disruptions of Al Qa'ida financing have been accomplished in counties such as the UAE, Pakistan, Afghanistan, and Indonesia.

- The FBI conducted a detailed financial investigation/analysis of the19 hijackers and their support network, following the September 11th attacks. This investigation initially identified the Al Qa'ida funding sources of the 19 hijackers in the UAE and Germany. The financial investigation also provided the first links between Ramzi Binalshibh and the 9/11 operation. A continuing investigation, in coordination with the PENTTBOMB Team, has traced the origin of the funding of 9/11 back to financial accounts in Pakistan, where high-ranking and well-known Al Qa'ida operatives played a major role in moving the money forward, eventually into the hands of the hijackers located in the U.S. As part of the 9/11 financial investigation, thousands of individuals and organizations were investigated in the U.S. and abroad to determine whether they played any part in supporting the hijackers or the operation. Although the vast majority of these individuals and organizations were cleared, this process of elimination resulted in numerous other quality terrorism investigations being initiated, as well as criminal charges against hundreds of individuals for fraud and other criminal activity.

- At the request of a foreign liaison service, TFOS traced financial transactions in a near real-time manner which led to the location of a terrorist cell and prevention of a terrorist act.

- Since 9/11, the United States has frozen $36.3 million in terrorist assets while other countries have frozen an estimated $97 million, for a total of over $133 million.

- U.S. authorities issued blocking orders on the assets of 281 terrorists, terrorist organizations, and terrorist supporters, effectively denying them access to the U.S. financial system.

- Federal law enforcement officials have arrested over 61 individuals, indicted 43 and convicted 12 in connection with terrorist financing investigations.

- U.S. Government agencies, to include the FBI's TFOS, deployed trainers and advisers on missions to countries around the world to assist with the drafting of legislation to combat terrorist financing, strengthen bank supervision in identifying suspicious transactions, and address other financial crimes and corruption.

- Since 9/11, over 120 countries have introduced new terrorist-related legislation and approximately 80 countries established Financial Investigation Units.

Saudi Arabia and the War on Terrorism

Following the 9/11 attacks, it became apparent that the role of Non-Governmental Organizations (NGOs) and charitable organizations, as a source of funding for terrorist groups, needed closer scrutiny. This included the role of Saudi Arabia and its citizens in the support of terrorism, both directly and indirectly, through the financial support of these charitable organizations.

The Kingdom of Saudi Arabia has taken proactive measures to deter global terrorism. In 1995, the bombing of Khobar Towers occurred in Saudi Arabia. In 1996, the Kingdom established a joint Counter-Terrorism Committee with the United States to share information on al-Qa'ida. In the wake of September 11, Saudi Arabia has increased its counterterrorism efforts with the following initiatives:

- Saudi Arabia has put new laws and regulations in place for all charitable groups, ensuring that they are audited to prevent the flow of funds to entities other than charity.

- Saudi Arabia has further strengthened its laws and regulations regarding money laundering. These efforts include new rules concerning the verification of customers' identities as well as restrictions on non-residents' ability to open accounts in the country.

- Saudi Arabia and the United States maintain a Counter-Terrorism Committee comprised of intelligence and law enforcement personnel who meet regularly to share information and resources and develop action plans to root out terrorist networks.

- In March 2002, Saudi Arabia and the US jointly blocked the accounts of Bosnia and Somalia branches of Al-Haramain Islamic Foundation, and in the summer of 2002, jointly froze the assets of the Rabita Trust, and those of its director Wa'el Hamza Julaidan, an associate of Bin Laden who provided financial and logistical support to al-Qa'ida.

- Saudi Arabia has contributed to the break up of a number of al-Qa'ida cells, the arrests of key al-Qa'ida leaders and capture of al-Qa'ida members in Saudi Arabia.

Since the May 12, 2003 bombings of the three western compounds in Riyadh, Saudi Arabia, cooperation with the Kingdom of Saudi Arabia has improved. The FBI sent an investigative team to the Kingdom and worked with the law enforcement and intelligence services to conduct the appropriate post incident investigation and evidence collection. Cooperation with the Saudi Arabian government continues on this and other terrorism investigations.

The USA PATRIOT Act and Other Legislation

Our efforts to combat terrorism have been greatly aided by the provisions of the PATRIOT Act. The success in preventing another catastrophic attack on the U.S. homeland would have been much more difficult, if not impossible, without the Act. It has already proved extraordinarily beneficial in the war on terrorism, and our opportunities to use it will only increase. Most importantly, the PATRIOT Act has produced greater collection and sharing of information within the law enforcement and intelligence communities.

Title III of the Act, also known as the International Money Laundering Anti-Terrorist Financing Act of 2001, has armed us with a number of new weapons in our efforts to identify and track the financial structure supporting terrorist groups. Past terrorist financing methods have included the use of informal systems for transferring value in a manner that is difficult to detect and trace. The effectiveness of such methods should be significantly eroded by the Act, which establishes stricter rules for correspondent bank accounts, requires securities brokers and dealers to file Suspicious Activity Reports or SARS, and certain money services to register with FinCEN and file SARS for a wider range of financial transactions.

There are other provisions of the Act that have considerably aided our efforts to address the terrorist threat including: strengthening the existing ban on providing material support to terrorists and terrorist organizations; the authority to seize terrorist assets; and the power to seize money subject to forfeiture in a foreign bank account by authorizing the seizure of a foreign bank's funds held in a U.S. correspondent account.

It is important for the Committee and the American people to know that the FBI is using the PATRIOT Act authorities in a responsible manner. We are making every effort to effectively balance our obligation to protect Americans from terrorism, with our obligation to protect their civil liberties.

Executive Branch Organizational Changes

Organizational changes that have taken place within the Executive Branch with respect to the investigation of terrorism financing include the execution of a Memorandum of Agreement (MOA) between the Department of Justice (DOJ) and the Department of Homeland Security (DHS) concerning terrorist financing investigations. The MOA addresses the importance of waging a seamless, coordinated campaign against terrorist sources of financing. It was signed by Attorney General Ashcroft and Homeland Security Secretary Ridge on May 13, 2003. Prior to this agreement, both the DOJ and DHS had separate terrorist financing task forces. Under DOJ, the FBI had the TFOS, which was discussed earlier. The DHS had the Bureau of Immigration and Customs (ICE) led Operation Green Quest (OGQ).

Pursuant to the MOA, OGQ ceased to exist as a program name as of June 30, 2003. Accordingly, the FBI was designated to lead terrorist financing investigations and operations. It was agreed that DHS would focus its activities on protecting the integrity of U.S. financial infrastructures. To that extent, the DHS implemented the ICE led Operation Cornerstone. Operation Cornerstone will identify vulnerabilities in financial systems through which criminals launder their illicit proceeds, bring the criminals to justice and work to eliminate the vulnerabilities.

The majority of the former OGQ case inventory was criminal cases, with no nexus to terrorism. These cases were converted from OGQ to Operation Cornerstone. Those cases that had a nexus to terrorism that were investigated by the former OGQ are currently being assessed for transition to the appropriate FBI Joint Terrorism Task Force (JTTF). Ongoing and future Operation Cornerstone investigations that develop links to terrorism will be referred to the FBI through the TFOS. The ICE and TFOS are coordinating investigative initiatives that will enable the ICE to identify financial systemic vulnerabilities and which will enable the TFOS to identify ties to terrorism and terrorist financing. In addition, there is a liaison from ICE assigned to TFOS, and investigators from ICE will be represented on the JTTFs.

Terrorism represents a global problem. The solution is grounded in what would have been considered prior to 9/11, unprecedented international cooperation and coordination. The threat it poses must always be considered imminent. In addition to considerable financial investigative expertise, addressing terrorism and the finances that support and propagate it requires the ability to both implement proactive and preventive approaches to disrupt and dismantle as well as the ability to conduct highly reactive immediate response financial investigations to address potential imminent threats. As stated herein and in conjunction with more and more of the international community and other aspects of the US Government, the FBI has made considerable progress toward achieving and implementing these abilities.

Again, I offer my gratitude and appreciation to you, Madam Chair Collins, Senator Specter, and the Governmental Affairs Committee, for dedicating your time and effort to this issue and I would be happy to respond to any questions.

STATEMENT OF R. RICHARD NEWCOMB, DIRECTOR
OFFICE OF FOREIGN ASSETS CONTROL
U.S. DEPARTMENT OF THE TREASURY
BEFORE THE
COMMITTEE ON GOVERNMENTAL AFFAIRS
UNITED STATES SENATE
HEARINGS ON TERRORISM FINANCING: ORIGINATION, ORGANIZATION AND PREVENTION
JULY 31, 2003

Madam Chairman, members of the Committee, thank you for the opportunity to testify on OFAC's efforts to combat terrorist support networks that threaten United States citizens and property worldwide. It's a pleasure to be here. Please allow me to begin with a brief general overview of the problem, as I see it.

Foundations of Terrorist Financing and Support

The threat of terrorist support networks and financing is real, and it has been our mission to help identify and disrupt those networks. The vast majority of the world's Muslims are peaceful, though a committed, vocal, and well-organized minority is competing to mobilize a new generation in the tools and trade of Jihad.

There is much we know about how such radical Islamic terrorist networks were established and still thrive. Wealthy and influential individuals and families based in the Middle East have provided seed money and support to build a transnational support infrastructure that terrorists have used for their purposes. This network, fueled by deep-pocket donors and often controlled by terrorist organizations, their supporters or those willing to look the other way, includes or implicates banks, businesses, NGOs, charities, social services organizations, schools, mosques, madrassas, and affiliated terrorist training camps and safe houses throughout the world.

The terrorist networks are well-entrenched and self-sustaining, though vulnerable to U.S., allied and international efforts applying all tools at our disposal. Looking forward, please allow me to explain how we have come to this view and present the strategy, being implemented in coordination with other Federal agencies including the Departments of Defense, State, Justice, Homeland Security, the FBI, the intelligence community and other agencies, to choke off the key nodes in the transnational terrorist support infrastructure.

OFAC Mission and Experience on Counterterrorism

The primary mission of the Office of Foreign Assets Control ("OFAC") of the U.S. Department of the Treasury is to administer and enforce economic sanctions against targeted foreign countries and foreign groups and individuals, such as terrorists and terrorist organizations and narcotic traffickers, which pose a threat to the national security, foreign policy or economy of the U.S. OFAC acts under general Presidential wartime and national emergency powers, as well as specific legislation, to prohibit transactions and freeze (or "block") assets subject to U.S. jurisdiction. Economic sanctions are intended to deprive the target of the use of its assets and deny the target access to the U.S. financial system and the benefits of trade, transactions and services involving U.S. markets, businesses and individuals. These same authorities have also been used to protect assets within the U.S. jurisdiction of countries subject to foreign occupation and to further important U.S. nonproliferation goals.

OFAC currently administers and enforces 26 economic sanctions programs pursuant to Presidential and Congressional mandates. Active enforcement of these programs is a crucial element in preserving and advancing the foreign policy and national security objectives that underlie these initiatives that are usually taken in conjunction with diplomatic, law enforcement and occasionally military action. In 1977, the Congress passed the International Emergency Economic Powers Act ("IEEPA"), which serves as the primary statutory authority for a Presidential declaration of a national emergency in peacetime for the purpose of imposing economic sanctions.

Many "country-based" sanctions programs are part of the U.S. government's response over time to the threat to U.S. national security and foreign policy posed by international terrorism. The Secretary of State has designated seven countries - Cuba, North Korea, Iran, Libya, Iraq, Sudan and Syria - as supporting international terrorism. Most of these countries are subject to comprehensive economic sanctions, including: Cuba (1963); Iran (1979 and again in

1987); Libya (1986); and Sudan (1997). Comprehensive sanctions against Iraq, originally imposed in 1990, were recently lifted although the national emergency remains in place. Comprehensive sanctions against North Korea, originally imposed in 1950, were lifted in 2000, except with respect to North Korean imports and "Weapons of Mass Destruction" blockings. Syria is not subject to comprehensive sanctions; however, certain financial transactions involving all terrorism list countries including Syria are regulated.

The origins of OFAC's involvement in the fight against terrorism stem from the initial conception of terrorism as being solely state-sponsored. OFAC's mandate in the realm of terrorism was to compile available evidence establishing that certain foreign entities or individuals were owned or controlled by, or acting for on behalf of, a foreign government subject to an economic sanctions program. Such entities and individuals become "specially designated nationals," ("SDNs") and are subject to the same sanctions as the foreign government to which they are related.

Authorities to Target Non State Organizations, Individuals and Entities

In January 1995, the President used the IEEPA authorities to deal with the threat to U.S. foreign policy and national security posed by terrorists who threaten to disrupt the Middle East Peace Process. This marked the beginning of the use of IEEPA sanctions authorities to target terrorists, terrorist groups and their sources of fundraising. This action, implemented through Executive Order 12947, opened the door to new programs and expanded the use of economic sanctions as a tool of U.S. foreign policy to target groups and individuals, as well as foreign governments. During the late 1990s, IEEPA authorities were used to issue additional Executive orders imposing sanctions on Al-Qaeda, and Usama bin Ladin. These E.O.s also provide authority to designate and sanction entities or individuals that are owned or controlled by, act for or on behalf of, or that provide material or financial support to Al-Qaeda or Usama bin Ladin.

Following this model, in October 1995, during a speech at a UN 50th anniversary celebration, the President announced the concept of adapting E.O. 12947 to target significant foreign narcotics traffickers centered in Colombia, i.e., the Colombian drug trafficking cartels. That IEEPA program, under E.O. 12978, began with the President identifying four Cali Cartel drug kingpins, and has expanded into a key tool in the fight against the Colombian cartels. As of today, 14 Colombian drug kingpins, 340 entities, and 470 other individuals associated with the Cali, North Valle, and North Coast cartels' and their business empires have been designated as Specially Designated Narcotics Traffickers ("SDNTs") under E.O. 12978.

Building on the successes of the Colombian cartels Program under E.O. 12978, in December 1999, Congress enacted the Foreign Narcotics Kingpin Designation Act ("Kingpin Act"), originally introduced by Senators Coverdell and Feinstein, modeled on IEEPA and OFAC's SDNT program. It provides a statutory framework for the President to impose sanctions against foreign drug kingpins and their organizations on a worldwide scale. Like the terrorism program under E.O. 12947 and the SDNT program under E.O. 12978, the Kingpin Act is directed against the individual or entity and their support infrastructure, not against the countries in which they are imbedded. Since the first list of kingpins was issued under that authority, 38 foreign drug kingpins (these are in addition to the 14 Colombian drug kingpins designated under E.O. 12978), 11 derivative companies, and 15 derivative individuals have been designated.

The Congress, in 1996, passed the Antiterrorism and Effective Death Penalty Act ("AEDPA"). AEDPA makes it a criminal offense to: (1) engage in a financial transaction with the government of a country designated as supporting international terrorism; or (2) provide material support or resources to a designated Foreign Terrorist Organization (FTO).

Currently, 36 FTOs are subject to OFAC-administered sanctions. These FTOs have been designated by the Secretary of State in consultation with the Secretary of the Treasury and the Attorney General. Under the AEDPA and OFAC's implementing regulations, U.S. financial institutions must maintain control over all funds in which an FTO has an interest and report those actions to OFAC. OFAC is the coordination point with State and Justice on FTO designations and also has responsibility for coordinating with the financial community, the FBI, State, and other Federal agencies in implementing the prohibitions of the AEDPA.

Authorities in Response to September 11th

The President harnessed these economic powers and authorities in launching the war against terrorism. In response to the terrorist attacks of September 11, and pursuant to the powers available to the President under IEEPA, President Bush issued Executive Order 13224, "Blocking Property and Prohibiting Transactions with Persons Who Commit, Threaten to Commit, or Support Terrorism" declaring that the acts of grave terrorism and the threats of terrorism committed by foreign terrorists posed an unusual and extraordinary threat to the national security, foreign policy, and economy of the United States. E.O. 13224, as amended, authorizes the Secretary of the Treasury, in consultation with the Department of State, Department of Justice and the Department of Homeland Security, to implement the President's authority to systemically and strategically attack terrorists, terrorist organizations and terrorist support networks.

This order prohibits U.S. persons from transacting or dealing with individuals and entities owned or controlled by, acting for or on behalf of, assisting or supporting, or otherwise associated with, persons listed in the Executive Order. Those designated and listed under the Executive Order are known as "Specially Designated Global Terrorists", or SDGTs. Violations of the E.O. with respect to SDGTs are subject to civil penalties; and if the violation is willful, persons may be criminally charged. The Executive Order also blocks "all property and interests in property of [designated persons] that are in the United States or that hereafter come within the United States, or that hereafter come within the possession or control of United States persons[.]"[1]

The PATRIOT Act, passed in October 2001, amends IEEPA to provide critical means and authority to OFAC to counter terrorist financing. The Act has enhanced OFAC's ability to implement sanctions and to coordinate with other agencies by clarifying OFAC's authorities to block assets of suspect entities prior to a formal designation in "aid of an investigation." This critical authority helps prevent the flight of assets and prevents the target from engaging in potential damaging behavior or transactions.

Prior to the passage of the PATRIOT Act, OFAC was wary of relying on classified information under IEEPA programs, because, unlike the Antiterrorism and Effective Death Penalty Act of 1996, IEEPA did not contain a provision explicitly authorizing submission of classified information to a court, in camera and ex parte, upon a legal challenge to a designation. The new PATRTIOT Act authority has greatly enhanced our ability to make and defend designations by making it absolutely clear that OFAC may use classified information in making designations without turning the material over to an entity or individual that challenges its designation.

Rolling FTO's into SDGT's Makes War on Terrorist Infrastructure Global

On November 2, 2001, the U.S. took a significant step in the War on Terrorism when the Secretary of State, in consultation with the Secretary of the Treasury and the Attorney General, utilized the new authorities in E.O. 13224 to designate 22 Foreign Terrorist Organizations (FTOs) as Specially Designated Global Terrorists (SDGTs). This action expanded the War on Terrorism beyond Al-Qaeda and the Taliban and associated individuals and entities to include Hamas, Hizballah, the FARC, the Real IRA and others. As then recognized by the State Department, this action created a truly global war on terrorism and terrorist financing and demonstrated our commitment to continue and expand our efforts against all terrorist groups posing a threat to the United States, our citizens, our interests, and our allies. Currently, there are 36 FTOs which are also designated as SDGTs.

To date, the U.S. has designated 281 individuals and entities as SDGTs pursuant to E.O. 13224. 202 of these entities are associated with either Al-Qaeda or the Taliban which provides the basis to notify these names to the UN for listing pursuant to United Nations Security Resolutions (UNSCRs) 1267, 1333, 1373, 1390 and 1455. The United States has worked diligently with the UN Security Council to adopt international resolutions reflecting the goals of our domestic executive orders and providing the mechanisms for UN member states to freeze terrorist-related assets.

Using Designation Authorities in Cooperation with International Partners

The emerging international threat of Al Qaeda in the 1990s necessitated OFAC's participation in the U.S. government's focus on developing information and strategies against terrorist financing and infrastructures. In that context, it was clear that the cooperation of foreign governments, including Saudi Arabia, Kuwait and the UAE, would be critical in impeding the flow of funds to terrorists.

Having developed an understanding of how terrorist support networks operate, we began direct engagements with allies. For example, in June 1999, an OFAC delegation met with Finance Ministry, Intelligence and Law enforcement officials in Saudi Arabia, Kuwait and the UAE. The purpose of the trip was to find answers to certain questions we were unable to resolve to our satisfaction and to put officials on notice that cooperation on these issues was critical. We were clear that U.S. interest in these issues would continue.

In these meetings and others held subsequently in the region, we shared information and asked questions. Through the discussions, we identified areas where we could work together. These areas included strengthening the weak regulatory authorities over financial institutions and discussing the possibility for creating new oversight for charities. These proposals were met with assurances of cooperation, but we understood that getting assistance on these issues would be a serious challenge because it represented a change in policies and structures within governments and societies.

Importantly, in efforts to crack down on support for terrorists and terrorist fundraising, we have always made clear the intent of the U.S. government to deal with these issues cooperatively. A key element of our strategy and engagement was to take open, decisive action with host governments against several high impact targets. The designation and blocking of assets of high-profile supporters of terrorist groups could deter others, forcing key nodes of financial support to choose between public exposure of their support for terrorist activity or their good reputation. We believed this approach could also be effective against banks, business, NGOs and other institutions.

We traveled to Saudi Arabia again in January 2000. The purpose was again to communicate that the U.S. wanted to work with Saudi officials jointly in efforts to crack down on support for terrorists and terrorist fundraising. At the time however, we did not have many of the tools necessary to sufficiently back up threats with action; especially, in cases where the target was assessed as intransigent. This is the strategy that has been in place since September 11th as one of the means of deterring and disrupting terrorist financing. The tools Congress and the President have given us since September 11th have enhanced our ability to deliver this message and carry out this strategy.

Post 9-11 Efforts

After the 9-11 attacks, President Bush rallied the international community to unite in the war on terrorism. The international community, including our allies in the Persian Gulf, joined us and have committed to fully cooperating on all fronts against Al-Qaeda and its supporters. On a regular basis, for example, the United States works cooperatively with Saudi authorities on issues relating to the war on terrorism. In some areas, cooperation is routine and systematic; in other areas, especially those touching on aspects of terrorist financing and infrastructure, which touches on all aspects of government, coordination is more complex.

Following up on our previous trips and other U.S. efforts, OFAC visited Saudi Arabia and several other states in the region in December 2001 and January 2002. In Saudi Arabia, we met with an inter-agency delegation to discuss terrorist financing and to explore areas of mutual concern. Specifically, we discussed some possible joint U.S.-Saudi public actions to deny individuals and entities we suspected were supporting terrorism access to international financial markets and to prevent U.S. and Saudi citizens from having dealings with them. We also discussed Saudi efforts to strengthen regulatory oversight of charities and other charitable fundraisers, and steps taken by the Saudi Arabian Monetary Authority (SAMA) to tighten-up banking controls and improve compliance efforts.

In addition, we held meetings with a small group of private Saudi citizens and leaders of the Jeddah Chamber of

Commerce (JCCI). The purpose was to explore the charitable giving practices amongst its membership and encourage actions that would ensure that charitable funds are not ultimately channeled to terrorist activity. Later in January 2002, the JCCI announced that a task force would be set up to develop a comprehensive financial and administrative system for the nation's charities.

On March 11, 2002, Treasury Secretary O'Neill and Saudi authorities announced the joint designation of the Somalia and Bosnia-Herzegovina offices of the Al Haramain Foundation, a Saudi-based NGO with offices throughout the world. In addition to on-going law enforcement and intelligence cooperation, this effort marked an expansion of U.S.-Saudi cooperative efforts to act against the terrorist support networks. Based on evidence that these two branch offices were providing support to Al-Qaeda, these entities were forwarded to the UN Sanctions Committee for inclusion under the UNSCR 1333/1390 list.

In May 2002, an OFAC delegation returned to Saudi Arabia to continue the on-going dialogue on issues related to terrorist finance and infrastructure. During this trip, we were informed that the Saudi Government planned to significantly enhance its oversight of charitable organizations to prevent their exploitation by supporters of terrorism. Several months later, on September 6, 2002, the United States acted again with Saudi Arabia and jointly referred to the UN Sanctions Committee Wa'el Hamza Julaidan, an Al-Qaeda co-founder who was a leader of several terrorist-affiliated NGOs.

In October 2002, Saudi authorities announced that a full review was conducted of its charitable organizations and issued new guidelines, including one which mandates reporting to the Saudi Foreign Ministry of all charitable activities outside of Saudi Arabia. Shortly thereafter, on December 3, 2002, Saudi authorities publicly announced the establishment of a High Commission for oversight of all charities. Saudi authorities also reported that a process was being developed to establish operational procedures to track all donations to and from charities.

In addition to these actions, SAMA enhanced its scrutiny of the financial system. As part of this effort, in February 2003, SAMA reported that it had launched a program to train judges and investigators on legal aspects of terrorist financing and money laundering, international requirements for financial secrecy, and methods followed by criminals to exchange information.

Effect of May 12, 2003 Riyadh Attacks

On May 12, 2003, homicide bombers affiliated with Al-Qaeda struck three residential compounds in Riyadh, Saudi Arabia, killing thirty-four including nine Americans. Saudi authorities responded with new resolve in fighting the war on terrorism and carried out a number of actions to capture, kill or arrest suspected terrorists operating in Saudi Arabia.

Marking a recognition of the seriousness of the challenges on terrorist finance and infrastructure issues, Saudi authorities announced that charitable organizations would no longer be authorized to provide funds outside of Saudi Arabia other than through highly-controlled and government supervised channels. Additionally, Saudi authorities announced that Al Haramain was closing operations in as many as ten countries outside Saudi Arabia. The U.S. continues to monitor the status of these announced efforts and to express our critical interest in cooperating to maximize possibilities for effectiveness.

In June 2003, Saudi authorities announced that SAMA distributed a circular to all banks and financial institutions in Saudi Arabia requiring the full and immediate implementation of nine new policies and procedures applicable to charitable and welfare institutions. The new rules include requirements that all accounts of a single organization be consolidated into one account, that depositors provide banks with sufficiently verifiable identification, and that cash withdrawals be strictly prohibited.

To implement these new rules, SAMA reported that it intends to verify compliance through on-site inspections by SAMA officials, receipt of regular compliance reports, and certification by external auditors. The new rules take into account the Saudi Banking Control Law, SAMA's regulations, the Financial Action Task Force (FATF) 40 Recommendations, the FATF 8 Special Recommendations on Terrorist Financing, and applicable UN Security Council resolutions.

The United States supports all efforts reported by Saudi authorities to improve efforts to prevent the flow of charitable funds to terrorist activity. Joint efforts, including the designation of senior Al-Qaeda leadership based in Saudi Arabia like Wael Hamza Julaidan, demonstrate the willingness of Saudi authorities to cooperate on high impact financing and infrastructure targets. These actions by Saudi authorities present the U.S. with opportunities to cooperate in improving, verifying, and evaluating progress. We must continue to engage Saudi authorities in areas where we believe improvements can be made, and continue to demonstrate that we are steadfast in our determination to eliminate the threat posed by the terrorist networks.

As efforts to improve oversight of charities continue, we believe we should seek to cooperate closely in three key areas: (1)-programmatic: (2) personnel; and (3) financial. Specifically, it is critical that we continue to follow up with Saudi authorities to measure whether 1) the true goals and objectives of charities are what they purport to be; 2) whether leadership and staff are appropriately vetted and not committed to any dual-purposes; and 3) whether the means that are used to raise and move funds are transparent.

Additionally, we must continue our dialogue with wealthy individuals, families and merchants to ensure that they are taking all necessary precautions to prevent charitable donations from supporting terrorist activity. In instances where we have strong reason to believe that some elements are not doing enough, we must pursue more stringent measures, which we believe, may force others to become more vigilant in ensuring that funds are not provided for terrorist activity. Looking forward, Saudi Arabia and other important partners continue to indicate their willingness to cooperate in joint efforts, and we remain committed to ensuring that maximum efforts are made to achieve tangible results.

Multilateral Actions Against Al-Qaeda and other Terrorist Infrastructure

Reflecting the broad range of mechanisms by which terrorist groups, particularly Al-Qaeda, receive financial and other material support, OFAC has effectively implemented the President's designation authority against a variety of targets. These range from using targeted economic sanctions to disrupt the terrorist financing operations of an international "hawala" network as well as a more traditional banking network, to disrupting the activities of several key NGOs in supplying financing and other services to Al-Qaeda. Information available to the US Government indicates that these actions have disrupted Al-Qaeda's support network and OFAC continues its efforts to plan, prepare and implement actions, which will impact on the ability of terrorists and their networks to provide material, financial and logistical support for future terrorist strikes. For examples of some of these actions, please see Appendix 1.

Due to the transnational nature of the terrorist infrastructure, support and cooperation with our allies is a critical part of making U.S. designation actions successful. By developing and establishing authorities and procedures for entities associated with Al-Qaeda and the Taliban to be submitted to the UN, we have begun to institutionalize on a global scale the importance of sanctions as a critical tool against the terrorist support networks. We continue to work with our allies in making designations against Al-Qaeda's infrastructure that may be notified to the UN.

Towards a Strategic Effort and "Key Nodes" Approach

Over the next six to twelve months, OFAC is seeking to significantly expand its efforts and the impact of the implementation of the President's authorities under E.O. 13224 by adopting a more systematic approach to evaluating the activities of major terrorist organizations in various regions. This approach will focus on identifying "key nodes" that sustain the abilities of terrorist organizations to remain operational, despite successful actions by the U.S. and its allies to capture, kill and arrest terrorist cell members, leaders and operational planners.

In furtherance of this end, OFAC initiated a collaborative effort with the Department of Defense to develop information and strategies against terrorist financing and infrastructure. Before OFAC's secure facility was operational, DOD agencies to include the Office of Naval Intelligence (ONI), in addition to the Financial Crimes Enforcement Network (FINCEN), generously provided space and support to OFAC personnel that was critical to OFAC efforts immediately following the 9-11 attacks. Since this time, OFAC staff have continued liaison relationships with several DOD agencies and combatant commands. As a result of this effort, OFAC has gained wider access to information and expertise critical in carrying out the President's authorities under EO 13224.

Specifically, in October 2002, OFAC began a joint project with the U.S. Pacific Command (USPACOM) and other DOD elements that identified terrorist support networks in Southeast Asia and selected key nodes, or priority targets, in these networks. The project's geographic scope included four countries – Indonesia, the Philippines, Malaysia and Singapore – and eight terrorist or Islamic extremist groups. The project focused special attention on Jemaa Islamiyah (JI), the Abu Sayyaf Group (ASG), and the Moro Islamic Liberation Front (MILF), because of their relative importance in the region and threat to U.S. interests.

For JI, which subsequently carried out the Bali bombings and has strong ties to Al-Qaeda, the project identified the key leaders, fundraisers, businessmen, recruiters, companies, charities, mosques, and schools that were part of its support network. Thus far, we have imposed sanctions against two of these key nodes, and are coordinating action against several others.

This process is the model that OFAC is seeking to continue and expand in collaborative efforts with DOD agencies including ONI and the combatant commands. Next week, I will be visiting USEUCOM headquarters and meeting with the Chief of Staff, to lay the groundwork to continue a joint project including USEUCOM and OFAC Officers. We also hope to begin projects with the Central (USCENTCOM) and Southern (USSOUTHCOM) Commands shortly thereafter. Working with DOD Commands and other DOD agencies provides OFAC and its DOD partners a force multiplier that brings together a variety of counterterrorism tools and resources to enhance opportunities for future efforts.

Taking a regional approach along with the various command's areas of responsibility, the effort will seek to identify and isolate key nodes in the transnational terrorist support infrastructure in the respective areas of responsibility. This approach seeks to provide the opportunity to cripple an entire organization at one time through OFAC's implementation of the President's authority in coordination with possible actions of other U.S. departments and agencies and in cooperation with our allies.

We have already taken steps to implement this approach in some regions. OFAC analysts are currently working with DOD agencies, including analysts from the Office of Naval Intelligence (ONI), to fully identify the terrorism support infrastructure in the Horn of Africa. In this region, shipping and related drug smuggling activities appear to be strengthening the terrorist networks in this area. Working with ONI provides OFAC the opportunity to work with analysts with unique expertise in areas otherwise less accessible to OFAC.

In the Southern Command area of responsibility, Narco-Terrorists in Colombia are one of the major targets. On October 31, 2001, three Colombian guerrilla-terrorist organizations that had previously been determined to be Foreign Terrorist Organizations - the FARC (Revolutionary Armed Forces of Colombia), the AUC (United Self-Defense Forces of Colombia) and the ELN (National Liberation Army) - were added to the list of global terrorists under E.O. 13224. On June 1 of this year, President Bush named two of those organizations - the FARC and the AUC - as foreign drug kingpins under authority of the Foreign Narcotics Kingpin Designation Act, thus, effectively recognizing them as narco-terrorists.

Although the structure, goals, and international ties of these groups are significantly different from those of the Islamic extremist terrorist organizations linked to Al-Qaeda and Hamas, these Colombian narco-terrorist organizations are still dependent upon cash or other media of exchange, such as drugs-for-guns, to sustain their guerrilla and paramilitary forces. Thus, although their key nodes may be more difficult to isolate in a meaningful sense for the effective application of OFAC's economic sanctions, they are not immune. We expect that some aspects of these organizations and their support structures will be found to be susceptible to OFAC actions.

For a description of the graphical representations of a key nodes approach that could be applicable to a terrorist support network in any region, please see Appendix 2.

Summary

The funds necessary for a terrorist organization to carry out an attack often are minimal, but the support infrastructure critical for indoctrination, recruitment, training, logistical support, the dissemination of propaganda and other material support requires substantial funding. The President's powers under IEEPA, E.O. 13224, as well as other legislation provide the United States with authorities that are critical to attacking the unusual and extraordinary threats posed by the transnational terrorist support networks. OFAC's effectiveness in implementing these authorities requires strong coordination with other U.S. departments and agencies and support from U.S. allies.

Terrorist organizations including Al-Qaeda, Egyptian Islamic Jihad, Jemaa Islamiyah, Al-Ittihad Al-Islamiyya, Hamas, Hizballah and others rely on their infrastructure for support and to shield their activities from scrutiny. The secretive nature of their activities and their frequent reliance on charitable, humanitarian, educational and religious cover are vulnerabilities OFAC can exploit by making designations under E.O. 13224. Decisive action against high impact targets deters others, forcing key nodes of financial support to choose between public exposure of support for terrorist activity or tarnishing their reputation, to the detriment of their business and commercial interests.

Looking forward, OFAC seeks to continue coordinating with other U.S. agencies as efforts are expanded to impede the activities of terrorist organizations. By duplicating the approach to Southeast Asia in coordination with USPACOM, we plan to identify and isolate key nodes in the transnational terrorist support infrastructure through a regional approach reflecting the areas of responsibility of the military commands. This approach seeks to enhance the coordination of OFAC's actions with those of other U.S. departments and agencies and in cooperation with allies.

Appendix 1

Al-Barakaat network: Shortly after September 11, 2001, OFAC identified the Al-Barakaat Network as a major financial operation that was providing material, financial, and logistical support to Usama Bin Laden, Al-Qaeda, and other terrorist groups. The work done by OFAC led to President Bush's November 7, 2001 announcement of the freezing of assets of the Al-Barakaat Network. In the announcement, the President was joined by the Secretary of the Treasury, the Secretary of State and the Attorney General. As a result of that action, Barakaat's cash flow--nearly $1.4 billion in less than two years--was severely disrupted. Al Ittihaad Al Islamiya--the Somali militia closely tied to Al Qaeda and a major beneficiary of the funds moving through Barakaat—also suffered a crippling loss of income.

Nada-Nasreddin network: OFAC worked closely with its partners in the Caribbean and Europe for nearly a year to unearth the Muslim Brotherhood backed network of financial houses and investment firms used by the European and Caribbean-based Al-Qaeda supporters, Yousef Nada and Ahmed Idris Nasreddin. These companies were then publicly designated by the U.S. and notified and listed at the UN in November 2001 and August 2002, significantly disrupting their activities. Cooperative efforts made by international partners including Italy, Switzerland, Luxembourg, and the Bahamas were critical in making this action successful.

Benevolence International Foundation (BIF) and Global Relief Foundation (GRF) Blocking in aid of Investigation: On December 14, 2001, the U.S. Treasury Department blocked in aid of investigation both BIF and GRF in Chicago, Illinois. OFAC, in coordination with the FBI in Chicago, blocked the business records and bank accounts of BIF and GRF, pending further investigation by OFAC. GRF filed for injunctive relief in U.S. District Court on January 28, 2002. BIF filed its complaint in U.S. District Court on January 30, 2002. On October 17, 2002, OFAC designated GRF pursuant to E.O. 13224 and on November 18, 2002, designated BIF. The district court rejected GRF's motion for a preliminary injunction on June 11, 2002. This decision was affirmed by the Seventh Circuit on December 31, 2002. On February 25, BIF's civil suit against the US Government was voluntarily dismissed with prejudice and without costs. On July 3, 2003, GRF filed a petition for *writ of* *certiorari* with the Supreme Court. Both BIF and GRF were notified and listed at the UN.

Designation of Holy Land Foundation (HLF), Beit al-Mal, and al-Aqsa Islamic Bank: On December 4, 2001, the U.S. Treasury Department designated Holyland Foundation ("HLF"), Beit al-Mal Holdings, and al-Aqsa Islamic Bank pursuant to E.O.s 13224 and 12947. HLF was also added to the EU's list of terrorists in June 2002. On March 8, 2002, HLF filed its complaint in U.S. District Court. On May 31, 2002, OFAC redesignated HLF. On August 8, 2002, the district court denied HLF's motion for a preliminary injunction on all counts and granted summary judgment to the government as to most of HLF's claims, including its due process, First Amendment, and Religious Freedom Restoration Act claims. On June 20, 2003, the D.C. Circuit upheld the district court's ruling in full. On February 6, 2002, OFAC received a petition from Beit al-Mal for removal from the SDGT list. On June 7, 2002, al-Aqsa submitted a petition to OFAC for removal from the SDGT list. Both cases are under review.

Kuwaiti Charities: On January 9, 2002, Treasury designated the Pakistani and Afghan branches of the Revival of Islamic Heritage Society (RIHS) and the Afghan Support Committee (ASC) as entities supporting the Al-Qaeda network. The RIHS is a Kuwaiti-based charity with offices in Pakistan, Afghanistan and throughout the world. The Peshawar, Pakistan office defrauded donors to fund terrorists, including inflating the number of orphans it was ostensibly supporting with the names of fictitious or dead children in order to obtain additional funds from the RIHS Kuwait headquarters. The additional money was then diverted to Al-Qaeda terrorists. ASC located in Jalalabad, Afghanistan, solicited donations from local charities in Arab countries by falsely asserting that the funds collected were destined for orphans and widows. In reality, the financial chief of the ASC served as the head of organized fundraising for Usama Bin Laden and turned over the funds collected by the ASC to Al-Qaeda operatives. These entities were notified and listed at the UN.

G7 Joint Designation: On April 19, 2002, the United States, along with the other G7 members, jointly designated nine individuals and one organization. Most of these groups were European-based Al-Qaeda organizers and financiers of terrorism. Because of their Al-Qaeda links, all ten of these names were notified and listed at the UN.

U.S.-Central Asia Joint Designation: On September 6, 2002, the United States, Afghanistan, Kyrgyzstan, and China jointly notified and listed at the UN the Eastern Turkistan Islamic Movement, an Al-Qaeda-linked organization active in parts of South and Central Asia.

Jemaa Islamiyya: On October 23, 2002, the United States designated the Southeast Asia-based terrorist group, Jemaa Islamiyya, the perpetrator of the deadly attacks on a nightclub in Bali on October 12th. In the subsequent request of the United Nations to also designate this group for its ties to the Al-Qaeda organization, the U.S. joined Australia, Indonesia, Singapore, and 46 other countries, including all the members of ASEAN and the EU, in notifying and listing Jemaa Islamiyya's at the UN. This represents the most widespread show of support to initiate a designation at the UN to date.

Three Chechen Groups: On February 28, 2003, the United States designated three Chechnya-based terrorists groups responsible for the Moscow theater siege. In the subsequent request to the UN for notification and listing these groups based on their ties to the Al-Qaeda organization, the U.S. was joined by UN Security Council members France, Russia, China, the UK, Spain, and Germany.

Cooperation with European Union Member States: On February 26, 2002 and May 3, 2002, the United States joined the Spanish Government and designated more than 20 ETA related operatives. These names were not notified to the UN. On August 8, 2002 joined the Italian Government in designating several Al-Qaeda related individuals which were notified to and listed at the UN. In addition, on June 6, 2003, the U.S. joined Italy and Germany in designating 17 Al-Qaeda individuals which were notified to the UN.

Appendix 2

Anatomy and Disruption of Terrorism Support Networks

The attached four charts lay out OFAC's theory regarding how we currently employ and could expand the use of sanctions authority to disrupt the financial and support networks of several prominent terrorist groups.

Charts 1 and 2 are examples of the various steps of the funding process. Donors provide money to a variety of intermediaries often acting on behalf of charitable organizations to collect funds. The charitable organizations, in turn, use the funds both for legitimate humanitarian efforts, but also either wittingly or unwittingly allow some funds to be siphoned off by facilitators who serve as the conduit to the extremist groups. Facilitators frequently are employees of the charitable organization with close ties to the extremist group or members of the extremist group with responsibility for liaising with charitable organizations.

Chart 3 is a model of a terrorist support network with the key nodes highlighted that we believe economic sanctions could effectively impact. These include financial, leadership, and influence nodes. Influence nodes can include individuals and institutions that provide spiritual or other guidance, or serve as recruitment centers.

Chart 4 shows theoretically how designation and isolation of the key nodes identified in Chart 3 will sever critical ties within the overall network and thereby disrupt its overall functioning.

Model of the Origin and Flow of Funds to Extremist Groups

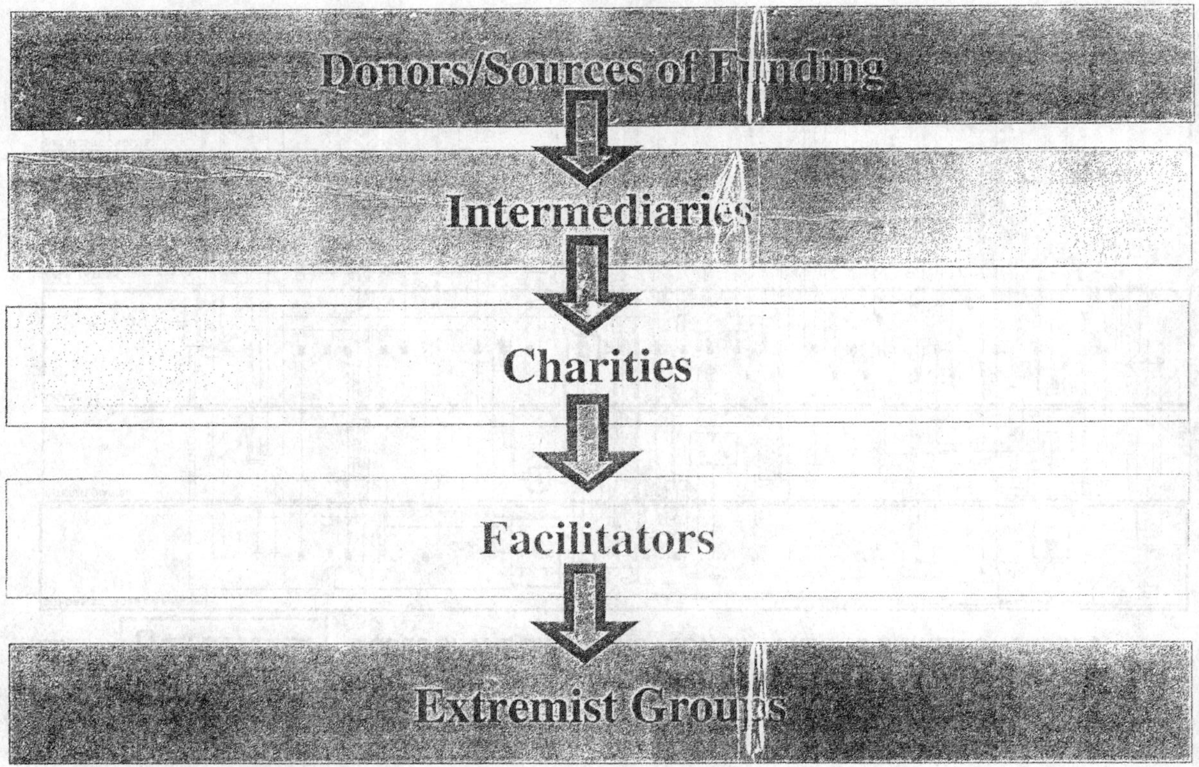

LARGER entities represent the key nodes of the network

Entities in a GREEN box are financial targets.

Entities in a RED box are leadership targets.

Entities in a BLUE box are influence targets.

CHART #2

MODEL OF THE ORIGIN AND FLOW OF FUNDS TO EXTREMIST GROUPS

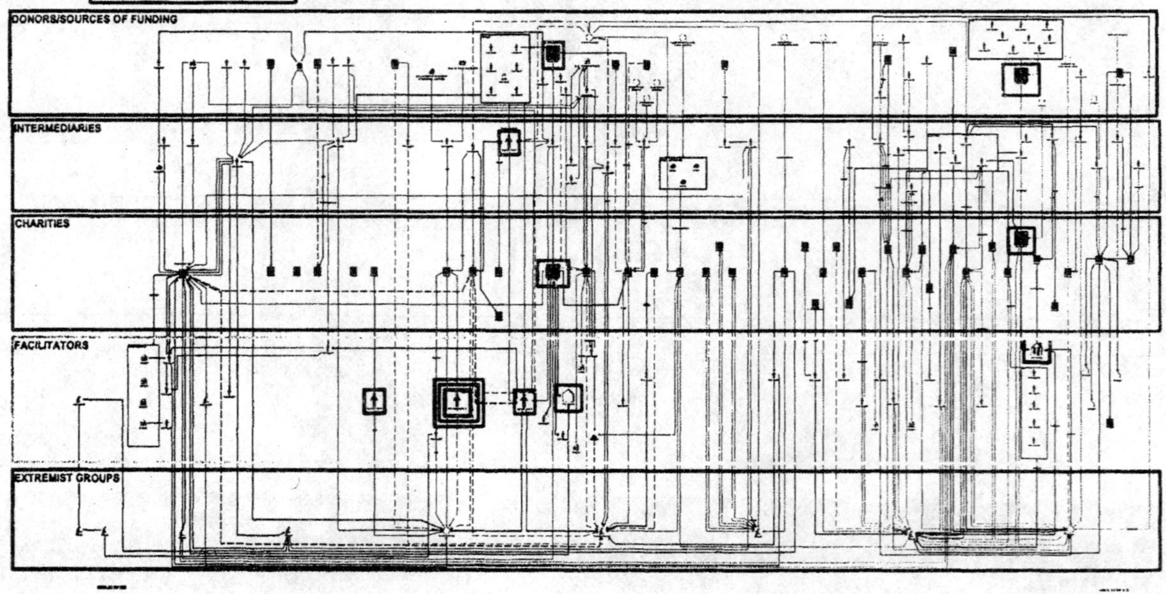

CHART #3

KEY NODES OF A MODEL TERRORIST NETWORK

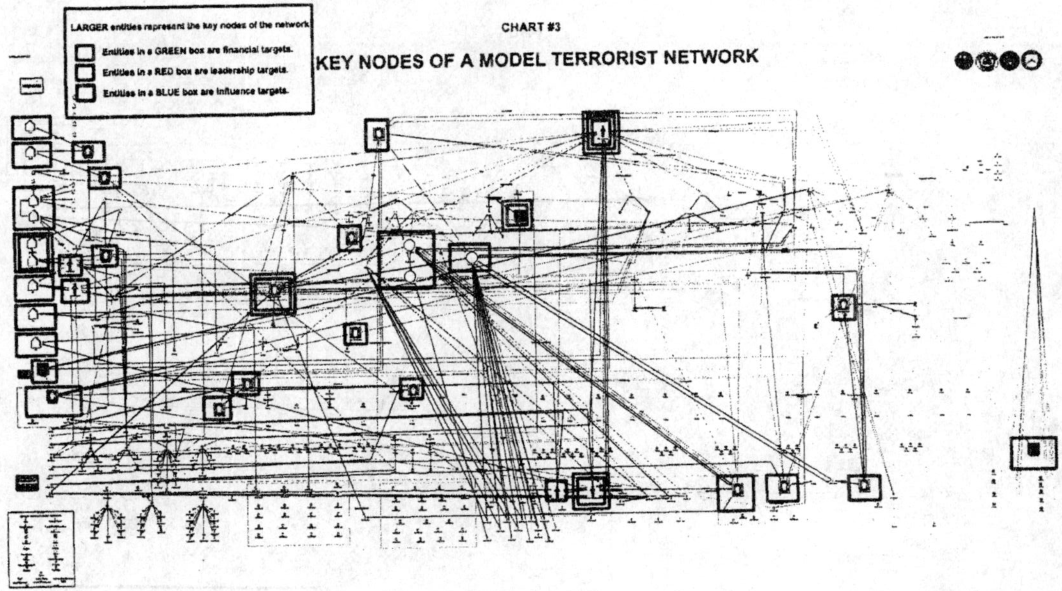

CHART #4

MODEL TERRORIST NETWORK WITH NODES REMOVED

LARGER entities represent the key nodes of the network.

- Entities in a GREEN box are financial targets.
- Entities in a RED box are leadership targets.
- Entities in a BLUE box are influence targets.

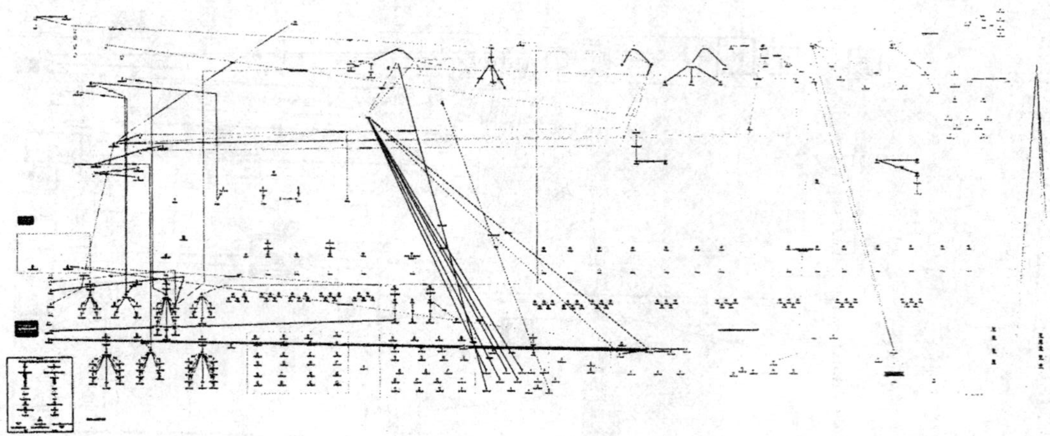

SAUDI SUPPORT FOR INTERNATIONAL TERRORISM: BACKGROUND AND CURRENT DEVELOPMENTS

Testimony by Dr. Dore Gold, President of the Jerusalem Center for Public Affairs and former Israeli Ambassador to the United Nations

U.S. Senate Committee on Governmental Affairs, Thursday, July 31, 2003

Nearly two years ago on September 11, 2001, most well-informed observers about the Middle East were shocked to hear that 15 out of the 19 hijackers who carried out the attacks on the World Trade Center and the Pentagon were Saudi citizens. It was equally surprising that the mastermind of the worst terrorist attack on the United States in its history, Osama bin Laden, was born and raised in Saudi Arabia. This curiosity and wonder about the Saudi role in the attack came up once more with the release of the September 11 report by the U.S. Congress and its disclosure of "incontrovertible evidence" linking Saudis to the financing of al-Qaeda operatives in the United States.

For decades, terrorism had been associated with states like Libya, Syria, or Iran. Saudi Arabia had been a pro-Western force during the Cold War and had hosted large coalition armies during the 1991 Gulf War. Saudi Arabia had not been colonized during its history, like other Middle Eastern states that had endured a legacy of European imperialism. This background only sharpened the questions of many after the attacks: What was the precise source of the hatred that drove these men to take their own lives in an act of mass murder?

In a series of articles appearing in the Egyptian weekly, *Ruz al-Yousef* (the *Newsweek* of Egypt), this past May, Wael al-Abrashi, the magazine's deputy editor, attempted to grapple with this issue. He drew a direct link between the rise of much of contemporary terrorism with Saudi Arabia's main Islamic creed, Wahhabism, and with the financial involvement of Saudi Arabia's large charitable organizations:

> "Wahhabism leads, as we have seen, to the birth of extremist, closed, and fanatical streams, that accuse others of heresy, abolish them, and destroy them. The extremist

religious groups have moved from the stage of *Takfir* [condemning other Muslims as unbelievers] to the stage of 'annihilation and destruction,' in accordance with the strategy of Al-Qa'ida – which Saudi authorities must admit is a local Saudi organization that drew other organizations into it, and not the other way around. All the organizations emerged from under the robe of Wahhabism."

"I can state with certainty that after a very careful reading of all the documents and texts of the official investigations linked to all acts of terror that have taken place in Egypt, from the assassination of the late **president Anwar Sadat** in October 1981, up to the Luxor massacre in 1997, Saudi Arabia was the main station through which most of the Egyptian extremists passed, and emerged bearing with them terrorist thought regarding *Takfir* – thought that they drew from the sheikhs of Wahhabism. They also bore with them funds they received from the Saudi charities."

(Middle East Media Research Institute, Special Dispatch Series - No. 526 - Saudi Arabia, June 20, 2003)

Thus, while some Western commentators have sought to explain the roots of al-Qaeda's fury at the U.S. by focusing on the history of American policy in the Middle East or other **external** factors, a rising number of Middle Eastern analysts have concentrated instead on **internal** Saudi factors, including recent militant trends among Saudi Arabia's Wahhabi clerics and the role of large Saudi global charities in terrorist finance. This requires a careful look at how Saudi Arabia contributed to the ideological roots of some of the new wave of international terrorism as well as how the kingdom emerged as a critical factor in providing the resources needed by many terrorist groups.

Historical Roots

The particular creed of Islam practiced in Saudi Arabia, which is known in the West as Wahhabism, emerged in the mid-18th century in Central Arabia from the teachings of Muhammad ibn Abdul Wahhab. This Arabian religious reformer sought to rid Islam of foreign innovations that compromised its monotheistic foundations and to restore what he believed were the religious practices of the 7th century at the time of the Prophet Muhammad and his immediate successors. He established a political covenant in 1744 with Muhammad bin Saud, according to which he received bin Saud's protection and in exchange legitimized the spread of Saudi rule over a widening circle of Arabian tribes. This covenant between the Saudi royal family and Wahhabism is at the root of modern Saudi Arabia.

In retrospect, Wahhabism was significant for two reasons. First, it rejuvenated the idea of the militant *jihad*, or holy war, which had declined as a central Islamic value to be applied universally. Under the influence of Sufism, for example, *jihad* had also evolved into a more spiritual concept. Second, Wahhabism became associated with a brutal history of political expansion that led to the massacre of Muslims who did not adhere to its tenets, the most famous of which occurred against the Shiites Muslims of Kerbala in the early 18th century and against Sunni Muslims in Arabian cities, like Taif, during the early 20th century. These Muslims were labeled as polytheists and did not deserve any protection. The highest spiritual authority of Islam during this period, the Sultan-Caliph of the Ottoman Empire, regarded the Wahhabis as heretics and waged wars against them in defense of Islam.

Yet it would be a mistake to focus on Wahhabism alone as the ideological fountainhead of the new global terrorism. Modern Saudi Arabia in the 1950s and 1960s hosted other militant movements that had an important impact, as well. For reasons of regional geopolitics, King Saud, King Faisal, and their successors provided sanctuary to elements of the radical Muslim Brotherhood from Egypt, Sudan, Jordan, and Syria. Some were provided Saudi stipends. Others were given positions in the Saudi educational system, including the universities, or in the large Saudi charities, like the Muslim World League, that was created in 1962. For example, Egyptian President Abdul Nasser had the Muslim Brotherhood ideologue, Sayyed Qutb, executed in 1966; his brother, Muhammad Qutb, fled to Saudi Arabia and taught at King Abdul Aziz University in Jiddah. He was joined in the 1970s by one of the heads of the Muslim Brotherhood from Jordan, Abdullah Azzam. In 1979, both taught Osama bin Laden, a student at the university.

Saudi Arabia's global charities, like the Muslim World League, permitted the spread of the new militancy that was forged from the cooperation between the Wahhabi clerics and the Muslim Brotherhood refugees. After 1973, these charities benefited from the huge petrodollar resources dispensed by the Saudi government, which undoubtedly helped them achieve a global reach. Abdullah Azzam headed the office of the Muslim World League in Peshawar, Pakistan, when it served as the rear base for the war against the Soviet occupation of Afghanistan. He was joined by his student, bin Laden, who with Saudi funding also set up the Mujahidin Services Center (Maktab Khadmat al-Mujahidin) for Muslim volunteers who came to fight the Red Army. After Moscow's defeat in Afghanistan, this office became al-Qaeda.

Thus, the Saudi charities became instrumental for the continuing global *jihad*. Bin Laden's brother-in-law, Muhammad Jamal Khalifa, ran the offices of the International Islamic Relief Organization (IIRO), a Muslim World League offshoot, in the Philippines. Local intelligence agencies suspected that it served as a financial conduit to the Abu Sayyaf organization. Muhammad Zawahiri, brother of bin Laden's Egyptian partner, Ayman Zawahiri, would eventually work for IIRO in Albania. Indeed, IIRO would eventually be suspected of involvement in terrorist threats in India, Kenya, and to Russian forces in Chechnya.

Ideological Roots of the New Terrorism

These developments seem far beyond the horizon of the Israeli-Palestinian conflict, but not completely, for a careful examination of the religious sources of some of the worst suicide bombings against the State of Israel by the Hamas organization leads also to Saudi Arabia. Looking at Hamas websites, this very month, one finds Saudi clerics prominently featured as providing the religious justification for suicide bombings. Of 16 religious leaders cited by Hamas, the largest national group backing these attacks are Saudis. The formal Saudi position on suicide bombings, in fact, has been mixed. To his credit, the current Saudi Grand Mufti, Sheikh Abdul Aziz bin Abdullah Al al-Sheikh, has condemned these acts. Yet at the same time, Saudi Arabia's Minister for Islamic Affairs, Sheikh Saleh Al al-Sheikh, has condoned them: "The suicide bombings are permitted...the victims are considered to have died a martyr's death."

The Hamas-Saudi connection should not come as a surprise. Hamas emerged in 1987 from the Gaza branch of Muslim Brotherhood which, as noted earlier, had become a key Saudi ally during previous decades. When Hamas spiritual leader Sheikh Ahmed Yasin was let out of an Israeli prison in 1998, he went to Saudi Arabia for medical treatment and Crown Prince Abdullah made a high-profile visit to his hospital bedside. Bin Laden had made the fate of Sheikh Yasin an issue for his al-Qaeda followers as well. In his 1996 "Declaration of War," he listed Sheikh Yasin's release from prison as one of his demands or grievances.

Saudi support for suicide bombings has wider repercussions. Other militant Islamic movements cite Saudi clerics to justify their activities – from the Chechen groups battling the Russians to Iraqi mujahidin (al-jam'ah al-salifiyah) fighting the U.S. army in western Iraq. In order to evaluate the significance of these religious rulings, it is necessary to focus on the stature of these various clerical figures.

For example, just after the September 11 attacks, it is true that many Saudi government officials condemned them. But there were other voices as well. Shortly thereafter a Saudi book appeared on the Internet justifying the murder of thousands of Americans, entitled *The Foundations of the Legality of the Destruction That Befell America.* The Introduction to the book was written by a prominent Saudi religious leader, Sheikh Hamud bin Uqla al-Shuaibi. He wrote on November 16, 2001, that he hoped Allah would bring further destruction upon the United States. Al-Shuaibi's name appears in a book entitled the *Great Book of Fatwas,* found in a Taliban office in Kabul. Sheikh al-Shuaibi appears on the Hamas website, noted earlier, as a religious source for suicide attacks. He appears on the website of the Islamic militants fighting the U.S. army in western Iraq as well. His ideas had global reach.

The question that must be asked is whether a religious leader of this sort is a peripheral figure on the fringes of society or whether he reflects more mainstream thinking. In fact, al-Shuaibi had very strong credentials. Born in 1925 in the Wahhabi stronghold of Buraida, he was a student of King Faisal's Grand Mufti, Sheikh Muhammad ibn Ibrahim Al al-Sheikh. Al-Shuaibi's roster of students read like a "Who's Who" of Saudi Arabia, including the current Grand Mufti and the former Minister of Islamic Affairs and Muslim World League secretary-general, Abdullah al-Turki. When al-Shuaibi died in 2002, many central Saudi figures attended his funeral. In short, he was mainstream. His militant ideas about justifying the September 11 attacks were echoed by Sheikh Abdullah bin Abdul Rahman Jibrin, who actually was a member of the Directorate of

Religious Research, Islamic Legal Rulings, and Islamic Propagation and Guidance – an official branch of the Saudi government.

Financial Support for the New Global Terrorism

As already demonstrated, Saudi Arabia erected a number of large global charities in the 1960s and 1970s whose original purpose may have been to spread Wahhabi Islam, but which became penetrated by prominent individuals from al-Qaeda's global *jihadi* network. The three most prominent of these charities were the International Islamic Relief Organization (an offshoot of the Muslim World League), the World Assembly of Muslim Youth (WAMY), and the Charitable Foundations of al-Haramain. All three are suspected by various global intelligence organizations of terrorist funding.

It would be incorrect to view these charities as purely non-governmental organizations. At the apex of each organization's board is a top Saudi official. The Saudi Grand Mufti, who is also a Saudi cabinet member, chairs the Constituent Council of the Muslim World League. The Saudi Minister of Islamic Affairs chairs the secretariat of WAMY and the administrative council of al-Haramain. All three organizations have received large charitable contributions from the Saudi royal family that have been detailed in Saudi periodicals.

The earliest documented links between one of these charities and terrorists was found in Bosnia. It is a handwritten account on IIRO stationery from the late 1980s indicating the use of this charity's offices for the support of militant actions. But the strongest documented cases that demonstrate the ties between Saudi Arabia's global charities and international terrorism are related to Hamas. These ties were alleged already in the mid-1990s when a Hamas funding group received instructions to write letters of thanks to executives of IIRO and WAMY for funds it had received. In 1994, President Clinton made a brief stopover in Saudi Arabia during which he complained about Saudi funding of Hamas. These charges about Saudi Arabia bankrolling Hamas have become even more vociferous in recent years.

The Saudis have been equally vociferous in their denials. Crown Prince Abdullah's foreign policy advisor, Adel al-Jubeir, asserted on CNN's "Crossfire" on August 16, 2002: "We do not allow funding to go from Saudi Arabia to Hamas." More recently, Foreign Minister Prince Saud al-Faisal told the Saudi daily *Arab News* on June 23, 2003, that since the establishment of the PLO as the sole legitimate representative of the Palestinian people, the Saudi Kingdom only sends funding through the PLO. He denied that the Saudis finance Hamas.

Yet during Israel's Operation Defensive Shield last year, a whole array of documents was uncovered which show these repeated Saudi denials to be completely baseless. One of the strongest pieces of evidence came from a handwritten letter written in Arabic by the current Palestinian Prime Minister, Mahmud Abbas (Abu Mazen), on December 30, 2000, to Prince Salman, governor of Riyadh and a full brother of King Fahd. Abbas complained that Saudi donations in the Gaza Strip are going to an organization called al-Jamiya al-Islamiya (the Islamic Society), which Abbas explained "belongs to Hamas." He wanted the funds for Fatah.

Al-Jamiya al-Islamiya was not just a Hamas front, supporting positive social programs and secretly diverting funds to military activity. Even its showcase activities were reprehensible. For example, at a kindergarten graduation involving some of its 1,600 Palestinian pre-schoolers, children wore uniforms and carried mock rifles. Others re-enacted the lynching of Israelis or other terrorist attacks. Thus, the Saudis were not only funding the current generation of terrorism but also the next generation as well.

There were other documents linking Saudi institutions to terrorist financing. An actual IIRO document was found that detailed how $280,000 was to be allocated to 14 Hamas front groups. Checks made out to well-known Hamas fronts from the corporate account of al-Rajhi Banking and Investment at Chase Manhattan Bank were also uncovered. Al-Rajhi Banking and Investment was one of the largest Saudi banking networks which serviced the Saudi charities. Its head, Sulaiman al-Rajhi, headed the family that established the SAAR (the acronym for his name) foundation in Herndon, Virginia, which was raided last year by U.S. federal agents because of suspected terrorist links.

There were other conduits for terrorist funding that were disclosed. Spreadsheets of the Saudi

Committee for Aid to the al-Quds Intifada were found. These lists, that detailed the movement of moneys to the families of suicide bombers, were significant. Saudi spokesmen tried to distance themselves from this activity by arguing that they helped these families through international aid organizations. Yet it became clear from the spreadsheets that these contributions were given through a specifically Saudi organization that was headed by the Saudi Minister of the Interior Prince Naif. Indeed, at the top right-hand side of the spreadsheet found in the West Bank, the name "Kingdom of Saudi Arabia" stands out. In the words of Secretary of State Colin Powell, this kind of support "incentivized" the suicide terrorist attacks.

The Hamas case demonstrated the mode of operation of Saudi charities in support of terrorism. It was significant for those investigating other cases of global terrorism, including al-Qaeda, since very often these groups shared the same funding mechanisms. As a case study, it is particularly useful, since it is the best-documented case of how the Saudis used their charities to back militant activities.

Current Situation

Most of the documents discovered in the West Bank and Gaza Strip were dated from the year 2000. Saudi diplomats argued that after September 11, 2001, they had turned over a new leaf. For example, in October 2002, the Royal Embassy of Saudi Arabia in Washington released a statement detailing the steps they had taken to keep better track of what the charities were doing. The Saudi statement asserted that since September 11, 2001, "charitable groups have been closely monitored and additional audits have been performed to assure that there are no links to suspected groups."

Yet, the very same month the newest Saudi assurances were provided in Washington, one of the top leaders of Hamas, Khaled Mashal, was invited to Riyadh for a WAMY conference. So while in Washington the press corps was told that there were no longer any ties between the Saudi charities and suspected groups, in Riyadh, one of the three main Saudi charities was hosting the leader of one of the suspected groups, Hamas, that had been labeled by the U.S. government as an international terrorist organization. According to a captured Hamas document that detailed Khaled Mashal's visit to Saudi Arabia, he actually had been invited by Crown Prince Abdullah himself. While Hamas had refused at the time to stop its suicide attacks, nonetheless, Saudi officials reassured Mashal of continuing support.

A new context for the issue of Saudi funding of terrorist groups was created when President Bush issued the "Roadmap to a Permanent Two-State Solution to the Israeli-Palestinian Conflict" on April 30, 2003. Besides requiring difficult measures by Israelis and Palestinians alike, the new Bush administration plan specifically called on Arab states in its first phase to "cut off public and private funding and all other forms of support for groups supporting and engaging in violence and terror." In short, Saudi Arabia had to come under the roadmap, as well. Meeting the leaders of Saudi Arabia, Jordan, Egypt, and Bahrain at Sharm el-Sheikh on June 3, 2003, President Bush announced that they had committed themselves to use all means to cut off assistance to any terror group.

It might have been expected that Saudi Arabia would adhere to this firm U.S. policy. On May 12, 2003, Saudi Arabia itself was struck by a triple suicide bombing that led to 35 fatalities, including 9 Americans. Having denied that there was an al-Qaeda presence in the Saudi kingdom, the Saudi government began uncovering al-Qaeda cells and munitions in Riyadh, Mecca, Medina, Jidda, and in the northern al-Jawf area. Having provided the ideological and financial basis for the growth of al-Qaeda and its sister organizations, including Hamas, Saudi Arabia found that the fire they had ignited was coming back to burn them as well.

Unfortunately, while the Saudis appear to be taking their own domestic threat seriously, there is no indication that they have scaled back their support for Hamas. The Israeli national assessment is that Saudi Arabia today funds more than 50 percent of the needs of Hamas and the Saudi percentage in the total foreign aid to Hamas is actually growing. Saudi Arabia continues to aid the families of suicide bombers. It helps dual-use charities and charities that funnel funds directly to military activities against Israel.

At present, Hamas has agreed to a temporary truce with Israel called a *hudna*, but it is vigorously seeking to rebuild its operational infrastructure, including an effort to increase the quantity and quality of Qassam rockets launched against Israelis towns. Muslim writers have argued in the past that a *hudna* is to be maintained until the balance of power improves for the Muslim side. Funding Hamas today jeopardizes the present cease-fire between Israel and the Palestinians and increases the likelihood that Hamas will return to militant action.

It is instructive to recall that in 1995, Saudi Arabia's National Guard headquarters was struck by pro-bin Laden forces, as well. Domestic threats in the mid-1990s did not cause the Saudis to halt their assistance to *jihadi* groups abroad, like Hamas or the Taliban, in the past. Riyadh appears able to draw a distinction between acts of domestic subversion and international terrorist activities, which are seen as part of the global *jihad.*

Conclusions

This testimony was intended to disclose the critical role of Saudi Arabia in providing ideological and financial support for the new terrorism. While most of the evidence presented here comes from the specific case of Hamas, the modus operandi adopted in the Hamas case is probably applicable to other parts of the global terrorist network as well. This is especially true of the critical role of Saudi Arabia's global charities in sustaining many similar militant organizations from Indonesia to central Russia. While Saudi spokesmen have provided repeated assurances that they have cleaned up these activities, their denials with respect to terrorist funding do not stand up against the documented evidence that has accumulated in the last two years.

The Saudi government faces hard dilemmas. It has recently taken disciplinary action against some of its most extreme religious leaders. But traditionally, the Saudis need the backing of their clerics to legitimize their regime; that is the heart of the Saudi-Wahhabi covenant that dates back to the 18th century. Yet the Saudis also need the ultimate protective shield provided by the United States. In order to sustain this, they have spent huge sums of money for public relations firms and influence-brokers. But the time has come to tell the Saudis that they have to make a choice. After September 11, there has to be zero tolerance for terrorist funding and other forms of terrorist support.

The stakes involved are not just a question of public relations or Arab-Israel point-scoring in Washington. The West needs to come to an understanding with the Islamic world based on mutual respect and tolerance. The radicalization of the Middle East being promoted by the Saudis undermines that goal and threatens to substitute instead a vision of perpetual militancy and conflict. For that reason, what is at stake is nothing less than the security of the United States and its allies, as well as the question of whether the Middle East moves in the direction of hope and peace or relapses into a state of continuing strife.

Saudi Minister of Interior Prince Nayef bin Abdel-Aziz, November, 2002;

- “We put big question marks and ask who committed the events of September 11 and who benefited from them…**I think they [the Zionists] are behind these events**…I cannot still believe that 19 youths, including 15 Saudis, carried out the September 11 attacks with the support of bin Laden and his Al-Qa`ida organization. It’s impossible. I will not believe that these people have the power to do so horrendous an attack.”

Abdallah Bin Matruk Al-Haddal - Ministry of Islamic Affairs, January, 2002;

- "…bin Laden waged an Islamic Jihad; he defended the oppressed people in Afghanistan. He expelled the Soviet Union [from Afghanistan] …**Men like bin Laden will not allow the Islamic world to bow down under the infidel enemies' tyranny, under the tyranny of the U.S**…"

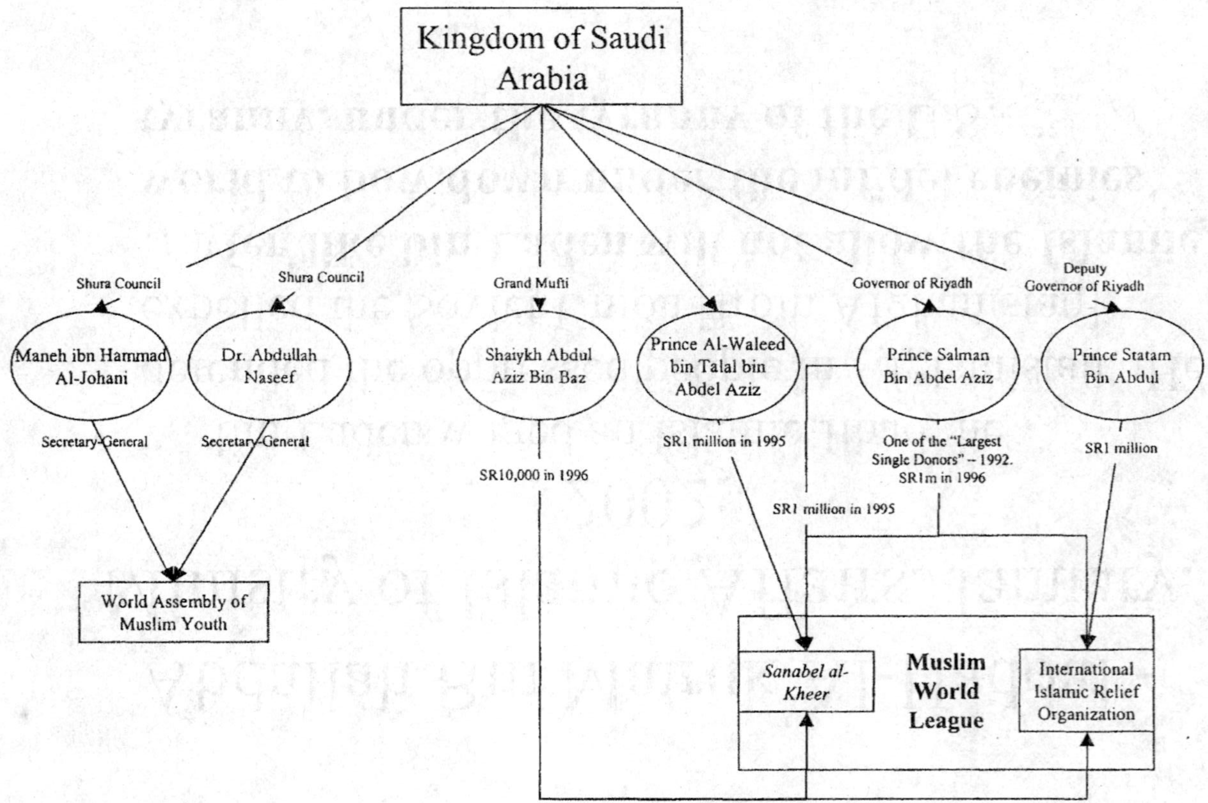

Kingdom of Saudi Arabia
Shura Council
Shura Council
Grand Mufti
Governor of Riyadh
Deputy Governor of Riyadh
Maneh ibn Hammad Al-Johani
Dr. Abdullah Naseef
Shaiykh Abdul Aziz Bin Baz
Prince Al-Waleed bin Talal bin Abdel Aziz
Prince Salman Bin Abdel Aziz
Prince Statam Bin Abdul
Secretary-General
Secretary-General
SR10,000 in 1996
SR1 million in 1995
One of the "Largest Single Donors" – 1992. SR1m in 1996
SR1 million
SR1 million in 1995
World Assembly of Muslim Youth
Sanabel al-Kheer
Muslim World League
International Islamic Relief Organization

DOCUMENTS OF MUJAHEDEENS – KHALIL ABDEL AZIZ

PIX. KHALIL ABDEL AZIZ, TEACHER FROM SAUDI ARABIA

11th Grade Saudi Textbook Distributed in the United States;

- **"... the Summons to Islam in its initial stages was confronted by this when factions of the Jews strove to oppose it and deceive it by various treacherous and perfidious methods, violating their agreement with the Messenger of Allah. Allah responded to their deception by slaughtering them, cleansing the land of their evil and filth**. The word of Truth was exalted, victories followed one after another and booty came continuously to the Muslims..."

Saudi Source of Inspiration for Hamas Suicide Bombing

المركز الفلسطيني للإعلا

الصفحة الرئيسة   من نحن؟   للاتصال بنا   خريطة الموقع   July 10, 2003

في هذا القسم

- الفتاوى الفقهية
- دراسات وبحوث
- كتب وإصدارات

الفتاوى والتأصيل الشرعي

مواضيع خاصة بالعمليات الاستشهادية

- الإرهاب الإسرائيلي وشرعية المقاومة والعمليات الاستشهادية
- سنة الله الماضية في الكون والحياة...
- بيان رابطة علماء فلسطين يناشد الإخوة المزارعين إخراج زكاة الزيتون ، و لمحافظة على أرضهم ، و الدفاع عنها
- التحالف مع أمريكا لضرب العراق أو أي قطر عربي أو إسلامي خيانة لله و رسوله و للمؤمنين و حرام شرعا
- بيان من هيئة علماء السودان نصراً للمجاهدين على أرض فلسطين
الجمعة 22 محرم 1423هـ الموافق 5 أبريل 2002م
- نداء للمسلمين لنجدة إخوانهم في فلسطين .. لم يبق للأمة من مخرج شرعي إلا الجهاد ودعم صمود شعبنا المسلم
الشيخ سفر بن عبد الرحمن الحوالي
- فتوى فضيلة الشيخ سليمان بن ناصر العلوان في العمليات الاستشهادية
- فتوى العلامة الدكتور يوسف القرضاوي حول مشاركة النساء في العمليات الاستشهادية
- ملف خاص : شرعية العمليات الاستشهادية
- فتوى بشأن العمليات الفدائية الاستشهادية صادرة عن مجمع الفقه الإسلامي – السودان
- فتوى صادرة عن رابطة علماء فلسطين في حكم العمليات الاستشهادية
- فتوى الشيخ عبد الله بن منيع عضو هيئة كبار العلماء في السعودية : العمليات الاستشهادية في سبيل الله من أفضل أبواب الجهاد
- فتوى الشيخ محمد بن إبراهيم آل الشيخ مفتي السعودية الراحل
- فتوى شيخ الأزهر وعدد من علماء مجمع البحوث الإسلامية في مصر
- هل يُعتبر منتحرا من فجر نفسه بحزام ناسف وسط العدو؟ د. عجيل جاسم النشمي – الكويت
- العمليات الاستشهادية في ميزان الشرع , الكاتب: الشيخ سلمان العودة
- فتاوى العلماء :
  - الشيخ العلامة حمود العقلا الشعيبي .
  - الشيخ حامد بن عبدالله العلي .
  - الشيخ سليمان العلوان .
  - الشيخ محمد بن عبدالله السيف ـ مفتي المجاهدين في الشيشان ـ .

  ملف ورد
- الإصابة في طلب الشهادة , جابر بن عبد القيوم الساعدي الشامي أبو قتيبة

“The Foundations of the Legality of the Destruction that Befell America”

(ما كان الله ليذر المؤمنين على ما أنتم عليه حتى يميز الخبيث من الطيب)

التأصيل لمشروعية ما حصل لأمريكا من تدمير

تقديم

الشيخ العلامة حمودالعقلاء

و

الشيخ الفاضل علي الخضير

كتبه /عبدالعزيز بن صالح الجربوع

Fatwah Authorizing the Use of WMD

رسالة
في
حكم استخدام أسلحة الدمار الشامل
ضد الكفار

: كتبه

ناصر بن حمد الفهد

ربيع الأول - 1424

Saudi National Charities and the Financing of International Terrorism

	IIRO	WAMY	al-Haramain
	International Islamic Relief Organization	World Assembly of Muslim Youth	Charitable Foundations of al-Haramain
CHAIRMAN	Sheikh Abdul Aziz bin Abdullah Al al-Sheikh	Sheikh Saleh bin Abdul Aziz Al al-Sheikh	Sheikh Saleh bin Abdul Aziz Al al-Sheikh
TITLE	(Grand Mufti, Saudi Cabinet Member)	(Minister of Islamic Affairs, Saudi Cabinet Member)	(Minister of Islamic Affairs, Saudi Cabinet Member)
RELATION TO SAUDI GOVERNMENT	Chairman of Constituent Council of World Muslim League	Chairman of WAMY Secretariat	Chairman of al-Haramain Administrative Council
OFFICIAL SOURCES OF FUNDING	DONATIONS FROM SAUDI ROYAL FAMILY	DONATIONS FROM SAUDI ROYAL FAMILY	DONATIONS FROM SAUDI ROYAL FAMILY

The "Golden Chain"

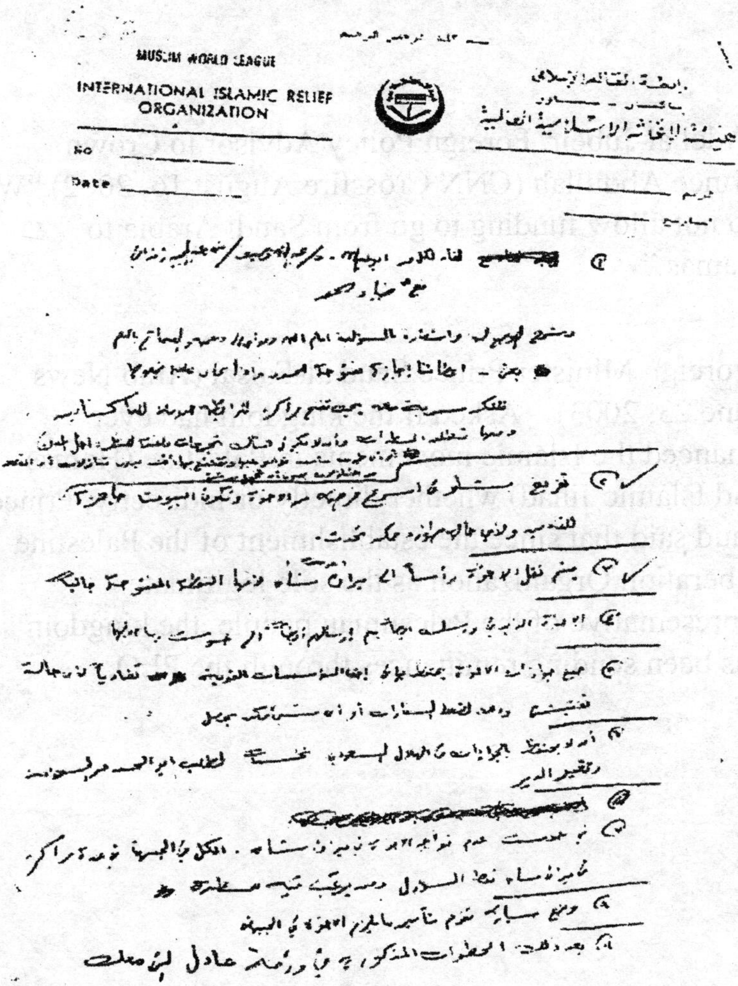

Saudi Denials of Terrorist Support for Hamas

•Adel al-Jubeir, Foreign Policy Advisor to Crown Prince Abdullah (CNN Crossfire August 16, 2002) "We do not allow funding to go from Saudi Arabia to Hamas."

•Foreign Minister Prince Saud al-Faisal (Arab News June 23, 2003) – Asked if the kingdom had ever financed the Islamic movements in Palestine (Hamas and Islamic Jihad) whether directly or indirectly, Prince Saud said that since the establishment of the Palestine Liberation Organization as the sole legitimate representative of the Palestinian people, the kingdom has been sending remittances through the PLO.

Abu Mazen Handwritten Letter to Prince Salman – Stop Funding Hamas!

50

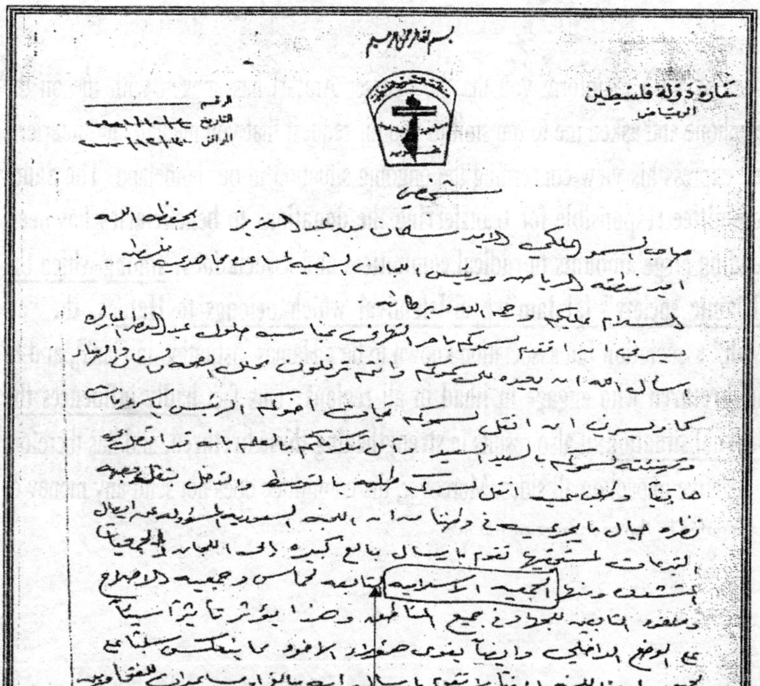

بسم الله الرحمن الرحيم

سفارة دولة فلسطين
الرياض

الرقم
التاريخ
الموافق

شخصي

صاحب السمو الملكي الأمير سلمان بن عبد العزيز يحفظه الله

السلام عليكم ورحمة الله وبركاته

The *al-Jam'iya al-Islamiya* society belonging to Hamas educates kindergarten children to violence and terrorism. It is referred to by Arafat as an example of one of the radical associations belonging to Hamas and supported by Saudi funds.

Abu Mazen Handwritten Letter to Prince Salman – Stop Funding Hamas!

I hereby wish to inform you that he [Yasser Arafat] has spoken with me on the telephone and asked me to transmit to you his request that you mediate and interfere, and express his view concerning the ongoing situation in our homeland. **The Saudi committee responsible for transferring the donations to beneficiaries has been sending large amounts to radical committees and associations, among which the "Islamic society" [al-Jam'iya al-Islamiya] which belongs to Hamas, the "al-Islah" association** [an association known to be a Hamas institution in Gaza], **and to the brethren who engage in jihad in all regions.** This fact **badly influences the internal situation**; it also results in **strengthening these brethren,** and has therefore a negative impact on all sides. Moreover, the committee does not send any money or assistance to the members of Fatah.

Islamic Society in Gaza – A Hamas Front

Islamic Society in Gaza – A Hamas Front

IIRO Disbursement of $280,000 to 14 Hamas Fronts

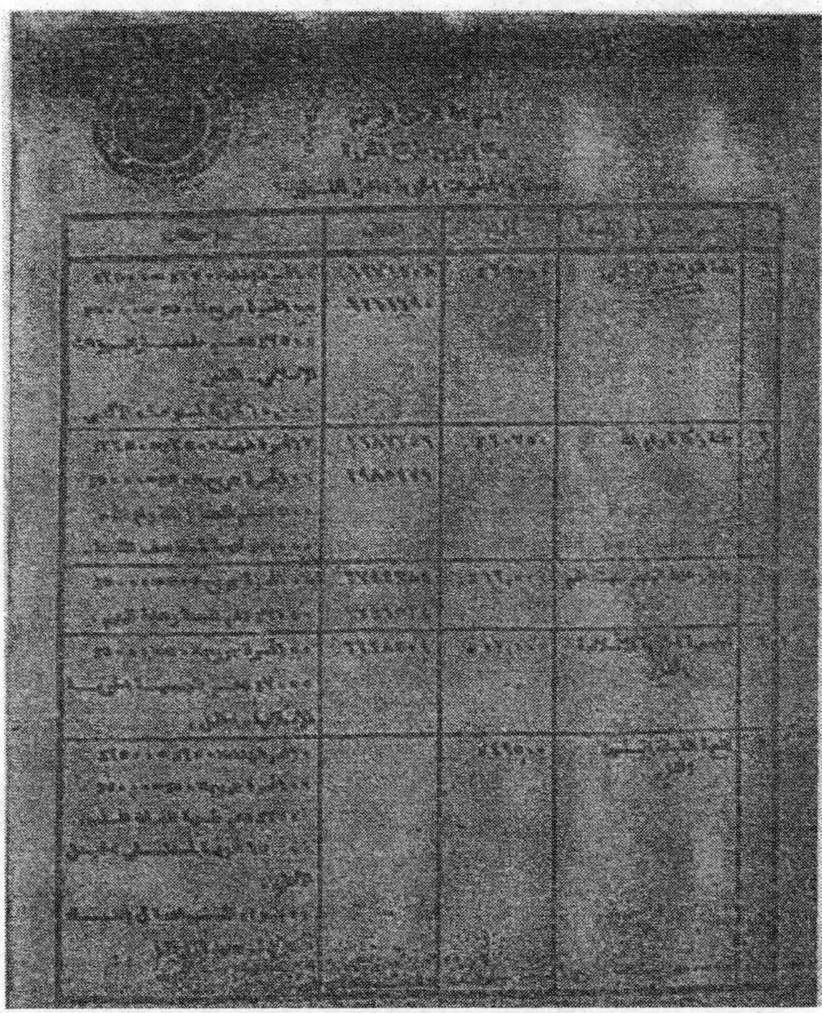

Saudi Chase Manhattan Check

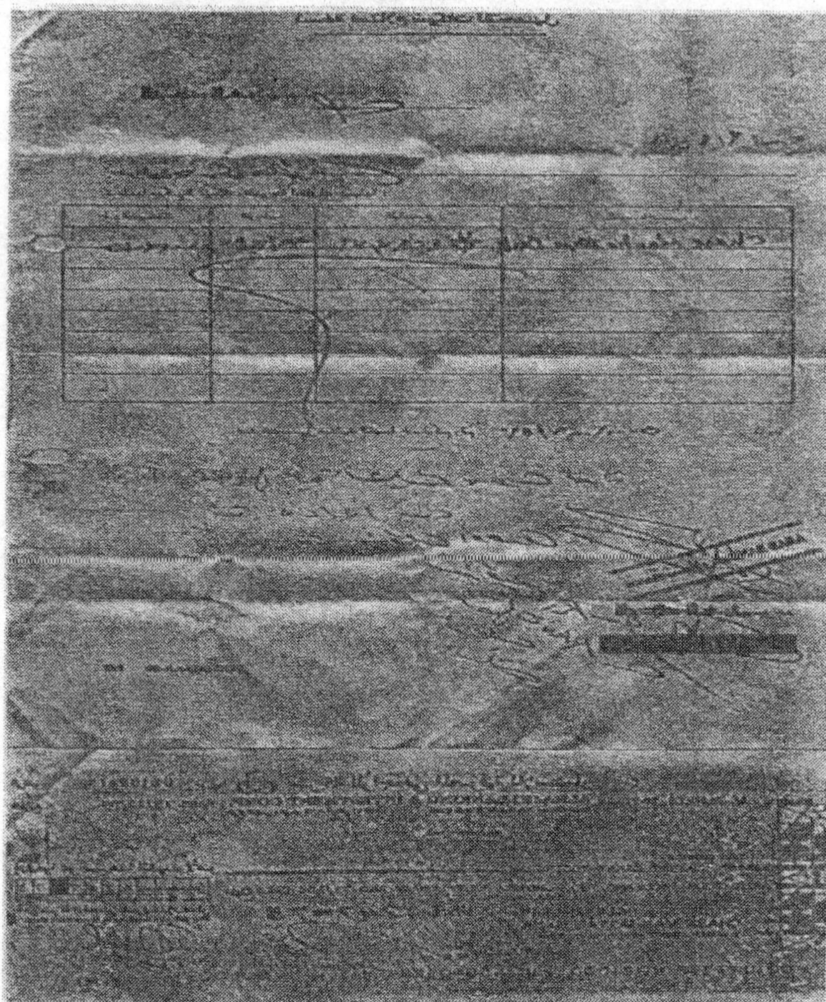

Saudi Committee for the Aid of the Al-Quds Intifada

المملكة العربية السعودية
اللجنة السعودية لدعم انتفاضة القدس
اللجنة العامة - الرياض

إجمالي المبلغ 2,040,000 ريال

شهداء انتفاضة القدس - الضفة الغربية (الدفعة العاشرة)

[illegible]	م	[illegible]	العمر	[illegible]	[illegible]	[illegible]	كيفية الاستشهاد	[illegible]	اسم الوكيل الشرعي	[illegible]	[illegible]	[illegible]
2195567974	1	عاطف احمد توفيق عارضة		9/12/2001	عرابة	جنين	قصف جوي وتصفية واغتيال	الغربي	[illegible]	939029147	القاهرة	20000
2195567975	2	[illegible]	39	10/25/2001	بيت لحم - مخيم عايدة		اطلاق النار في الرأس	الغربي	[illegible]	973675465	القاهرة	20000
2195567976	3	[illegible]	13	12/16/2001	الخليل - [illegible]		قصف صاروخي	الغربي	[illegible]	954582928	القاهرة	20000
2195567977	4	[illegible]	21	9/14/2001	نابلس		انفجار عبوة ناسفة	الغربي	[illegible]	990650121	القاهرة	20000
2195567978	5	[illegible]		9/12/2001	طمون	جنين	قصف جوي [illegible]	الغربي	[illegible]	983290813	القاهرة	20000
2195567979	6	[illegible]	34	8/20/2001	نابلس - مخيم بلاطة		اشتباك مسلح	الغربي	[illegible]	832383309	القاهرة	20000
2195567980	7	[illegible]	16	11/18/2001	جنين - [illegible]		[illegible]	الغربي	[illegible]	988137832	القاهرة	20000
2195567981	8	[illegible]	30	10/18/2001	بيت لحم		اغتيال	الغربي	[illegible]	911663107	القاهرة	20000
2195567982	9	[illegible]	23	8/5/2001	طولكرم		اغتيال	الغربي	[illegible]	953793871	القاهرة	20000
2195567983	10	[illegible]	23	8/22/2001	نابلس - مخيم بلاطة		اشتباك مسلح	الغربي	[illegible]	919430739	القاهرة	20000-
2195567984	11	[illegible]	39	10/20/2001	القدس		اطلاق النار في الصدر	الغربي	[illegible]	80768799	القاهرة	20000
2195567985	12	[illegible]	23	12/14/2001	الخليل - [illegible]		اشتباك	الغربي	[illegible]	980310171	القاهرة	20000
2195567986	13	[illegible]		7/29/2001	[illegible]	جنين	اغتيال [illegible]	الغربي	[illegible]	972155931	القاهرة	20000
2195567987	14	[illegible]	34	10/14/2001	قلقيلية		[illegible]	الغربي	[illegible]	904199627	القاهرة	20000
2195567988	15	[illegible]	32	9/9/2001	طولكرم - ارتاح		عملية استشهادية	الغربي	[illegible]	987092132	القاهرة	20000
2195567989	16	[illegible]	22	10/19/2001	بيت لحم - مخيم عايدة		قصف المنزل [illegible]	الغربي	[illegible]	977110634	القاهرة	20000
2195567990	17	[illegible]	25	11/27/2001	جنين - [illegible]		عملية استشهادية في العفولة	الغربي	[illegible]	950622811	القاهرة	20000
2195567991	18	[illegible]	35	10/31/2001	طولكرم		اغتيال [illegible]	الغربي	[illegible]	949910475	القاهرة	20000
2195567992	19	[illegible]	22	10/24/2001	رام الله - [illegible]			الغربي	[illegible]	944225929	القاهرة	20000
2195567993	20	[illegible]	34	10/20/2001	اريحا			الغربي	[illegible]	999608274	القاهرة	20000
2195567994	21	[illegible]	39	8/29/2001	الخليل - ترقوميا		رصاص بالرأس	الغربي	[illegible]	901147826	القاهرة	20000
2195567995	22	[illegible]	32	9/1/2001	نابلس		انفجار عبوة ناسفة	الغربي	[illegible]	980478223	القاهرة	20000
2195567996	23	[illegible]	29	12/9/2001	طولكرم - بيت ليد		اغتيال	الغربي	[illegible]	905396215	القاهرة	20000
2195567997	24	[illegible]		11/6/2001	مخيم جنين	جنين	[illegible]	الغربي	[illegible]	901874826	القاهرة	20000
2195567998	25	[illegible]	22	9/1/2001	الخليل		اشتباك مسلح	الغربي	[illegible]	951834710	القاهرة	20000
2195567999	26	[illegible]	30	8/5/2001	رام الله - [illegible]		عملية استشهادية	الغربي	[illegible]	81071908	القاهرة	20000
2195568000	27	[illegible]	20	11/6/2001	سلفيت - [illegible]		[illegible]	الغربي	[illegible]	904967448	القاهرة	20000
2195568001	28	[illegible]	25	9/16/2001	رام الله		اشتباك مسلح	الغربي	[illegible]	950055335	القاهرة	20000
2195568002	29	[illegible]	19	8/29/2001	طولكرم - [illegible]		اغتيال	الغربي	[illegible]	954730628	القاهرة	20000
2195568003	30	[illegible]	18	9/3/2001	الخليل		[illegible]	الغربي	[illegible]	973180634	القاهرة	20000
2195568004	31	[illegible]	25	11/11/2001	بيت لحم - [illegible]		انفجار عبوة ناسفة	الغربي	[illegible]	907377154	القاهرة	20000
2195568005	32	[illegible]		10/4/2000	[illegible]	جنين	رصاص حي في الصدر	الغربي	[illegible]	21965024	القاهرة	20000
2195568006	33	[illegible]	20	9/6/2001	طولكرم		قصف صاروخي / اغتيال	الغربي	[illegible]	963030812	القاهرة	20000
2195568007	34	[illegible]	55	10/24/2001	بيت لحم			الغربي	[illegible]	904685937	القاهرة	20000
2195568008	35	[illegible]	35	10/18/2001	بيت لحم		اغتيال	الغربي	[illegible]	908653469	القاهرة	20000
2195568009	36	[illegible]	28	10/21/2001	بيت لحم - [illegible]		[illegible]	الغربي	[illegible]	916743289	القاهرة	20000
2195568010	37	[illegible]	18	10/21/2001	جنين - [illegible]		[illegible]	الغربي	[illegible] **	940620453	القاهرة	20000

Report From the Website of the Royal Embassy of Saudi Arabia

Royal Embassy of Saudi Arabia
Information Office
Washington, D.C.

PRESS RELEASE
October 18, 2002

Saudi actions to crack down on terrorist financing:

- **Since September 11, all charitable groups have been audited to ensure that there are no links to suspected groups. Financial control mechanisms are required to ensure that evildoers cannot take advantage of these charitable groups in the future.**

Khaled Mishal Visits Riyadh

Roadmap

U.S. DEPARTMENT *of* STATE

A Performance-Based Roadmap to a Permanent Two-State Solution to the Israeli-Palestinian Conflict

At the outset of Phase I:

Security:
"Arab states cut off public and private funding and all other forms of support for groups supporting and engaging in violence and terror."

President Bush at Sharm El-Sheikh Summit:

"The leaders here today have declared their firm rejection of terror, regardless of its justifications or motives. They've also committed to practical actions to use all means to cut off assistance, including arms and financing to any terror group, and to aid the Palestinian Authority in their own fight against terror." (June 3, 2003)

Origins, Organization and Prevention of Terrorist Finance
Testimony

Jonathan M. Winer
Alston & Bird LLP
Former U.S. Deputy Assistant Secretary of State
International Law Enforcement

U.S. Senate Committee on Governmental Affairs
July 31, 2003

Mr. Chairman and Distinguished Members of the Committee:

I am honored to testify here today to share my views on terrorist finance, developed during my service as Deputy Assistant U.S. Secretary of State from 1994 through 1999, and most recently, in connection with my service on as a member of the Independent Task Force of the Council on Foreign Relations on Terrorist Finance chaired by Maurice R. Greenberg and directed by William F. Wechsler and Lee S. Wolosky. My testimony has been heavily informed by and is consistent with the report issued by that Task Force in the fall of 2002, whose recommendations I endorse. The views as expressed are my own, but the recommendations I make here parallel in large part those of the Task Force as regrettably few of the recommendations made almost a year ago have yet to become reality.

On the U.S. side, it is essential that the Administration declassify much of the information it may have regarding Saudi terrorist finance, starting with the matters pertaining to the September 11 attacks. With almost two years having passed since the attacks, it can do so without imperiling investigations: the terrorist financiers covered their tracks long ago. I spent years reviewing highly sensitive intelligence information pertaining to illicit finance. I do not find credible the assertions that have been made that declassifying information provided to Congress by the Administration more than a year ago would jeopardize U.S. national security. Sunlight is the best disinfectant. The people have a right to know about the trail of money that made it possible for the September 11 terrorists to murder our people. The material should be declassified.

As a second recommendation, let me emphasis how important it is that the government of Saudi Arabia make public what it knows regarding terrorist finance activities of some key Saudi Arabian businessmen as well as make public what it has done to seize the assets of and punish its terrorist financiers. It is deeply ironic that Saudi Arabia has demanded that the U.S. declassify and release portions of the September 11 report that reportedly discuss Saudi terrorist funding. The Saudi government itself continues to maintain secrecy about what it now knows about past financial support for terrorism on the part of Saudi businessmen. It similarly continues to maintain secrecy about its own actions, if any, against the assets of such businessmen.

The relationship between the U.S and Saudi Arabia has been sorely torn by September 11. If Saudi Arabia is to repair that relationship, as well as restore its image internationally, it needs to go beyond the public actions it is now taking against terrorists in Saudi Arabia, to take public actions against those who funded Al Qaeda, permitting the allocation of millions of dollars donated in the name of charity to Islamic terrorists who used them in the cause of mass murder.

Summary

Until the terrorist attacks of September 11, 2001, terrorist finance had remained a back-burner issue internationally, despite efforts by the U.S. to require countries to make it a serious crime and to prosecute it as a serious crime. Combating terrorist finance was especially minimalist in the Middle East, where no jurisdiction had taken substantial steps to discourage it, and few even had minimal anti-money laundering or financial transparency laws in place.

Since the attacks, international organizations, responding largely to US-led efforts, issued a series of measures mandating that jurisdictions curtail the passage of terrorist finance, including UN Security Council Resolution 1373, the FATF Eight Special Recommendations on Terrorist Finance, and significant initiatives by the G-8 and the European Union. Each of these resolutions made clear in broad terms that nations must take more action to inhibit the passage of terrorist finance through domestic financial institutions. These international efforts were supported by individual acts of legislation passed by numerous jurisdictions, including global financial centers such as the United Kingdom and United States, and states in the Middle East and southwest Asia previously known for minimal oversight of their financial sectors. The resolutions were passed in an effort to impede the passage of funds to terrorist groups in the Americas, Asia, Middle East and Western Europe.

During the first two years after the September 11 attacks, these initiatives have achieved modest successes. Several dozen nations have seized terrorist assets, together comprising more than $112 million, according to the UN terrorist monitoring group. Many more countries, including a number in the Middle East, have declared that despite diligent search, there have been no terrorist funds to be found. The U.S has shut down one substantial international hawala network, Al Barakaat. However, there is little evidence to date that new laws requiring alternative remittance houses to register, enacted in the U.S., Hong Kong and elsewhere, have yet had the desired effect of forcing such institutions to either submit to regulation and transparency or to shut down. While a substantial number of countries have enacted new laws and imposed new regulations to avoid name and shame lists, institutions licensed in poorly regulated jurisdictions still have substantially unimpeded access to the financial institutions and markets of New York, London, and Tokyo. Gold and diamond markets, hedge funds, and free-trade zones continue to abound, with few controls and open access to international wire transfer capabilities. In practice, while terrorist groups face new risks in laundering their money, they continue to have a variety of mechanisms by which to finance their activities, involving a range of both banking and non-banking financial institutions. Further progress in protecting against international terrorist finance is unlikely without international action to require customer identification and verification, know-your-customer, and the ability to trace funds across jurisdictions. Whether non-Islamic states with sophisticated financial services sectors will require the financial institutions they regulate to require such standards of their foreign counterparts, especially in the Middle East and Asia remains to be seen.

Much about the origin and history of recent terrorist finance remains veiled not only by the terrorists but also by ongoing investigative efforts and government secrecy. But one core fact should by now no longer be in dispute: Saudi Arabia has been the most significant source of terrorist funds for Al Qaeda. Accordingly, the response of Saudi Arabia to the terrorist finance problem remains at the center of an effective global response to terrorism. Although Saudi Arabia has now undertaken a series of actions to combat terrorist finance, it has yet to take a number of critically important public actions that will be essential for the further disruption of Al Qaeda's global operations. Steps that have been taken include Saudi disruption of operational cells and arrests or killings of more than 25 suspected members of al Qaeda; announcements that audits of Saudi based charities have been completed; condemnations of extremism and arrests of radical clerics. However, other major terrorist financiers continue to live in Saudi Arabia not visibly affected by enforcement activity.

For further progress against terrorist finance, both the U.S. and Saudi Arabia need to take further actions. Here at home, we need to centralize coordination and oversight of terrorist finance. The President should appoint a special assistant for terrorist finance, as was proposed last fall by the Council on Foreign Relations Task Force on Terrorist Financing. The U.S. should press the EU, the G-8, and all countries in the Middle East to criminalize all fundraising for Hamas, everywhere. The U.S. Treasury should use the Patriot Act Section 311 special designations to apply sanctions to designated foreign financial institutions that we know to have allowed themselves to be used for funneling terrorist funds, tailoring the sanctions to achieve the maximum impact on terrorist financing. We should be sharing greater information with the U.S. private sector regarding what we know and suspect about terrorist money laundering and finance. We should be intensifying our training efforts with other countries on specific strategies to counter terrorist finance. And when it comes to terrorist financiers, regardless of their location or their nationality, we should be prepared to name names and freeze assets, regardless of such political considerations as whether the terrorist financiers live in a large, oil producing Gulf State. As for Saudi Arabia, it needs to arrest terrorist financiers, freeze their assets, and announce these actions in public. Without substantial and visible public actions by Saudi Arabia against terrorist financiers, continued stress in the U.S.-Saudi relationship is not merely probable.

Funding Methods For Terrorism.

The methods employed by terrorist groups to garner illicit profits are varied, and each group routinely employs one or more mechanisms to raise funds, to place and layer funds, and to invest funds for terrorism. These include a mixture of ideological, religious, criminal, and business sources, which often mingle and merge, so that it becomes difficult to determine the provenance of any particular terrorist funds in any given case.

Terrorist funds for Al Qaeda have come not only from misapplied Islamic charitable contributions but also from investments in otherwise legitimate businesses, such as Al Barakaat's financial services and Telecommunications Empire. Traditional sources of funds for criminal organizations are also tapped, especially extortion. There also been a number of reports that businessmen paid Al-Qaeda operatives extortion money to prevent attacks on their business interests throughout the Middle East. The alleged payments were made to assuage Bin Laden, who reportedly threatened to initiate attacks against targets in politically moderate Middle Eastern states, such as Jordan and Saudi Arabia. Similarly, the tiny Abu Sayyaf Group (ASG), which controls sections of the southern Philippines and has close ties with a number of Middle Eastern terrorist groups, routinely demands monthly "revolutionary taxes" from local residents, businessmen, and white-collar workers. It also raises funds through kidnappings for ransom.

Terrorist groups are also linked to narcotics trafficking. The LTTE, a highly organized terrorist group centered in the northern and eastern coastal areas of Sri Lanka, reportedly has close ties to drug trafficking networks in Burma, and members of Hizballah are linked to drug trafficking in Lebanon. The Al-Qaeda network received millions of dollars per annum through the production and distribution of opium, which was smuggled through neighboring Central Asian states, or transported to distribution networks in East Africa. Many terrorist groups have also been linked to other criminal activities, including smuggling and counterfeiting operations. For instance, the Real IRA is active in smuggling assorted goods into Great Britain. In recent years the Real IRA established close links to British criminal groups to sell converted diesel fuel on the black market. Moreover the Real IRA established tobacco-smuggling operational links to east European mafia, and oversees counterfeit operations that produce pirated copies of compact discs and videocassettes. When these illicit profits are coupled with the millions of dollars raised by Irish communities in the United States, the Real IRA can easily afford to recruit new members, construct bomb-making facilities, procure light weaponry, and maintain close contact with other terrorist groups, especially in the Americas.

Funds raised through criminal activities are supplemented with private donations. Prior to Al Qaeda taking advantage of charitable contributions, this approach was undertaken by both Hamas and Hizbollah, which during the 1980 and 1990s received significant financial support from Palestinian émigrés in Western Europe and the US, and even greater support from wealthy Muslims within the Middle East in their course of their making of *zakat*, or charitable contributions. Since the onset of the Second Intifada in mid-2000, Muslim clerics and religious leaders from Lebanon, Sudan, Algeria, and Jordan publicly and routinely solicit Muslims to support suicide attacks against Israel by making donations to Hamas activists. The backing of religious leaders in the Middle East provides Hamas with spiritual support, and assures a sympathetic presence in mosques, which routinely collect funds for the movement. Efforts to combat terrorist finance schemes were bolstered by pledges from Kuwait, Bahrain and the United Arab Emirates to improve the monitoring of charitable donations. This may prove a difficult task. Intelligence agencies anticipate that the increased presence of U.S. troops in the Middle East may foster anti-US sentiment in the region, and increase donations to charities linked to Middle Eastern terrorist groups.

The growing sophistication and participation of Islamic investors in western finance has also provided an increased source of opportunity for terrorist finance. International investigations continue among securities regulators to determine whether international commodities and futures markets, customarily a secure means of conducting financial transactions with relative anonymity, were used by buyers who knew about the 11 September attacks in advance. In the days after the attacks on the U.S., financial regulators uncovered an unusual pattern of purchases in shares of a number of companies that fell 40% after the attacks, and other suspicious investments. Though no certain links have been made to members of terrorist organizations, at least one purchaser of the suspect investments reportedly left more than $2 million in profits uncollected after September 11, rather than claim the funds and thereby risk identification.

The extent to which nation-states continue to sponsor terrorist groups remains an open question. The Al-Qaeda network received significant passive and active support from more than one government in the region, and its support from wealthy Saudi Arabians is by now difficult to dispute based on documentation found on the hard drives of computers used by Al Qaeda operatives. U.S. officials continue to signal, with little public evidence to date, that Iraq may have provided support for some Al-Qaeda operations, including the attack on the USS Cole in October 2000. There are also reports that Iran has significantly increased funding to a number of Middle Eastern terrorist groups. In an attempt to radicalize the Palestinian peace process and establish an Islamic Palestinian state similar to its own, Iran has allegedly increased its financial support for Hamas through wire transfers in Jordan. According to public reports, the Iranian embassy in Damascus has been frequently used as a meeting place for members of Hamas and Iranian intelligence agents, suggesting ongoing cooperation among Syria, Iran and Hamas.

Role of The Muslim Brotherhood.

The Muslim Brotherhood ("Brotherhood") has played a central role in providing both the ideological and technical capacities for supporting terrorist finance on a global basis. Officially *Jamiat al-Ikhwan al-Muslimun,* literally translated as the Society of Muslim Brothers, the Muslim Brotherhood was founded as a religious and political organization in Egypt in 1928 by an pan-Islamicist, Hasan al-Banna. Early opposed to secular tendencies in Islamic nations, the organization has sought to foster a return to the original precepts of the Qur'an. It grew rapidly, establishing an educational, economic, military, and political infrastructure. Threatened by its power, Egypt's government banned the organization in 1948 and 1954. It has since existed largely as a clandestine but militant group, marked by its rejection of Western influences.

Elements of the Brotherhood reached Saudi Arabia and the other Gulf states following the Egyptian disaspora. Egyptian Salawfi Muslims involved in the Brotherhood came into closer contact with Saudi Wahabism, and the Brotherhood began to access to Saudi and other Gulf state funds through the zakat process. As a result, Islamic militants had access to revenue streams with no controls that they used to support Islamic associations, Islamic proselytizing, and in some cases, militant and terrorist activity. This Gulf State support, in which Kuwait has played a substantial secondary to Saudi Arabia's primary role, has likely been the most significant source of Al-Qaeda's funding.

As described by Kuwaiti liberal politician Abdallah Bishara, "Charitable associations of Kuwait, Saudi Arabia and other Gulf countries have invested huge sums in Afghanistan and its neighboring countries to create a structure of schools, Koranic seminaries, Islamic cooperatives, humanitarian associations, and social services networks that feed Islamic terrorism. This Islamic system is the rear echelon that supports Bin Laden. And this is why it becomes truly specious to try to check with a magnifying lens whether this money has indeed ended up in Bin Laden's pockets. What really counts is knowing that the military training camps in Afghanistan, Pakistan, Kashmir, and Chechnya that are under Bin Laden's authority are nurtured by that Islamic system which in its turn was created with money from the Gulf. You will not find a single cent in the possession of these organizations that did not come from the Gulf region. . . . If it were wanted to dry up the funding sources of terrorist organizations at the world level it would not be difficult, because they are all concentrated here in the Gulf region."

One example of the relationship of the Brotherhood to the development of Al Qaeda funding networks, as well as to the involvement of wealthy individuals from Gulf States, is he allegation that Al Taqwa, one of the Brotherhood's major financial mechanisms during the 1990's, received funds from Kuwait and the United Arab Emirates that were then transferred to its accounts in Malta and Lugano and then to the Bahamas. Another is the number of Islamic institutions based in Yemen with alleged ties to the Muslim Brotherhood alleged to act as incubators for terrorist training. These included the al-Baihani school in Aden, owned by a charity, now forcibly closed by Yemen's government, the private al-Iman university, run by Sheikh Abd al-Majid al-Zindani, a leader of the Islah party's radical wing, also temporarily closed, and the Dar Al-Hadith institute, located in a tribal region where Yemeni forces had been searching for suspected Al-Qaeda members, was closed. Last year, the government pushed through a bill unifying the education curriculum and abolishing the so-called scientific institutes - strict Islamic schools with connections to Sudan's erstwhile spiritual leader, Hassan al-Turabi, and, allegedly, Osama bin Laden

The Brotherhood's role in the development of other militant Islamic organizations is also illustrated by its relationship to the establishment of the Indonesian terrorist group Jemaah Islamiya, the JI, created with the aim of setting up an Islamic state in Indonesia. JI's founder has acknowledged being inspired by the Brotherhood in the goal of jihad as a means to the creation of an Islamic state in South East Asia covering Malaysia, Indonesia, Singapore and the southern Philippines. JI then received funding from wealthy Saudis affiliated with Al Qaeda. In turn, the Brotherhood's central financial mechanism,

Al Taqwa, established operations in Malaysia that linked to JI. According to the U.S. Treasury, the al Taqwa group, which was designated as terrorist financiers by Treasury on November 7, 2001, has long acted as financial advisers to Al Qaeda, with offices in Switzerland, Liechtenstein, Italy and the Caribbean, providing direct assistance to Osama bin Laden as well as investment advice and cash transfer mechanisms for Al Qaeda and other radical Islamic groups.

Separately, the Brotherhood has been characterized by the U.S. Treasury as the parent from which Hamas ultimately emerged. It also has been linked to a wide range of Islamic terrorist groups, including at various times over the past two decades, the Tamil Tigers, the Afghan mujahidin, the Kashmiri mujahidin, and wars of Islamic revival from Algeria to Egypt, Sudan to Saudi Arabia, Bosnia to Chechnya, Afghanistan to Kashmir, and Central Asia to Mindanao in the Philippines.

In summary, the Brotherhood spread both the ideology of militant pan-Islamicism and became the spine upon which funding operations for militant pan-Islamicism was built, taking funds largely generated from wealthy Gulf State elites and distributing them for terrorist education, recruitment, and operations widely dispersed throughout the world, especially in areas where Muslims hoped to displace non-Muslim or secular governments.

<u>International Efforts to Counter Terrorist Finance.</u>

The United Nations Convention for the Suppression of Financing of Terrorism was proposed eighteen months before 11 September 2001, but had received little serious attention. Forty-one states had signed the Convention, but only six had ratified the convention before September 2001. After 11 September 2001, in an effort to assure U.N. support for combating terrorist finance schemes, the UN Security Council unanimously adopted Resolution 1373 (UNSCR 1373), a binding document that requires all 189 U.N. member states to criminalize the use or collection of funds intended, or known to be intended, for terrorism; freeze immediately funds, assets or economic resources of persons who commit, attempt to commit, or facilitate terrorist acts and entities owned or controlled by them; prohibit nationals or persons within their territories from aiding or providing any aid to the persons and entities involved in terrorism; refrain from providing any form of support to entities or persons involved in terrorism; and deny safe haven to those who finance, plan, support, or commit terrorist acts, or provide safe havens.

Member states were required to submit progress reports, providing information as to how they have implemented Resolution 1373 by the end of 2001. The incomplete, and in some cases misleading responses provided a window of the distance yet required to combat terrorist finance by governments in some of the most vulnerable countries. For instance, UAE described as anti-terrorist legislation laws forbidding efforts to engage in armed overthrow of the governments of the UAE. Responses by Yemen and Oman were too vague to permit analysis of whether they had undertaken any substantial anti-terrorist efforts. During 2002, however, a number of countries, including most of those in the

Middle East other than Saudi Arabia, enacted comprehensive anti-money laundering and terrorist finance laws, which on paper at least fully implemented Resolution 1373.

At the community level, the European Union (EU) undertook several efforts against terrorist financing and money laundering in the wake of September 11. On 4 December 2001 the European Community adopted an amendment to Directive 91/308, its main anti-money laundering instrument, to expand reporting obligations to include attorneys, and require the oversight of funds channeled through exchange bureaus .The EU also froze the assets of terrorist groups, charities and individuals linked to terrorist finance schemes, established a counter-terrorist unit within Europol intended to work closely with US counterparts, and pledged to ratify a convention on mutual assistance in criminal matters during the course of 2002. The EU undertook plans to introduce a union-wide arrest warrant to replace the current extradition system between the countries. Within the EU, however, legal measures are generally not applicable until they have been undertaken by individual EU member states, many of which have been slow to take action curtailing illicit finance schemes. In other cases, some EU states have taken independent views of which groups activities are terrorist, and which are not subject to sanction. For instance, the EU has not frozen the assets of organizations affiliated with HAMAS, only funds destined for Izz al-Din al-Qassam, the military arm of Hamas. Investigators, however, routinely link the funding of Hamas militant activities to Hamas front organizations that claim to support only social activities in the Middle East.

The FATF responded to the September 11 attacks by explicitly adding terrorist finance to its existing remit to combat money laundering after a two-day meeting in Washington in late October 2001. It issued a series of Eight Special Recommendations dealing specifically with terrorist financing, which if systematically implemented and enforced, would have a substantial impact. The recommendations highlighted the level of work still be undertaken, asking countries to ratify the 1999 UN Convention for the Suppression of the Financing of Terrorism and UNSCR Resolution 1373; to criminalize the financing of terrorism, terrorist acts and terrorist organizations; freeze and confiscate terrorist assets; report suspicious transactions linked to terrorism; provide the greatest possible measure of assistance to enforcement agencies in other jurisdictions that investigate terrorist financing; impose anti-laundering requirements, such as licensing, on alternative remittance systems; strengthen customer identification measures in all wire transfers; and to ensure that non-profit organizations and charities are not misused to finance terrorism.

FATF member states pledged to implement the Eight Special Recommendations by June 2002, and develop a process of self-assessment to aide other states in implementing the new recommendations. This deadline, however, was not met, because of a lack of cooperation in the international financial community, especially from the Gulf States, none of whom have yet to implement the entire array of Eight Special Recommendations. In theory, the FATF could "blacklist" non-cooperative countries and call on its member states to implement sanctions, such as detailed inspections of accounts that contain funds from non-compliant jurisdictions or a reduction in bilateral and international aid programs. But to date, the FATF has not undertaken action to name and shame for failures to abide by terrorist finance recommendations.

After September 11, the International Monetary Fund (IMF) and the World Bank each pledged to assist in the campaign to cut terrorist funding. In November 2001, the IMF's International Monetary Financial Committee (IMFC) called on all countries to establish financial intelligence units and to increase information sharing across jurisdictions. The IMFC also agreed to counter terrorist financing by accelerating its program of offshore financial center assessments, and to work more closely with the FATF. The World Bank held a ministerial-level meeting in November 2001, and pledged to aid in capacity-building in states that are ill-equipped to regulate money laundering or terrorist financing and are unlikely to meet the new international standards. However, neither of these organizations has chosen to make financial transparency, including effective action against money laundering and terrorist finance, a conditionality on further lending activities.

At a closed meeting held in Monaco on 7 June 2002 members of the Egmont group, an informal organization composed of experts in financial intelligence from 78 countries, met to discuss on-going efforts to combat terrorist finance schemes. The frank discussions revealed a growing frustration toward a number of Gulf States for failing to track funds linked to al-Qaeda. Western regulators expressed marked concern over the failure by jurisdictions in the Middle East to provide assistance to enforcement agencies in other jurisdictions, confiscate terrorist assets, and impose licensing requirements on alternative remittance systems, especially hawaladars located throughout the region.

Efforts by Middle Eastern States to Curtail Terrorist Finance.

The well-publicized transfer of funds from financial institutions in the United Arab Emirates (UAE) to al-Qaeda cell members in the United States has caused the UAE to reverse years of inactivity, and pass legislation to combat financial crimes. In early October 2001 the UAE put into force the Law Regarding the Criminalization of Laundering of Property Derived from Unlawful Activity, and drafted legislation to criminalize hawalas. Individuals convicted of an irregular money transfer to finance kidnapping, piracy and terrorism in the UAE could receive a seven-year prison sentence and a $272,000 fine. Financial institutions are now obliged to report suspicious transactions and the Central Bank is authorized to freeze suspected assets up to seven days. A financial information unit is to be formed within the Central Bank, as well as a National Anti-Money Laundering Committee, chaired by the Governor of the Central Bank. Significant problems still plague financial institutions located in the UAE. There have been no convictions related to financial crimes in the emirates, and Western regulators remain skeptical over the ability of UAE to oversee transactions through hawala brokers. Notably, many bank tellers in the UAE are South Asian immigrant workers, for whom questioning or challenging of the local documentation of an UAE citizen could prove problematic.

UAE concrete action to assist in efforts to combat terrorist finance schemes over the fall and early winter of 2001 presaged other Middle Eastern states initiating nascent steps to combat terrorist finance schemes. In early 2002, Saudi officials invited the FATF into the Kingdom and instructed the appropriate authorities to assist in the preparation of regulations to curtail financial crimes. The Saudi Arabian Monetary Authority reportedly began monitoring 150 suspicious accounts at the request of US law enforcement officials. Western officials have expressed concerns, however, at pronouncements from Saudi officials who have stated that accounts held by Saudi nationals are only being monitored in financial institutions located outside of the Kingdom. Despite conflicting statements by U.S. officials, no one has yet identified any bank accounts related to terrorist finance schemes that have been frozen by Saudi officials. Other states in the Gulf have followed Saudi Arabia, mixing reform and denial. In late March 2002, for example, Oman issued an anti-money laundering law as part of a pledge to combat the financing of global terrorism. However, at the same time, authorities in Oman continue to contend that domestic financial institutions are not vulnerable to money-laundering, despite the reality that Oman abuts the Pakistan/Afghanistan/Iran/Europe drug smuggling route, and offers a sophisticated financial infrastructure to assist in the transfer of illicit assets out of the region.

Central Role of Saudi Arabia

In my judgment, based on the public information I have reviewed since the September 11 attacks, Saudi Arabian funders have constituted the preponderant sources of funds for the development of Al Qaeda, and a major source of funds for many other terrorist organizations, including Hamas. Notably, however, the public evidence regarding Saudi support of terrorists is both murky and voluminous. It is murky because only sparse evidence in the form of documents and witnesses has been made public regarding particular terrorist financiers by the U.S. or other governments since the September 11 attacks. It is voluminous in that most of the major elements of Al Qaeda have reported Saudi funding ties, and Saudi funds permeate the world of Islamic charities, supporting entities in the Middle East, South Asia, Southeast Asia, Europe and North America tied to terrorism. On a regional basis, such terrorist funding links include:

- In Pakistan, support for religious schools by Saudi charities that have become training grounds for Al Qaeda at a sufficiently dangerous level that President Musharref has requested such support to cease.
- In Afghanistan, Albania, Bosnia, and Chechnya, direct support for Islamic resistance by Saudi charities such as Khalid bin Mahfouz's and Yasin al Qadi's Muwafaq or Blessed Relief and Benevolence International, as well as providing direct support to Hamas for terrorist activities.
- In Europe, financial support for Mosques linked to Al Qaeda and/or the Muslim Brotherhood, in such countries as Germany, Italy and the United Kingdom. This has included funneling by Al Qaeda of funds from Saudi Arabia to front companies in Madrid, Spain between 1995 and 2001. The companies were allegedly controlled by Muhammad Galeb Kalaje Zouaydi, European chief financier for Al Qaeda, and a Syrian (not Saudi) national. Allegedly, hundreds of

thousands of dollars flowed from Saudi Arabia into the accounts of these companies and to Al Qaeda and other radical Islamicist groups.

- In the U.S., funding of numerous charities by Suleiman Abdul Al-Aziz al-Rajhi, a senior member of one of Saudi Arabia's most prominent families. These charities, largely based in Herndon, Virginia, are according to press reports under current investigation by the FBI and have been in turn linked to Muslim Brotherhood specially designated terrorist finance company Al-Taqwa.
- In the Philippines, funding by Khamil al-Shalifa, a brother-in-law of Osama bin Laden, of Abu Sayyaf and possibly of Jamaah Ismaliya in Indonesia.

<u>What's the Evidence for Terrorist Finance Involving Saudi Arabians?</u>

There are many data points regarding Saudi Arabia and Saudi Arabian persons as sources of funds for Al Qaeda and other terrorist groups, but little narrative material laying out and integrating the data into a cohesive account. Moreover, because of the scanty information that has been made public, it remains very difficult to determine the extent to which persons that have been publicly identified as linked to terrorist finance intentionally engaged in the activity, or provided funds that were then abused by others, or taken beyond authorized military purposes, such as funding Hamas or rebels in Chechnya, or always intended for Al Qaeda's general use.

Current public information about these strands includes:

The Golden Chain. A handwritten list found by the FBI in a raid of the Saudi charity Benevolence International in Sarajevo in March 2002 purports to specify 20 wealthy donors to Al Qaida, including "the bin Laden brothers" and "Baterji," an apparent reference to Adel Abdul Jail Baterjee.

The Spanish/Saudi Connection. Mohamed Galeb Kalaje Zouaydi, a Syrian-born businessman charged with financing the September 11 terrorist attacks, allegedly channeled 670,000 Euros to Al Qaeda cells in the U.S., Germany, Saudi Arabia, Belgium, China, Turkey, Jordan, Syria and the Palestinian territory. According to Spanish police, Zouaydi lived in Saudi Arabia from 1996-2000, where he collected funds for purportedly charitable purposes that he then used to fund Al Qaeda. These operations were in turn linked to the purchase of weapons from Kosovo Albanian guerrillas for bin Laden's operations in Afghanistan and financial support for a Yemenese who attempted to murder the Prime Minister of Yemen. In the fall of 2002, U.S. and Spanish investigators were quoted as expressing frustration with their inability to obtain information from the government of Saudi Arabia regarding the "hundreds of thousands of dollars" that flowed from Saudi Arabia into the accounts of the Spanish companies used as conduits for money to Al Qaeda and other radical Islamic groups.

Allegations Regarding Major Saudi Bankers and Businessmen. Press accounts have repeatedly identified a small number of potentially significant sources of terrorist funds from Saudi Arabia, although the limits to publicly available information continues to make an informed assessment possible of the involvement of any of these individuals in the alleged activity. Reported names include such persons as Yasin Al-Qadi (Muwafaq); Sheikh Saleh Kamel, chair of the Dallah Al Baraka Group; Khalid bin Mahfouz and possibly some of his relatives; the Al-Rajhi Family, including Saleh Abdul Aziz Al Rajhi; Wael Hamza Jelaidan (Rabita Trust); the Abdullatif Jamil Group of companies; and Adel Abdul Jalil Batterjee.

Allegations Regarding Major Charities. Saudi funds have supported Islamic charitable activities throughout the world, for Islamic centers, mosques, schools, health care facilities, food distribution, and housing. Some half a dozen of the most visible charities, including two of Saudi Arabia's largest, the International Islamic Relief Organization ("IIRO") and the World Muslim League, have repeatedly been linked to supporting terrorist organizations in areas well beyond the Persian Gulf. These include:

The IIRO. Established in 1978, the IIRO has branches throughout the world. Its official activities, as specified on its website, include building mosques, financing and administering schools and sponsoring orphans. Its alleged finance of terrorism include: (a) employment of Mahmoud Jaballah at its offices in Canada, who was arrested in 1999 (and again in 2001) for belonging to Al Jihad; (b) financial support through its office in Zamoanga City in the Philippines for secessionist Islamic militants in the southern region of the country, through Mohammad Jamal Khalifa, Osama bin Laden's brother-in-law; (c) alleged direction of planned attacks on U.S. consulates in Madras and Calcutta through the offices of IIRO Asia; (d) alleged support for the terrorists involved in the 1998 embassy bombings in Dar Es Salaam, Tanzania and Nairobi, Kenya, leading to it being closed by the Kenyan government.

Muwafaq or Blessed Relief. Muwafaq has allegedly forwarded millions of dollars to Al Qaeda for terrorist training and resistance in Afghanistan, Bosnia, and Chechnya, as well as to Hamas.

Benevolence International, an Islamic charity founded in 1987 and alleged in a federal indictment in Chicago to have supported Al Qaeda for more than a decade. The charity spent a reported $3.4 million on relief operations in 2000-2001 alone. The initial president and secretary of the organization was Adel Batterjee, a Saudi identified by federal investigators as the person referred to in the "Golden Chain" memorandum found at the raid by Benevolence International's headquarters in Sarajevo specifying Al Qaeda's principal financial benefactors. Benevolence International also has had interlocking directors and senior officers from the World Muslim League.

Al-Haramain Islamic Foundation. This charity is based in Riyadh, with offices in more than 50 countries. Of these offices, U.S. intelligence has found sufficient evidence of terrorist finance activity, shared with the Saudi government to secure the near-term closing of their operations. As with the IIRO, its official activities include building mosques, financing and administering schools and sponsoring orphans. It has been listed by the U.S. as a specially designated global terrorist organization as a result of its alleged assistance to the Egyptian terrorist group known as Gamma Al Islamia, as well as contacts with the Taliban, Osama bin Laden and Al Qaeda. In May 2003, Saudi Arabia asked the Al-Haramain Islamic Foundation to suspend its activities outside of Saudi Arabia until a security clearance mechanism to screen all personnel is implemented. The charity has closed offices in Croatia, Albania and Ethiopia, and the Saudis state that closures are underway in Kenya, Tanzania, Indonesia and Pakistan, although there are other reports that some Al-Haramain offices have closed and then reopened, including the one in Indonesia.

Rabita Trust. Based in Pakistan, with the mission of repatriating and rehabilitating Pakistanis stranded in Bangladesh and India after the partitions, the Rabita Trust was founded by the secretary general of the Muslim World League and funded by wealthy Saudis. It was listed as a specially designated global terrorist organization by the U.S. on October 12, 2001.

World Muslim League. One of the largest charities created by the Saudi royal family, World Muslim League personnel have reportedly worked for or with Al Qaeda in Bosnia and Kenya.

Wafa Humanitarian Organization. This Saudi-funded charity was based in Afghanistan and listed as a specially designated global terrorist organization by the U.S. on December 20, 2001. It allegedly was involved in efforts to develop a nuclear program for Al Qaeda.

What Measures Has Saudi Arabia Taken to Combat Terrorist Finance?

The May 2003 terrorist attacks in Saudi Arabia have been described by Saudi Prince Bandar as "our September 11," prompting recognition by the government that further anti-terrorist steps are still required, including greater attention to combating terrorist finance. Since then, domestic anti-terrorist efforts by the Saudis have substantially intensified, as have efforts by terrorists to carry out attacks within the Kingdom. As of mid-June 2003, Saudi Arabia reported to the U.S. government that it had arrested some terrorist financiers and is prepared to arrest more over the summer of 2003. The Kingdom is also moving forward with an anti-money laundering and terrorist finance law that it intends to have in place by the time of its first assessment by the Financial Action Task Force ("FATF"), currently scheduled to begin in September 2003. However, public information on the actual activities undertaken by Saudi Arabia to combat terrorist finance remains obscured in several of the most important areas. These include:

Arrests. There have been no publicly reported law enforcement arrests involving terrorist finance. There have been several cases in which Saudi Arabia reported seized assets at the request of the U.S. In its report to the UN, Saudi Arabia stated that it had no successful prosecutions pertaining to terrorist finance acts on the part of any Saudi person, inside or outside of Saudi Arabia. According to the U.S. Department of State, Saudi Arabia has had a small number of prosecutions for money laundering that originated from the filing of suspicious transaction reports. One Saudi official has informally stated that an unspecified number of terrorist financiers have been arrested as of June 16, 2003, although no public announcement of the arrests had been made by that date. The same official also stated that the assets of Yasin al-Qadi, a wealthy Jeddah businessman listed on the specially designated global terrorist list, had also been frozen, but this has not been stated publicly or verified to date.

Asset Freezes. In October 2001, U.S. Treasury officials reported that Saudi Arabia had agreed to block financial assets for groups associated with Al Qaeda. Earlier, there had been reports that Saudi Arabia had agreed in September 2001 to freeze a small number of bank accounts from the National Commercial Bank ("NCB") and Faisal al Islamic Bank, but that subsequent cooperation has been "inconsistent." On January 28, 2002, Saudi Arabia announced that it had "acted" against 150 suspected terrorist accounts, but did not specify what action had been taken. In February 2002, Saudi Arabia announced that it had frozen four bank accounts linked to suspected terrorists. According to the Associated Press, the announcement was the first time Saudi Arabia had acknowledged it had frozen any terrorist-related accounts, and came the same day Interior Minister Prince Nayef told the AP that no accounts had been frozen. On February 16, 2002, an unnamed senior source at SAMA stated that four accounts had indeed been frozen, and that each belonged to foreigners in Saudi Arabia rather than to Saudi citizens. According to the Saudi government, as of December 2002, it had frozen 33 accounts belonging to three individuals totaling $5,574,196. In a recent press release, Saudi Arabia has stated that it was also one of the first countries in the world to take action against terrorist finance when it froze the assets of Osama bin Laden in 1994.

Action Against Charities. In March 2002, the U.S. and Saudi Arabia announced a joint crackdown on a Saudi charity whose operations in Bosnia and Somalia have been linked to Osama bin Laden, agreeing to freeze the assets of two branches of Al-Haramain Islamic Foundation. According to press accounts, Al-Haramain had been used by the Saudi government as a conduit for relief aid sent to Afghanistan as recently as January 2002 and the group had close ties to senior Saudi officials. U.S. Treasury officials were reported as alleging that Al-Haramain employees in Somalia and Bosnia had been connected to terrorists for years, funneling money to a terrorist group by pretending the funds were going to build orphanages, Islamic schools and mosques. In the summer of 2002, Saudi Arabia also reportedly undertook joint action with the U.S. to freeze the assets of Wa-el Hamza Julaidan, a Saudi fugitive alleged to have funneled money to Al Qaeda, and a director of the Rabita Trust. On June 12, 2003, Adel Al-Jubeir, the foreign affairs advisor to the Crown Prince, announced that Saudi Arabia had "closed the door on terrorist financing and money laundering," through promulgating new regulations to prevent charities from giving money outside Saudi Arabia except under strict controls and oversight. According to a June 12, 2003 Saudi press release, the new regulations require:

- Identification and consolidation of all bank accounts of a charitable or welfare society into a single account for each such organization.

- Requiring identification of each depositor.

- A prohibition on cash withdrawals from any Saudi charity.
- On-site inspections of Saudi banks to determine that the rules regarding charities are being implemented.
- Prohibiting Saudi foundations from maintaining offices outside of Saudi Arabia.

In addition, in June 2003, Saudi Arabia was reportedly preparing to close an additional eight branches of Al-Haramain Islamic Foundation at the request of the U.S., after the U.S. provided it with detailed intelligence regarding the involvement of those branches in terrorist finance.

Identification of Terrorist Fronts. Since September 11, Saudi Arabia has reportedly worked with the U.S. to identify a network of more than 50 shell companies that Osama bin Laden used to move money through more than 25 countries around the world. The companies were identified as located in the Middle East, Europe, Asia and the Caribbean. According to Anthony Cordesman, Saudi Arabia has "quietly" provided information on suspect Saudi accounts in Switzerland, Liechtenstein, Luxembourg, Denmark and Sweden.

Other Activity. On June 12, 2003, the Saudi government announced that it had accelerated a national study of its school curriculum, undertaken by its Ministry of Education, in response to the May 12, 2003 terrorist attacks within Saudi Arabia. It stated that it had adopted two pilot programs in Jeddah and Riyadh, that if successful would then be adopted nationally. It further stated that it had organized a new joint U.S.-Saudi counterterrorism team, including persons from both its intelligence and law enforcement agencies, to work side-by-side to share information on terrorism in "real time" and to conduct joint operations.

Is Saudi Arabia Still Vulnerable to Terrorist Finance?

Although Saudi Arabia has taken a number of actions to create a legislative framework to combat terrorist finance, it remains a potential source of funds for terrorism due to a number of vulnerabilities that remain difficult for its government to address. These include:

Charities. Islamic charities funded by Saudi Arabians are estimated to receive about $3 billion to $4 billion annually, of which some 10% to 20% is sent abroad. Until recently, there was little to no regulation of these charities by the Saudi government. Regulations newly imposed in June 2003 to constrain new funding to overseas charitable activities may reduce this vulnerability, depending on the effectiveness of the oversight function and the intentions of key bureaucrats within the country's religious ministry. However, the Saudi government is poorly situated to oversee effectively the disbursement of funds that have already left the Kingdom prior to the new regulations.

Use of Currency. Saudis frequently use cash for monetary transactions rather than electronic payments through credit cards or ATM machines. Reportedly the U.S. Treasury in May 2002 expressed concern to Saudi authorities regarding "the growing use of cash" in the country, making tracing of terrorist funds more difficult.

Alternative Remittance Systems. Hawala transactions outside banks and licensed moneychangers are illegal in Saudi Arabia. Saudi Arabia has reported to the UN that such services outside licensed banks are criminalized. The State Department has reported that SAMA has investigated a number of such cases in recent years. SAMA officials have acknowledged that the financial system is porous and includes illicit currency dealers and traditional hawaladars that are difficult to police.

Support for Islamic Militancy. Saudi Arabia has provided a political and religious environment in which Islamic militancy has flourished. Saudi support for the Palestinians in the Arab-Israeli conflict, urbanization, the Saudi educational system, unemployment, and some themes within Wahhabi religious teachings, including attacks on Christians and Jews by some Islamic teachers, have contributed to the politicization and radicalization of some Saudi Muslims. The country's educational curriculum has long included anti-Christian and Jewish hate literature, as has material issued by the Saudi Ministry of Islamic Practices. In recent weeks, Saudi Arabia has arrested a small number of extremist Islamic clerics and announced that it has sent thousands of others to school for courses to discourage militancy and extremism. However, the strands of religious extremism in Saudi Arabia have been strong and militant pan-Islamic theology remains a significant element fueling terrorism.

Ambivalence Towards Terrorism Associated With Islamic Militancy. Saudi Arabia has long taken the position that terrorist finance has not been a problem and has not existed in Saudi Arabia. For example, the Saudi July 2002 report to the UN stated "no financial operations with terrorist aims have thus far come to light in the country." It also appears to reserve to itself a determination of what constitutes terrorist finance, albeit in ambiguous terms. In its Resolution 1343 report, Saudi Arabia advised the UN that "in the absence of a precise and unequivocal definition of terrorism endorsed by the international community," it can only freeze or seize funds on the basis of a request from the Minister of the Interior to the Minister of Finance, and confiscate funds only on the basis of a judgment issued by a Saudi court. Given Saudi Arabia's signature on most international treaties concerning terrorism, the statement could be viewed as a veiled articulation of a position that terrorism has yet to be precisely defined internationally, and therefore Saudi Arabia is free to decide who and who are not terrorist financiers.

Bureaucratic Schizophrenia. Public expressions of Saudi attitudes towards asset freezes have been inconsistent. In October 2001, the governor of SAMA, Hamad Sayari, stated that the country had frozen every account Saudi Arabia could find on the U.S. Treasury terrorist list, but it later appeared that Saudi Arabia took the position that there were no such accounts. In February 2002, Saudi Arabia announced freezing four terrorist-related accounts in February 2002. Three months later, Sayari's deputy at SAMA was reported as categorically denying freezing any bank accounts, either of individuals or corporate entities, relating to either money laundering or terrorism. According to a BBC account, the official, Muhammad Al-Jasir, stated that "not even a single bank account has been frozen in Saudi Arabia," noting at the same time that "this Jewish state has not been complying with the 40 recommendations made by the FATF," in an apparent suggestion that inadequate regulation of money laundering in Israel was a greater terrorist finance problem than any that might be posed by Saudi Arabia.

Externally Held Funds. There is little the government of Saudi Arabia can do regarding the billions of dollars in Saudi-owned capital held outside of the country, mostly in trusts and international business companies where the ownership of the assets is hidden behind nominees and agents. This vulnerability is one that can only be dealt with through a global effort by international organizations and other governments to strengthen implementation of know-your-customer principles and to continue focused intelligence acquisition targeting possible terrorist financiers.

Legal Regime Regarding Money Laundering. As of June 2003, Saudi Arabia has yet to create a comprehensive legal regime to combat money laundering, leaving only drug money laundering as a predicate offense.

Reporting. Although the Central Bank has issued guidelines requiring know your customer and suspicious activity reporting, the government's failure to publish statistics makes it difficult to know how comprehensively this regime has been adopted in practice.

Asset Freezes. The handful of accounts reported frozen by Saudi Arabia to date can be interpreted as the result of several likely factors: limited Saudi intelligence on terrorist finance, a failure of political will, a willful refusal to share information with the U.S., and/or a reluctance to provide the Saudi public with information about enforcement actions taken within the Kingdom.

Conflicts of Interest. The fox-guarding-the-chicken-coop problem in Saudi Arabia is potentially substantial. For example, a task force established by the Jeddah Chamber of Commerce and Industry ("JCCI"), to develop a comprehensive financial and administrative system for charity in Saudi Arabia, was funded and overseen by the Muslim World League ("MWL"). On the one hand, this is unremarkable, as the MWL is Saudi Arabia's largest state-funded charity. On the other hand, MWL has itself been repeatedly linked to terrorist finance, through the activities of some of its member organizations, including the Rabita Trust, placed by the Treasury on its list of specially designated terrorist organizations. Notably, the approach of MWL's leadership to terrorism at an ideological level has itself been ambivalent. For example, a group of scholars affiliated with the MWL issued a statement January 11, 2002 describing terrorism to be only "any unjustified attack by individuals, groups or states against a human being." According to the MWL, terrorism could include an attack on a person's "religion, life, property and honor," but excluded jihad, as "struggling against occupiers and colonial settlers who drive people from their land and against those who help them" is legitimate in Islam.

Corruption. Saudi Arabia has been slow to create a system of civil law that would provide a secure, stable foundation to permit people and businesses to secure property rights and resolve commercial disputes. Despite some progress against corruption, cronyism and local agents remain norms in government contracting, and foreign investment has remained minimal, making the country both dependent upon, and resentful of, the ruling family. Checks and balances are few, making it difficult to police elements of the population, either within the ruling class or elsewhere, who may provide financial support for extremism.

<u>What Further Steps Could Saudi Arabia Take To Reduce the Threat?</u>

Enact a FATF-Compliant Money Laundering Law. In the current environment, Saudi Arabia's agreement with the FATF to schedule an assessment in the fall of 2003 likely is evidence of the Kingdom's expectation that it will have a FATF-compliant money laundering law in place by that time. Its draft money laundering law, which has yet to be made public, currently remains under review by a Saudi religious council, one of the final stages prior to adoption.

Intensify Crackdowns on Persons Linked to Terrorism. Soon after the September 11 attacks, Saudi Interior Minister Prince Nayef bin Abdul Aziz reportedly warned that persons engaged in terrorist activities were "ill and cannot be accepted in Saudi society, even if they were part of us. Some organs of the body may become ill, but the sick organ is amputated." Since then, arrests of persons in Saudi Arabia linked to terrorism have taken place in waves, often following the provision of intelligence to the government of Saudi Arabia by the U.S. These arrests appear to have substantially accelerated since the May 2003 attacks. To date, such enforcement activity has largely focused on terrorist cells themselves. They must now focus on terrorist financiers.

Stringently Oversee Charities. The Saudi government appears determined to gain control over the uses of funds overseas raised by charities within the Kingdom as a matter of protecting its own national security. It also appears willing to work with the U.S. on shutting down particular foreign offices of Saudi charities when there is evidence to enable the Saudi government to make an adequate case for such closures with its own clerics. However, follow-through has been inconsistent. In case of Al Harmadain, for example, foreign offices have closed and reopened. To date, it remains uncertain whether oversight of charities within Saudi Arabia's borders yet extends to the actual activities in the field of Saudi-supported charities operating in the field. Oversight of the financial activities of firms operating in other countries can be difficult for governments in any context. For Saudi Arabia to do so regarding Islamic charities will require a sustained effort. Moreover, such an effort is extremely unlikely to succeed in the absence of the application of public sanctions to charities found to have engaged in prohibited activities.

Make Actions Against Terrorist Finance Public. Adel A. Al-Jubeir, the foreign affairs advisor to the Crown Prince responsible for communicating Saudi efforts regarding terrorist finance to the U.S. public, argues that the Kingdom has sought privacy in the past regarding problems such as terrorist finance, but now is moving towards greater transparency and disclosure to its own public given that public's desire to see the terrorists who have undertaken bombings within the Kingdom punished. Such public naming-and-shaming is essential. It remains, unfortunately, invisible in the area of terrorist finance, raising the question of whether enforcement activity is actually taking place. Saudi Arabia needs to let the world know when it has taken an action against a specific designated terrorist, rather than to speak in generalities only.

Continue to Assist the U.S. The U.S. government is best in the position to monitor Saudi international cooperation against terrorist finance by assessing the Saudi response to particular requests for information on the financial activities of suspected terrorist financiers, and its willingness to freeze assets of such persons or entities. One indicator of such cooperation would be agreement to provide access to suspected terrorist financiers and their agents and related documents to U.S. government investigators. Another would be to return to the U.S. any Saudis who have fled to Saudi Arabia to avoid U.S. legal proceedings or questioning.

Arrest and Seize Assets of Prominent Al-Qaeda Financiers. Saudi Arabia needs to take public action against the Saudis involved in the Golden Chain where there is evidence to show financial support for Al Qaeda after the time of Osama bin Laden's expulsion from Saudi Arabia in 1992. These actions need to include arrests and asset seizures.

Extradite Terrorist Financiers. Beyond arrests and asset seizures are trials and sanctions. To date, Saudi Arabia has refused (at least in public) either to try or to extradite persons involved in terrorist finance. Public trials of persons engaged in such activity, together with seizures of their assets, might act as a deterrent to other would-be terrorist financiers.

Close Financial Institutions Involved in Terrorist Finance. To date, Saudi Arabia has imposed sanctions on no financial institution it has licensed for involvement in handling the funds of terrorism. Suspension or revocation of license for negligence in handling terrorist funds would act as a significant deterrent and constitute an important indicator of Saudi political will against terrorist finance.

Prohibit All Forms of Terrorist Finance. The continued support by Saudi Arabia for Hamas creates a terrorism problem that goes well beyond the impact on the Arab-Israeli conflict, given the ties between Hamas and other terrorist groups. An important indicator would be statements and actions by the Saudi government demonstrating a commitment to combat all forms of terrorism and terrorist finance.

Demonstrate Full Implementation of Anti-Money Laundering and Terrorist Finance Laws. To date, the Saudi government has issued little information to demonstrate that its anti-money laundering and terrorist finance laws have actually been implemented and enforced. Publication of information on suspicious activity reporting, investigations, arrests, indictments, prosecutions and convictions, as well as regulatory sanctions, would be indicators that such laws are being enforced in practice.

Close Gaps in Existing Anti-Money Laundering Laws and Demonstrating Enforcement of Such Laws. Saudi Arabia has been studying proposed amendments to its existing anti-money laundering laws for more than year, but has yet to enact them.

Provide Public Data On Suspicious Transaction Reports. Existing SAMA guidelines require know your customer procedures and the provision by financial institutions of suspicious transaction reports to SAMA, but there is no evidence these guidelines are being enforced. Public information on suspicious transaction reporting could be one useful indicator that SAMA's anti-money laundering guidelines have been adopted in practice.

Provide Greater Transparency and Accountability Over Charities. The government of Saudi Arabia has announced its comprehensive regulation and supervision of its charities. Given such supervision, publication of detailed data regarding the sources and uses of such funds should be feasible, and could help demonstrate that controls and oversight are actually in place.

For further progress, Saudi Arabia must fully implement the oversight mechanisms it has put into place in theory and apply them to all levels of the population, including prominent Saudis. The government needs to communicate to the Saudi people that no support of Islamic militancy will be tolerated, whether directed inside the Kingdom or beyond, and whether connected to Al Qaeda, Hamas, or other organizations. Such a communication requires the arrest of the most prominent funders of Al Qaeda, based on existing documentation, together with the freezing and ultimately the confiscating of their assets.

Saudi Arabia's continued support for institutions run or managed by Hamas remains an especially significant and continuing terrorist finance problem. Saudi Arabia's official position is that the funds go solely to the "political wing" of Hamas, not terrorists, and are targeted to such institutions as the UN's High Commissioner for Refugees and the Red Crescent. As of yet, there is no public evidence that effective auditing mechanisms are in place to prevent such diversions in fact, despite Saudi Arabia's public assertions that audits of all of its charities have been completed within the Kingdom, as such diversions could readily take place within the Palestinian territories regardless of paper documentation made available in Saudi Arabia to authorities there.

Conclusion

The actions taken to date by the U.S. against terrorist finance have helped to result in real progress to impair the ability of terrorists to raise, transfer, and use money to carry out terrorist activities. Before September 11, few countries had laws to combat terrorist finance. Today, most do. Before September 11, few countries froze the assets of terrorists. Today, some have. Prior to September 11, the United Nations contribution against terrorist financing was marginal. Since, it has become significant and likely to be enduring. With that said, progress is not accelerating and in some areas, it may be flagging. The recommendations made last year by the Task Force on Terrorist Finance of the Council on Foreign Relations remain sensible and feasible. They merely require greater political will. Among the most important actions we could now take would be to:

- Designate a special assistant to the president for combating terrorist financing with the special mandate to lead U.S. efforts on terrorist financing issues. This work should not be done, as it is today, on a part time basis, or without the direct authority and centralized responsibility of the President and the NSC.
- Intensify multinational operational and policy coordination on border controls and identification of terrorist networks.
- Intensify efforts to develop comprehensive global regulation of alternative remittance systems such as hawaladars.
- Expand U.S. bilateral technical assistance programs in problem countries to assist in the creation of effective regulatory, enforcement and control regimes for financial institutions and charitable organizations.
- Undertake strengthened oversight of U.S. charities that send funds overseas.
- Use "special measures" under the Bank Secrecy Act as provided by the Patriot Act to cut off correspondent relations between foreign financial institutions with weak anti-money laundering practices and U.S. banks.
- Publicize what we know about foreign terrorist financiers – regardless of whether they happen to be prominent persons in Saudi Arabia or other allies – and take appropriate regulatory and enforcement action against them.

Testimony of

Steven Emerson
with Jonathan Levin

Before the

United States Senate Committee on Governmental Affairs

"Terrorism Financing: Origination, Organization, and Prevention:
Saudi Arabia, Terrorist Financing and the War on Terror"

July 31, 2003

Steven Emerson
Executive Director
The Investigative Project
5505 Conn. Ave NW #341
Washington DC 20015

Email:
stopterror@aol.com
phone 202-363-8602
fax 202 966 5191

Introduction

Terrorism depends upon the presence of three primary ingredients: Indoctrination, recruitment and financing. Take away any one of those three ingredients and the chances for success are geometrically reduced.

In the nearly two years since the horrific attacks of 9/11, the war on terrorism has been assiduously fought by the US military, intelligence and law enforcement. Besides destroying the base that Al Qaeda used in Afghanistan, the United States has conducted a comprehensive campaign in the United States to arrest, prosecute, deport or jail those suspected of being connected to terrorist cells. The successful prosecution of terrorist cells in Detroit and Buffalo and the announcement of indictments against suspected terrorist cells in Portland, Seattle, northern Virginia, Chicago, Tampa, Brooklyn, and elsewhere have demonstrated the resolve of those on the front line in the battle against terrorism. Dozens of groups, financial conduits and financiers have seen their assets frozen or have been classified as terrorist by the US Government.

One of the most sensitive areas of investigation remains the role played by financial entities and non-governmental organizations (ngo's) connected to or operating under the aegis of the Kingdom of Saudi Arabia.

Since the July 24 release of the "Report of the Joint Inquiry into the Terrorist Attacks of September 11, 2001," the question of what role Saudi Arabia has played in supporting terrorism, particularly Al Qaeda and the 9/11 attacks, has come under increasing scrutiny. The redaction of a 28 page classified section dealing with Saudi Arabia has raised even more questions about the exact role and oversight exercised by Saudi officials over non-profit groups and even members of the Royal Family in supporting terrorism.

To be sure, there are those in the Saudi government who are genuinely committed to stopping support for terrorism. At the same time, it must be recognized that the level of institutionalized support for terrorist movements has been so pervasive and sustained during the past 20 years that the centers of terrorist gravity within Saudi Arabia have assumed an independence of their own. Even for those officials who sincerely desire to break the terrorist connections, their power and influence over other members of the regime is limited. In the end, decisions by Saudi Arabia are made either by consensus, meaning there has to be agreement at the lowest common denominator, or are made as fiats by officials who control specified ministries.

While key Saudi governmental officials have publicly denounced terrorism and pledged to support the United States in the battle against worldwide Islamic militancy, the pattern of support to terrorism generated by financial and "humanitarian" conduits operating with the permission or support of the Saudi regime raise serious questions as to whether Saudi Arabia is prepared to or capable of genuinely cracking down.

The author would like to thank the following individuals for their input, assistance, and research in the preparation of this testimony: Tamar Tesler, Matthew Epstein, Evan Kohlmann and Erick Stakelbeck.

Using an elaborate network of mosques, schools, "charitable" and "humanitarian" organization, and even official diplomatic facilities, Saudi Arabia has for years fostered the growth and spread of a militant doctrinal interpretation of Islam. The ideology of Wahhabism has been exported not only throughout the Middle East but throughout the world resulting in the indoctrination of anti-American, anti-Christian, anti-Semitic and anti-western hatred among new generations of militant Islamic youth. Moderate and secular Muslims are also targeted. Indeed, in looking at the numbers of terrorist victims worldwide at the hands of Islamic extremists during the past decade, the largest number of victims have been fellow Muslims killed or wounded by militant Islamic groups.

It is imperative to point out at the outset that the terrorism of Osama bin Laden and the extremism of Wahhabism do not equal Islam. The vast majority of Muslims are not tethered to terrorism or extremism but rather seek a peaceful co-existence like members of other religious denominations. Rather it is only a small Islamic extremist minority that seeks to impose its views on the rest of the Muslim world. But because of the vast financial resources generated by years of petrodollar sales by Saudi Arabia, extremists have been able to disproportionately exercise influence in Muslim communities.

Coupled with its virtually unlimited financial resources, the Wahhabi *dawah* invariably leads to acts of terror against non-Muslims and moderate Muslims alike.

In an effort at damage control, the Saudi Arabian Embassy in Washington, DC issued a statement just hours after the Joint Committee Report's publication. The press release was a speech by Saudi Ambassador Prince Bandar Bin Sultan praising Saudi efforts in the War on Terrorism:[1]

> Since September 11, Saudi Arabia has questioned over 1,000 individuals, arrested more than 500 suspects and succeeded in extraditing *Al-Qaeda* members from other countries to face justice. The Kingdom has audited its charities and enacted strict financial control measures to ensure that evildoers cannot take advantage of the generosity of our citizens. Bank accounts of suspected individuals have been frozen and some of the most stringent banking regulations implemented. Saudi Arabia today has one of the toughest counter-terrorism laws and regulations in the world.
>
> Cooperation between our two countries in fighting terrorism is excellent in all areas and has never been greater.[2]

Directly citing the Joint Inquiry report, Prince Bandar wrote:

> In a 900-page report, 28 blanked-out pages are being used by some to malign our country and our people. Rumors, innuendos and untruths have become, when it comes to the Kingdom, the order of the day.

---

[1] Press Release From Embassy of Saudi Arabia, "Saudi Ambassador Responds to Reports of Saudi Involvement in 9-11," July 24, 2003. http://saudiembassy.net/press_release/releases/03-PR-0724-Bandar.htm.

[2] Press Release From Embassy of Saudi Arabia, "Saudi Ambassador Responds to Reports of Saudi Involvement in 9-11," July 24, 2003. http://saudiembassy.net/press_release/releases/03-PR-0724-Bandar.htm.

> It is my belief that the reason a classified section that allegedly deals with foreign governments is absent from the report is most likely because the information contained in it could not be substantiated. Saudi Arabia has nothing to hide. We can deal with questions in public, but we cannot respond to blank pages.[3]

Therein lies the problem: The refusal by Saudi officials to admit that they have a problem.

For years, components of Saudi charities have been used to funnel money or divert resources to terrorist organizations. However, the Saudi Government has refused to reign in these groups or acknowledge the flow of funds to terrorist movements.

In a June 2003 news conference at the Saudi Embassy in Washington, DC, Adel al-Jubeir, Foreign Affairs Advisor to Crown Prince Abdullah, said the Saudi Government "implemented new rules and regulations…which lay out what Saudi Arabia has done. It is now not legal for a Saudi charity to have offices outside Saudi Arabia."[4] Asked later whether Saudi charities had complied with these new regulations, al-Jubeir said, "I hope so." Al-Jubeir also stated, "**if the United Nations is headquartered in New York, is America responsible for everything the U.N. does?** Of course not."

The indifference to the role of Saudi-supported, headquartered, or sanctioned charities in monies flowing to terrorist groups is embodied by Saudi representatives like al-Jubeir, who refuse to categorically and unequivocally condemn terrorism. Asked whether the Saudi government views Hamas as a terrorist organization, al-Jubeir replied, "Anytime you take the life of innocent people, that's unacceptable; that's terrorism. Anytime you try to fight for your independence, that's a liberation movement."[5]

When asked, "**Why not say, 'we condemn Hamas for this act of terrorism?'**" al-Jubeir responded:

> Well, again, we have condemned terrorism in all its forms, regardless of where it takes place.
>
> **I think that the prime minister of Israel has to think very seriously about his policies.**[6]

When asked whether the Saudi government funded Hamas, al-Jubeir replied, "**A lot of the institutions may be run or managed by the political wing of Hamas. That may be the case; I'm not an expert on this. But we do not fund terrorism.**"[7]

In one major respect, I agree with the statement made by Saudi officials that the 28 page section, to the extent it does not jeopardize sensitive intelligence sources and methods, should be made public.

---

[3] Press Release From Embassy of Saudi Arabia, "Saudi Ambassador Responds to Reports of Saudi Involvement in 9-11," July 24, 2003. http://saudiembassy.net/press_release/releases/03-PR-0724-Bandar.htm.
[4] News Conference, Saudi Embassy, June 12, 2003.
[5] News Conference, Saudi Embassy, June 12, 2003.
[6] News Conference, Saudi Embassy, June 12, 2003.
[7] News Conference, Saudi Embassy, June 12, 2003.

But we should also realize that a major body of evidence, documentation, and information exists showing the role of Saudi connected groups in facilitating extremism and terrorism. Some of this information is in the public domain; other information will be revealed for the first time in this hearing. Often, the connections are not neatly compartmentalized, largely because of the intricate and complex ways in which terrorist funding has been laundered to terrorist groups. Still, other times, the evidence shows that non-governmental organizations carry out, to a large degree, activities that are totally legitimate and legal; indeed it is the very external legitimacy of these groups that provide the perfect cover to siphon off, divert or launder financial support or provide cover to terrorist cells. It should also be stated that some of the components of Saudi groups may be operating independently of their central apparatus.

"Follow the money" was the famous advice of protagonist Deep Throat in the Watergate Scandal nearly 3 decades ago. In this testimony, I have set out to follow the money trail of terrorist financing.

Either by omission or commission Saudi Arabia has failed to reign in the network of charities and religious organizations that have fueled some of the most violent terrorist organizations in the world, including *Al-Qaeda* and Hamas. The paper trail of Saudi money, funneled through a network of charities and religious organizations, leads to some of the most violent terrorist groups in the world, including Al-Qaeda and Hamas. For reasons of political expediency, undue diplomatic sensitivities and a desire to protect the Saudi-American relationship, there has been an unwillingness on the part of the US Government to fully tackle the problem of Saudi support for terrorism in the past. It is hoped that by shining a light on to this problem that has been swept under the proverbial rug for too long, there will be a new willingness on the part of the US Government to fully utilize all of its levers in investigating, prosecuting, and bringing to justice those who have enabled terrorists to carry out their murderous deeds. At the same time, by bringing into sharp focus the role of state supported institutions in facilitating terrorism, perhaps those Saudi forces that are genuinely opposed to terrorism will be empowered to act once and for all.

Saudi Textbooks

A reviewed selection of textbooks used in Saudi schools actively engender fundamental distrust of and opposition to non-Muslims and the West.

- PBS's Frontline program ran a report in which it analyzed two Ministry of Education textbooks used in Saudi middle-schools. According to Frontline the books, published in 2000, "are part of the official curriculum for Saudi students and are a fundamental part of their education. Approximately 35% of school studies is devoted to compulsory Saudi religious education."[8]
    - An extract from one of the books was titled, "The Victory of Muslims Over Jews." *Hadith* narrated by Abi Hurira: "The last hour won't come before the

[8] http://www.pbs.org/wgbh/pages/frontline/shows/saudi/etc/textbooks.html, accessed July 29, 2003.

Muslims would fight the Jews and the Muslims will kill them so Jews would hide behind rocks and trees. Then the rocks and tree would call: oh Muslim, oh servant of God! **There is a Jew behind me, come and kill him**..."[9]

Teachings of the *Hadith*

1) **It's fate decided by Allah that the Muslims and Jews will fight till the end of the world.**

2) The ***Hadith*** **predicts for the Muslims God's victory over the Jews.**

3) The victory for the Muslims because they are right, and whoever is right is always victorious, even though most people are against him.

4) God grants victory to the Muslims if they have a true will, if they unite, hold on to God's *sharia*, if they go by God's ruling, if they are patient.

...

7) **Jews and Christians are the enemies of believers. They will never approve of the Muslims—beware of them.**[10]

The Saudi government distributes textbooks to schools in the United States. Many of these books are virulently anti-Semitic, glorify violence, and provide religiously-based justification for *Jihad*. The reviewed textbooks, except as noted, are headed "Kingdom of Saudi Arabia / Ministry of Education / The Ministry of Education has Determined the Content of / This Book and Printed it at its own Expense." All books are marked, "Distributed Free. Not For Sale."

Selected excerpts from these books include:

- 4th Grade, Principles of the Arabic Language (Book 2) – "Under the Shihada [martyr] is the sword which indicates *Jihad* in the way of Allah, for Truth."[11]
- 5th Grade, Principles of the Arabic Language contains a grammatical exercise saying "**God loves the *Mujahideen***."[12]
- 6th Grade, Principles of the Arabic Language, Book 1 – After a reading on the Battle of Badr, a number of fill-in-the-blank questions were asked, including, "The *Mujahideen* ___ in the way of Allah."[13]
- 7th Grade, Principles of the Arabic Language, (Book 9) – The grammatical examples and exercises include the following:[14]

o "The Palestinian *Mujahideen* are steadfast in the face of the enemy."

---

[9] http://www.pbs.org/wgbh/pages/frontline/shows/saudi/etc/textbooks.html, accessed July 29, 2003.
[10] http://www.pbs.org/wgbh/pages/frontline/shows/saudi/etc/textbooks.html, accessed July 29, 2003.
[11] 4th Grade, Principles of the Arabic Language (Book 2), Kingdom of Saudi Arabia, Ministry of Education, Riyadh, 1991.
[12] 5th Grade, Principles of the Arabic Language, Kingdom of Saudi Arabia, Ministry of Education, 1997.
[13] 6th Grade, Principles of the Arabic Language, Book 1, Kingdom of Saudi Arabia, Ministry of Education, Riyadh, 1993.
[14] 7th Grade, Principles of the Arabic Language, (Book 9), Kingdom of Saudi Arabia, Ministry of Education, Riyadh, 1993.

- "[The poet] Iliya Abu Madi said:

  Say to the Jews and their adherents
  Flashes of desires have deceived you
  Palestine is not common land
  Given to who wants to dwell there
  Do not consider it a homeland for you
  It has never been a homeland for you."[15]

- 7th Grade, Tawhid Class (Book 5) – Tawhid means, "Proclaiming the unity of Allah." The Saudis use this word to describe the teachings of the predominant Wahhabi sect. The subtitle of the textbook is "of the Sheikh of Islam Muhammad Abd al-Wahhab (May God have mercy of him)." Abd al-Wahhab is the founder of Wahhabism.

  - **The book asks, "What is learned from the *Hadith*?" and teaches, "The curse of Allah be upon the Jews and the Christians."**[16]

- 8th Grade Principles of the Arabic Language (Book 6) – One grammatical exercise on conjugating a class of verbs runs as follows:

  - "I said to my sister:

    We have triumphed over our unjust enemy.
    The mothers shouted with joy at the safe return of their soldier sons.
    Our two armies wiped out the enemy and won a great victory.
    The Muslims achieved a great victory.
    The female *Mujahideen* won by the grace of God."

  - "The two commanders said to the troops:

    You are fighting for our dignity, and making your nation last forever.
    You, oh sister, are always leading your sons to victory.
    Oh, female *Mujahideen*, you have obtained from us the best praise.
    Oh, commanders, you two are always in our thoughts.
    Oh, soldiers, return to your sons safe and sound.
    Oh, sister, say, 'Praise be to Allah for this clear-cut victory.'"[17]

- 8th Grade Principles of the Arabic Language (Book 6) - One grammatical example is "**No one will be absent from *Jihad* except for the sick.**"[18]

---

[15] 7th Grade, Principles of the Arabic Language, (Book 9), Kingdom of Saudi Arabia, Ministry of Education, Riyadh, 1993.
[16] 7th Grade, Tawhid Class (Book 5), Kingdom of Saudi Arabia, Ministry of Education, Riyadh, 1996.
[17] 8Th Grade Principles of the Arabic Language (Book 6), Kingdom of Saudi Arabia, Ministry of Education, Riyadh, No date.

- 9th Grade, *Hadith* Syllabus (Book 11) is published by the Saudi Government's General Presidency for Girls Education.[19]
    - o "***Jihad* in the way of Allah is the apex of Islam in terms of exertion and sacrifice of your life.**"
    - o "What is learned from the *Hadith*: ***Jihad* is the best of pious actions after faith in Allah.**"
    - o "**Why is *Jihad* one of the best of pious actions?**"
- 11th Grade, Religious Commentary:[20]

> **Since friendship with infidels is forbidden in the religion of Allah,** no one will do this unless he has a sickness in his heart. There are hypocrites who profess Islam, but their hearts are sick and empty of faith. They are afraid of the infidel and fear them. They take their side, and appoint them over the Muslims to confirm their victory over the Muslims.
>
> Since the hypocrites love the infidels and take them as friends, **the believer must do the opposite and love his believing brother, make friends with him, and show him affection and love. He must show the infidels rudeness and violence, and wage *Jihad* in the way of Allah** without fear of the Infidels and hypocrites, or terror of their arms and numbers.

- 11th Grade, Religious Commentary (Book 12):[21]

> O you who believe! **Take not the Jews and the Christians as *Auliya'* (friends, protectors, helpers, etc.), they are but *Auliya'* to one another. And if any amongst you takes them as *Auliya'*, then surely he is one of them.** Verily, Allah guides not those people who are the *Zalimun* (polytheists and wrongdoers and unjust).

- o Later under, "Explanation of Phrases," the book explains that:
    - "Take not the Jews and the Christians as *Auliya'* [means] That is, **no one of you should take one of the Jews and Christians as a *wali* who he loves, associates closely with, appoints, supports and fraternizes with."**
    - "And if any amongst you takes them as *Auliya'*, then surely he is one of them: Because **full friendship entails going over to their religion, and friendship with a few leads to many. Then slowly by degrees, he is their slave/worshipper."**

- 11th Grade, Reading Comprehension (Book 14) - In a chapter dealing with the victory of the Arabs over the Persian Empire:[22]

---

[18] 8Th Grade Principles of the Arabic Language (Book 6), Kingdom of Saudi Arabia, Ministry of Education, 1996.
[19] 9th Grade, *Hadith* Syllabus (Book 11), Kingdom of Saudi Arabia, Ministry of Education, 1995.
[20] 11th Grade Religious Commentary, Kingdom of Saudi Arabia, Ministry of Education , Riyadh, 1995.
[21] 11th Grade Religious Commentary (Book 12), Kingdom of Saudi Arabia, Ministry of Education, 1997.
[22] 11th Grade Reading Comprehension (Book 14), Kingdom of Saudi Arabia, Ministry of Education, 1995.

- "Do not forget that Allah was with them against their polytheist enemies, and that **he who died on *Jihad* in the way of Allah achieved martyrdom. How great a reward is Paradise!"**
- "If we are in fact Muslims, **readiness and preparation for *Jihad* in the way of Allah is a duty for the nation and its citizens.**"
- "[Below a photograph of a hand grenade] **The Kingdom participates with the Arabic and Islamic Institute for War Factories, in both heavy and light weapons, out of an awareness of its responsibility to share in preparing the forces of Muslims and Arabs to defend our holy places and Arab and Islamic lands, and awareness of its belief in the holy *Jihad* for the sake of exalting the word of the One God and the victory of the Religion."**

- 11th Grade, Reading Comprehension (Book 16)[23]
  - From the introduction – "For example, **the Summons to Islam in its initial stages was confronted by this when factions of the Jews strove to oppose it and deceive it by various treacherous and perfidious methods, violating their agreement with the Messenger of Allah. Allah responded to their deception by slaughtering them, cleansing the land of their evil and filth.** The word of Truth was exalted, victories followed one after another and booty came continuously to the Muslims."
  - Later – "This is **Zionist colonialism whose danger is unequalled in the pages of ancient and modern colonialism,** because it blocks – on every side – the progress of fifty million who two million exploit. The exploitation does not cease in the long or short run; it increases and grows larger with time. **Open and hidden forces collaborate with it,** including those who call this blatant distortion a balance in preparations and material between the Arab world and **the Zionist gang.**"

- 11th Grade, *Hadith* and Islamic Culture (Book 13) - The book discusses a *Hadith* attributed to Muhammad on the day Mecca fell to Muslim forces, "No [more] *hijra* but *Jihad* and good intention."[24]
  - Under "Precepts:"

    ***Jihad* will last until Judgment Day.**

    He who is not waging *Jihad*, must resolve on *Jihad* in his heart.
  - And later, ***"Jihad* is not a temporary duty for a certain time.** On the contrary, **it is a perpetual duty as long as man is on this earth, and as long as man wavers between faith in Allah and disbelief in Him, between the True Path and the False Path, and between truth and falsehood."**

---

[23] 11th Grade, Reading Comprehension (Book 16), Published by the Saudi government's General Presidency for Girls Education, Riyadh, 1995.

[24] 11th Grade *Hadith* and Islamic Culture (Book 13), Kingdom of Saudi Arabia, Ministry of Education, 1995.

- 11th Grade, Literature and Texts (Book 15)[25]
  - The second part: "**Showing the truth about the Jews and the Jewish conspiracy, and the alliance of these people with the English, because in [the Jews'] hands is the power of money, because they pretended weakness, that they are an oppressed people** who desire to return to – what they allege is – their land."

Saudi Clergy

Several members of the Saudi clergy propagate religious radicalism. Interviewed in November 2002, the Saudi Minister of Interior Prince Nayef bin Abdel-Aziz charged:

> We put big question marks and ask who committed the events of September 11 and who benefited from them...**I think they [the Zionists] are behind these events**...I cannot still believe that 19 youths, including 15 Saudis, carried out the September 11 attacks with the support of bin Laden and his Al-Qa`ida organization. It's impossible. I will not believe that these people have the power to do so horrendous an attack.[26]

Speaking on *Al-Jazeera* in January 2002, Abdallah Bin Matruk Al-Haddal, a Saudi preacher from the Ministry of Islamic Affairs, characterized Osama Bin Laden as a victimized hero:

> ...bin Laden waged an Islamic Jihad; he defended the oppressed people in Afghanistan. He expelled the Soviet Union [from Afghanistan] ...**Men like bin Laden will not allow the Islamic world to bow down under the infidel enemies' tyranny, under the tyranny of the** U.S...There is no doubt that Usama bin Laden waged Jihad against the infidels, against the aggressor and the oppressor. America does not want Islamic principles [to exist] on the face of this planet...**The nation who gave rise to Osama bin Laden is a strong and great nation. It is the nation of the future...I don't believe that the attack on America [on September 11th] was perpetrated by bin** Laden or the Muslims...**It is a continuation of the Jewish deception and the Jewish-Zionist wickedness which infiltrates the U.S.**[27]

Shaykh Abdulaziz Bin Baz is the late Grand Mufti of the Kingdom of Saudi Arabia. As Grand Mufti, Bin Baz served as the official religious voice for the Saudi Kingdom. Though Bin Baz has been attacked by some Salafi Muslim radicals as a *munafiq* (traitor) for his cooperation with the Saudis, while alive, Bin Baz was himself often a militant proponent of confrontation with the West.

In his book, The Ideological Attack, Bin Baz affirmed:

> Yes, the Muslims in general...are all subject to a great ideological attack from the various nations of kufr [infidels] from both the east and

---

[25] 11th Grade Literature and Texts (Book 15), Published by the Saudi government's General Presidency for Girls Education, Jiddah 1995.

[26] http://www.ain-alyaqeen.com/issues/20021129/feat6en.htm.

[27] *Al-Jazeera* (Qatar), "The Opposite Direction," January 22, 2002.

> the west. The severest and most serious of these attacks are: the attack of the christian crusaders; the Zionist attack; [and] the communist and atheistic attack.[28]

Bin Baz continued:

> [T]he attack of the Christian crusaders is today at its most intense...The Muslim whose mind has not been corrupted cannot bear to see the infidels wielding authority...[t]herefore such a Muslim strives his utmost to expel and distance them—even if he has to sacrifice his own life, or his most cherished possession for this cause.[29]

The cleric also had harsh words for the parallel alleged "Zionist plot" against Islam:

> The Jews scheme and crave after possessing the Muslim lands, as well as the lands of others. They have fulfilled some of their plans and continue striving hard to implement the rest of them.[30]

The Saudi Red Crescent

The Saudi government has allocated millions of dollars to the Red Crescent, an organization engaged in charitable works around the world. However, a review of SRC activities reveals their active role in supporting the *mujahideen* in Afghanistan in during the confrontation against the Soviets in the 1980s. Recent activities of the SRC suggest a lack of government oversight for an organization charged with providing humanitarian relief.

The Annual budget statement from the Saudi Ministry of Finance details the revenues and expenditures of public corporations whose budgets are annexed to the Saudi national budget. As listed in Royal Decree Number Three, the revenues and expenditures of the Saudi Red Crescent Society totaled SR206,840,000 [$55.1 million by today's conversion rate];[31] for the year 2000 the total was SR238,346,000 [US $63,558,933.33];[32] for the year 2002 the total was SR249,055,000 (US $66,414,666.67).[33]

Historical

In a 1989 interview, Sheikh Abdullah Azzam, co-founder of *Al-Qaeda* and spiritual mentor to Osama bin Laden, said the Saudi Red Crescent sent money to the *Mujahideen*. Azzam also identified Wael Jalaidan as the head of the Saudi Red crescent during the Afghan *Jihad*. When asked, "Who donates to the *Mujahedeen*?" Azzam replied:

> ...The **Saudi Red Crescent** and the Saudi Relief Agency headed by Salman Abdel 'Aziz, has a budget of 100 million riyal per year. These

[28] Bin Baaz, Shaykh Abdul-Azeez, The Ideological Attack, Message of Islam Publications; Hounslow, UK, 1999.
[29] Bin Baaz, Shaykh Abdul-Azeez, The Ideological Attack, Message of Islam Publications; Hounslow, UK, 1999.
[30] Bin Baaz, Shaykh Abdul-Azeez, The Ideological Attack, Message of Islam Publications; Hounslow, UK, 1999.
[31] Ministry of Finance, "Budget Statement from Ministry Of Finance," December 29, 1998.
[32] Ministry of Finance and National Economy, "Budget for Fiscal Year 2000," December 20, 1999.
[33] Ministry of Finance and National Economy, "Budget for Fiscal Year 2002," December 8, 2001.

> two Saudi organizations are under one headed [by] **Wa'il Jlaydan, who happens to be head of the Red Crescent** as well. He was a representative of the University of King Abdel Aziz in Saudi Arabia in the United States, and left it to become the head of the Red Crescent.[34]

Additionally, Jalaidan was head of the Peshawar, Pakistan branch of the Muslim World League (MWL).[35]

In a 1999 interview with *Al-Jazeera* television, Osama bin Laden discussed the assassination of Abdallah Azzam ten years earlier and the founding of *Al-Qaeda*. Bin Laden recalled, **"We were all in one boat, as is known to you, including our brother, Wa`il Julaidan."**[36]

Jalaidan also headed the Rabita Trust, an organization whose assets were frozen October 12, 2001 by the United States government.[37] **Jalaidan's personal assets were frozen September 6, 2002.**[38]

The Arab Volunteers in Afghanistan, a documentary of the Arab-Afghans, repeatedly refers to the active role that the SRC played in the Afghan *Jihad*. Quoting founder Mohammed Loay Bayazid,[39] the author writes:

> I came from Peshawar with Walid Jalidan [Wa'il Julaidan] and Abi l-Bara'. We were on our way to Sadda. Since, however, the place was new and we were not familiar with it we ended up in **Parachinar, where the ambulances of the Saudi Red Crescent were stationed. They had been sent there by Walid Jalidan and waited at the *Jihad* Hospital that belonged to the Da`wa Committee.** Walid Jalidan continued with them and three cars to Al-Fath whereas I returned with Abi l-Bara' to Sadda.

He continued later,

> ...the area where you are going to work is notorious for the anti-Mujahidin stance of its people who will report things to the enemy. **You are not coming with an ordinary bike. These machines resemble more tanks.** The moment you appear with them they will be destroyed by planes.
>
> I said, well, if that happens we shall ask God's pardon, and if not, we shall do our work.
>
> **We got them into the country in the name of the Mujahidin via the Saudi Red Crescent. May God reward the Ambassador, Abu**

---

[34] GIV Interview with Abdullah Azzam. March, 10, 1999.

[35] *Rose Al-Yusif*, "Usama BinLaden - A Millionair[sic] Finances Extremism in Egypt and Saudi Arabia," May 17, 1993. See also: Muhammad, Basil. *Al-Ansaru l'Arab fi Afghanistan*. The Committee for Islamic Benevolence Publications; ©1991. *Page 26*.

[36] Office of Public Affairs, United States Treasury Department, "Treasury Department Statement on the Designation of Wa'el Hamza Julidan," September 6, 2002.

[37] Executive Order 13224 Blocking Terrorist Property and a Summary of The Terrorism Sanctions Regulation, US Department of the Treasury Office of Foreign Assets Control.

[38] Executive Order 13224 Blocking Terrorist Property and a Summary of The Terrorism Sanctions Regulation, US Department of the Treasury Office of Foreign Assets Control.

[39] "Government's Evidentiary Proffer Supporting the Admissibility of Co-Conspirator Statements." United States of America v. Enaam M. Arnaout. United States District Court Northern District of Illinois, Eastern Division. Case #: 02 CR 892. January 31, 2003. Page 21.

> Muhammad (Taufiq `Alamdar). He helped very much in getting them in. So the work began.[40]

Taufiq Alamdar was Saudi Ambassador to Pakistan during the 1980s.[41]

The Straits Times writes that:

> ...Saudi funds flowed to Azam and the Makhtab at [sic] Khidmat or Services Center, which he created in 1984 to service the new recruits and receive donations from Islamic charities.
>
> Donations from **Saudi Intelligence, the Saudi Red Crescent, the World Muslim League and private donations from Saudi princes and mosques were channelled [sic] through the Makhtab**."[42]

According to USA Today number two *Al-Qaeda* leader Ayman al-Zawahiri joined the Red Crescent in 1985 to aid the *Mujahideen* in Afghanistan.[43]

Contemporary Activity

- According to a report filed by United Press International in 1995, Ayman al-Zawahiri, *Al-Qaeda's* second-in-command and spiritual mentor of Osama bin Laden, presented himself as a representative of the Red Crescent and raised $500,000 in the San Francisco area.[44] Zawahiri was head of extremist group Islamic *Jihad* that bombed the Egyptian Embassy in Pakistan in 1995 and a failed plot to break a number of terrorists out of an Egyptian prison.[45]

- According to the Pakistani newspaper The News, Two Sudanese members of the Saudi Red Crescent, Muhammed Ali Syed and Bashir Babar Qadim, were arrested in early 1996 in connection to the 1995 Egyptian Embassy bombing in Pakistan. The two Sudanese were teachers at Ummul Qura'—a religious educational institution funded by the Saudi Red Crescent—but had recently switched posts to work in Faisalabad.[46]

- According to Vancouver Sun Canadian court documents reveal that Essam Marzouk spent five years (1988-1992) transporting wounded Afghans to Pakistan as an ambulance driver for the Red Crescent.[47] He was accused of the ex-supervisor of an *Al-Qaeda* training camp, Marzouk is currently serving a fifteen-year prison sentence in Egypt for his membership in the outlawed al-*Jihad*.[48]

- According to one news report from Sarajevo, Boumediene Lakhdar and Nechle Mohamed, two *Al-Qaeda* members arrested in 2001 for planning terrorist attacks

---

40 Basil Muhammad, The Arab Volunteers in Afghanistan (*al-Ansar i-Arab fi Afhanistan*).
41 BBC, "Other Reports; Large Saudi Cash Donation to Resistance Leader," May 26, 1984.
42 The Straits Times, "The Making of a Terrorist," September 23, 2001.
43 USA Today, "Family, Friends Tell of the Man Behind bin Laden," October 12, 2001.
44 United Press International, "Bin Laden Underling Raised Money in US," October 11, 2001.
45 United Press International, "Bin Laden Underling Raised Money in US," October 11, 2001.
46 The News, "Pakistani Police Hold Two Sudanese in Egypt Embassy Blast Case," February 1, 1996.
47 The Vancouver Sun, "CSIS Questioned Alleged Terrorist," November 15, 2001.
48 The Vancouver Sun, "CSIS Questioned Alleged Terrorist," November 15, 2001.

against the U.S. and British Embassies in Sarajevo, were administrators for the Red Crescent.[49]

- In October 2001, Pakistan's military regime ordered eighty-nine Arab and Muslim relief workers deported for possible links to *Al-Qaeda*.[50] Among the NGOs targeted were the Saudi Red Crescent and another Saudi organization, the International Islamic Relief Organization (IIRO).[51]

- In May 2002, the London-based Arabic newspaper *Al-Sharq Al-Awsat* interviewed Mansur al-Suwaylim, brother of deceased Chechen *Jihad* leader Samir Salih Abdallah al-Suwaylim, AKA "Khattab." In the interview al-Suwaylim said:

> ...He decided to join the Afghan *Jihad* in 1987, immediately after the month of Ramadan. He was 17 years old. He established close relations with the mujahidin before leaving. Thus he **took two documents with him to help introduce him when he left Saudi Arabia. One document was from the director of the Mujahidin Service Office in Al-Dammam and the second from a person who had a special status with the official in charge of the Saudi Red Crescent in Pakistan.**[52]

- On January 6, 2003, Federal Prosecutors filed a Santiago Proffer in the case United States of America v. Enaam Arnaout. Enaam Arnaout is the former Executive Director of the Benevolence International Foundation (BIF).[53] The U.S. government named BIF a Specially Designated Global Terrorist (SDGT) Organization on November 19, 2002.[54] Excerpts of the proffer include:[55]

> ...Abu Hassan al Madani (Wael Julaidan) is a leader of a relief organization that also provided logistical support to Bin Laden.* **A letter on MWL [Muslim World League]/IIRO [International Islamic Relief Organization] letterhead recounting a meeting discussed attacks being launched from "League" offices and that passports should not be kept with the Saudi Red Crescent because Julaidan was returning to Saudi Arabia.**
>
> ...
>
> Included in this file is a letter to Abu Rida on the **letterhead of the Saudi Red Crescent agency requesting that weapons be inventoried**...At the bottom of the letter is a note from Usama Bin Laden to "Abu Al Hasan" (Wael Juleidan) stating that Bin Laden's group has an extreme need for weapons. *Id.*

---

[49] ONASA, Sarajevo, "ONASA Carries Biographies of Six Algerians Handed Over to the US Officials,".January 18, 2002.
[50] AP, "Pakistan Deporting 89 Arab Aid Workers," October 6, 2001.
[51] AP, "Pakistan Deporting 89 Arab Aid Workers," October 6, 2001.
[52] *Al-Sharq al-Awsat*, Saudi Arabia: Khattab's Brother Interviewed on Khattab's Life, Death In Chechnya," May 2, 2002.
[53] State Department, "FBI Arrests Head of Chicago-Based International Charity Organization; Charges Include Perjury Relating to Alleged Terrorist Activity," May 1, 2002.
[54] Executive Order 13224 Blocking Terrorist Property and a Summary of The Terrorism Sanctions Regulation, US Department of the Treasury Office of Foreign Assets Control.
[55] "Government's Evidentiary Proffer Supporting the Admissibility of Co-Conspirator Statements." United States of America v. Enaam M. Arnaout. United States District Court Northern District of Illinois, Eastern Division. Case #: 02 CR 892, January 6, 2003.

A report by Dr. Abdullah Azzam titled "Journey of Maktab Khadamat Al-*Mujahideen*" discusses issues related to MK including publishing *Al Jihad* magazine and providing support to the *Mujahideen*. Ex. 103. It concludes by noting that the **"Islamic foundations contributed in the *Jihad*ist arena through the financial support of the fronts and of the Arab lions in the Maktab Al-Khadamat," noting that at the forefront LBI and the Saudi Red Crescent, among others.**[56]

* NOTE FROM PROFFER:

A dispute broke out between two relief organizations in late 1988 (after *Al-Qaeda* had been founded), including the Saudi Red Crescent Society of which Julaidan was president...(The memoranda from the time indicate that the "Saudi Benevolence Committee (Adel Baterji)" was the main financier of the humanitarian project in dispute and took sides with Julaidan.) The dispute was submitted to secret arbitration before Dr. Fadhl (a leading Islamic Scholar for the al Jihad organization headed by Ayman al Zawahiri) and Abu Hajer al Iraqi, both of whom served on the fatwah committee of *Al-Qaeda*...Among other things, Julaidan had accused the opposing party (Ahmed Said Khadr, a/k/a "Abdel Rahman al Kanadi") of having suspicious contacts with non-Islamic agencies.[57]

- According to the Chicago Tribune, when Yasin al-Qadi was asked about his recent philanthropic donations, he "cited the Saudi Red Crescent society."[58] The US government named Yasin al-Qadi a Specially Designated Global Terrorist (SDGT) on October 12, 2001.[59]

Saudi High Commission for Relief

The Saudi High Commission for Relief was founded by Saudi Prince Selman bin Abdul-Aziz, mayor of Riyadh and son of Abdul Aziz ibn Saud, the founder of Saudi Arabia, in 1993.[60] The Saudi High Commission for Relief was actively providing humanitarian relief in Bosnia in the early 1990s. According to the Boston Globe, "the High Commission says it has given more than $600 million in aid and has cared for war orphans and paid utility bills for impoverished Bosnian families. Its Sarajevo

---

[56] "Government's Evidentiary Proffer Supporting the Admissibility of Co-Conspirator Statements." United States of America v. Enaam M. Arnaout. United States District Court Northern District of Illinois, Eastern Division. Case #: 02 CR 892, January 6, 2003.
[57] "Government's Evidentiary Proffer Supporting the Admissibility of Co-Conspirator Statements." United States of America v. Enaam M. Arnaout. United States District Court Northern District of Illinois, Eastern Division. Case #: 02 CR 892, January 6, 2003.
[58] Chicago Tribune, "Saudi Businessman Denies Terrorist Dies," October 14, 2001.
[59] Executive Order 13224 Blocking Terrorist Property and a Summary of The Terrorism Sanctions Regulation, US Department of the Treasury Office of Foreign Assets Control.
[60] USA Today, "US, Saudis Plan to Shut Down Charity's Branches," March 11, 2002.

headquarters cost an estimated $9 million, and includes a mosque, classrooms, a library, restaurants, and a sports hall."[61]

- According to Bosnian reports, "The *ul-Mujahidin* members began to come to BiH back in 1992, via Croatia and Herzegovina, using **identity cards from humanitarian organizations**. Most frequently, these phony humanitarian workers came through the Kuwaiti Rebirth of Islam Mission, the Saudi IGASSE; TWR and **Saudi High Commission**, the Egyptian Humanitarian Relief Agency and the Third World Agency"[62]

- In October 2001, the U.S. and British Embassies in Sarajevo were closed due to an imminent terrorist threat against them.[63] The same month, six men accused of plotting attacks against the Embassies and other targets were arrested.[64] The six men were moved to Guantanamo Bay in January 2002.[65] According to Boston Globe, one of the men, Sabir Lamar, worked for the Saudi High Commission.[66]

  In January 2002, with American support, the Bosnian government began investigating several charitable organizations operating in the former Yugoslavia. As reported by the Boston Globe Bosnian officials stated, "At the top of the list…is an organization called the Saudi High Commission for Relief of Bosnia and Herzegovina."[67]

- A month later, in February 2002, U.S. peacekeeping troops in Bosnia raided the offices of the Saudi High Commission. The Boston Globe reported that the raid found "**computer hard drives with photographs of the World Trade Center before and after its collapse, files on pesticides and crop dusters and information about how to make fake State Department badges.**"[68] Former FBI analyst Matthew Levitt has said, "**investigators have been unable to trace about $ 41 million donated to the charity.**"[69] According to The Boston Globe, other files found at the High Commission "**contained photographs of U.S. military installations, plans for crop dusters, and information about the production of pesticides.**"[70]

---

[61] Boston Globe, "Fighting Terror / A War on Manuy7 Fronts, Saudi Group; Charity's Files Hold US Data, Bosnians Say," February 17, 2002.
[62] http://www.pogledi.co.yu/izetbegovic/articles/6-2001.php, Accessed July 27, 2003.
[63] http://www.usatoday.com/news/world/2002/03/22/embassy.htm, accessed July 27, 2003.
[64] http://news.bbc.co.uk/1/hi/world/europe/1767554.stm, accessed July 27, 2003.
[65] http://news.bbc.co.uk/1/hi/world/europe/1767554.stm, accessed July 27, 2003.
[66] Boston Globe, "Fighting Terror / Islam, Roundup Religious Conflict; Saudi 'Charity' Troubling to Bosnian Muslims," January 27, 2002.
[67] Boston Globe, "Fighting Terror / Islam, Roundup Religious Conflict; Saudi 'Charity' Troubling to Bosnian Muslims," January 27, 2002.
[68] USA Today, "US, Saudis Plan to Shut Down Charity's Branches," March 11, 2002.
[69] USA Today, "US, Saudis Plan to Shut Down Charity's Branches," March 11, 2002.
[70] Boston Globe, "Fighting Terror / A War on Manuy7 Fronts, Saudi Group; Charity's Files Hold US Data, Bosnians Say," February 17, 2002.

Bosnian officials were quoted as saying the Commission's offices were raided due to "'illegal activities' that were 'not in accordance with the Saudi High Commission's humanitarian mission.'"[71]

- The Boston Globe also reported that "according to some officials...**the files contained information that could pertain to biological warfare, but U.S. officials cautioned that the information was inconclusive.**"[72]
- Jane's Intelligence writes:

> The [Saudi High] commission is opaque; whether it is a Saudi government body, an NGO, or a private organisation has never been made clear, although it is the focus of considerable interest among intelligence agencies. In 1994, Abdul Hadi al-Gahtani, a Saudi who was director of the commission in Zenica, was accused of the murder of the British aid worker, Paul Goodall. Al-Gahtani escaped police custody, and a Bosnian court later convicted him in absentia of Goodall's murder.[73]

The Muslim World League

In May 1962, in an effort to strengthen Saudi presence in regional affairs and dilute Egypt's influence, King Faysal of Saudi Arabia sponsored a pan-Islamic conference in Mecca. The objectives of the conference were to (1) promote cooperation among Muslim states, (2) counter Soviet and communist threats in the Arab world, and (3) mobilize the Muslim world to oppose the state of Israel. The Mecca meeting resulted in the creation of the Muslim World League (*rabitat al-'alam al-Islami*).[74]

According to former Secretary General of MWL, Dr. Abdullah Naseef:

> The establishment [of MWL] came in a decision approved by the first General Islamic Conference held under the auspices of Saudi Arabia in Makkah in Dhul-Hijjah, 1381/1962. The conference was attended by a large number of Islamic leaders, Ulema [clerics], and intellectuals from various countries and continents.[75]

Since its founding, the League has functioned as the quasi-official religious missionary and propaganda arm of the Saudi Kingdom. In March 1997, **Secretary General Abdullah Al-Obaid thanked King Fahd for his continued support, noting that the Saudi government had officially provided more than $1.33 billion in financial aid to MWL since 1962.**[76] In 1997, Prince Majid bin Abdel Aziz, emir of the Mecca province,

[71] Boston Globe, "Fighting Terror / A War on Manuy7 Fronts, Saudi Group; Charity's Files Hold US Data, Bosnians Say," February 17, 2002.
[72] Boston Globe, "Fighting Terror / A War on Manuy7 Fronts, Saudi Group; Charity's Files Hold US Data, Bosnians Say," February 17, 2002.
[73] Jane's Intelligence Review, "Islamist Groups Take Root in the Balkans," January 1, 2002.
[74] Al-Rasheed, Madawi, A History of Saudi Arabia, Cambridge Univeristy Press 2002. Page 132.
[75] http://www.wamy.org/english/conferences/speech3.htm. July 1, 2003.
[76] Monthly Newsletter of the Royal Saudi Embassy in Washington D.C. March 1997. http://www.saudiembassy.net/publications/news_letter/NL_97/nl_97_03.html.

attended a meeting of the MWL Constituent Council in Saudi Arabia and delivered a speech on behalf of King Fahd:

> Since its unification under King Abdel Aziz, may God grant him mercy, the kingdom of Saudi Arabia has devoted its concern to Muslim affairs, and proffered its hand to assist Muslims wherever they may be....**the kingdom has sponsored many such conferences and meetings. Foremost amongst them, is the Muslim World League which today we regard—thanks be to God—as an outstanding Muslim body devoted to the spreading of the Islamic call**...Islamic unity must be cornerstone of co-operation to which we aspire. It's the source of strength, and the secret of our potency.[77]

Muhammad Ibn Ibrahim Ibn Uthman Ibn Jubair was Chairman of the Saudi Shura Council[78] and a member of the MWL Jurisprudence Council until he died in January, 2002.[79] The **Deputy Chairman of the Saudi Shura Council, Dr. Abdullah Naseef, is a former Secretary General of the MWL.**[80]

On its current website, MWL lists its main objectives as "to disseminate Islamic Dawah and expound the teachings of Islam. To defend Islamic causes in a manner that safeguards the interests and aspirations of Muslims, solves their problems, **refutes false allegations against Islam, and repels inimical trends and dogma which the enemies of Islam seek to exploit in order to destroy the unity of Muslims and to sow seeds of doubt in our Muslim brethren**."[81]

There have been credible reports and intelligence that MWL has assisted Islamic militants with financial and organizational assistance. According to intelligence sources, bin Laden's mentor, **Shaykh Abdallah Azzam, was first sponsored by the Muslim World League in the early 1980's to open and head a relief agency in Peshawar, Pakistan that would aid arriving Arab-Afghan warriors.**[82] The **Peshawar MWL branch office was also led for a time by Wa'il Jalaidan.**[83] **The Peshawar office was financed by Osama bin Laden, and later was subsidized by large donations from the Kingdom of Saudi Arabia.**[84] In addition, the **Egyptian MWL branch** office served as the "**third route to the Al-Ansar House in Jedda,**" **one of Bin Laden's "guest houses"** used to funnel recruits to terrorist training camps.[85]

In February 2000, **Jalaidan was appointed to the Board of Trustees of the Rabita Trust (another financial arm of MWL in Pakistan) and served as its Director**

---

[77] *Ain al-Yaqeen*, "At the Opening of the Muslim World League Meeting: The Custodian of the Two Holy Places Calls for Islamic Solidarity to Overcome Obstacles," December 15, 1997.
[78] http://www.saudiembassy.net/gov_profile/consult.html, accessed July 29, 2003.
[79] http://www.saudiembassy.net/gov_profile/consult.html, accessed July 29, 2003.
[80] http://www.saudia-online.com/Shura%20Council.htm.
[81] "About the Muslim World League." http://www.arab.net/mwl/about.htm.
[82] Muhammad, Basil. *Al-Ansaru l'Arab fi Afghanistan*. The Committee for Islamic Benevolence Publications; ©1991. *Page 193*.
[83] *Rose Al-Yusif*, "Usama BinLaden - A Millionair[sic] Finances Extremism in Egypt and Saudi Arabia," May 17, 1993.
[84] Muhammad, Basil. *Al-Ansaru l'Arab fi Afghanistan*. The Committee for Islamic Benevolence Publications; ©1991. *Page 193*.
[85] *Rose Al-Yusif*, "Usama BinLaden - A Millionair[sic] Finances Extremism in Egypt and Saudi Arabia," May 17, 1993.

General.[86] Soon thereafter, U.S. officials sent a confidential memorandum to UN police forces in southeastern Europe titled "Secret: US office only-Release to UNMIK [the U. N. administration in Kosovo]."[87] The document **named MWL representative Wael Jalaidan as an associate of Osama bin Laden and stated that Jalaidan had directly assisted bin Laden's efforts to "move money and men to and from the Balkans."**[88] MWL's Rabita Trust itself was named a Specially Designated Global Terrorist (SDGT) Organization by the U.S. government on October 12, 2001.[89]

The International Islamic Relief Organization (IIRO) in Saudi Arabia

The IIRO was established in 1978 and is headquartered in Jeddah, Saudi Arabia.[90] IIRO is a major financial branch of the Muslim World League (MWL). According to Dr. Ahmed Mohammed Ali, Secretary General of the MWL, the MWL provides "humanitarian assistance" through the arms of IIRO.[91]

According to Dr. Farid Qurashi, IIRO's former general supervisor,[92] "IIRO was the first relief organization to enter Bosnia-Herzegovina and the Balkan region. From the very beginning of the Bosnia war, we were there to help."[93] According to a Serbian news source, IIRO in Bosnia (AKA "IGASA,") was managed primarily by three men: Abdel Aziz Zaher (AKA Abu Anas), Jamal Al-Jibouri (AKA Abu Mahmoud al-Iraqi), and Djamel Lamrani (AKA Abu Musab al-Djazairi). Zaher was expelled from his residence in Belgrade at the beginning of 1993 after being tied not only to IIRO, but also to two other international Muslim organizations suspected of aiding armed fundamentalist militant groups: *Al-Rabita Al-Alami Al-Islamiyya* (the Muslim World League) and the Sanabil Relief Agency. During the following Serb official inquiry into Zaher, **investigators reportedly discovered PLO Force 17 terrorist training manuals in the Belgrade offices of Sanabil Relief.**

As reported by one Serbian news source, beginning in 1992, **Zaher's top lieutenant at IIRO, Jamal Al-Jibouri was allegedly personally responsible for general oversight of a massive logistics operation to provide Muslim militants in the Balkans with weapons and ammunition.**[94] According to documents published by one Serbian website, www.truthinmedia.org **Serb troops had found an IIRO identification card on the body of a killed Arab-Afghan guerilla in Bosnia.**[95] According to Compass Newswire At the time, the IIRO issuing bureau in Peshawar was being run by senior Egyptian *Al-*

---

[86] Office of Public Affairs, United States Treasury Department. "Treasury Department Statement on the Designation of Wa'el Hamza Julidan." September 6, 2002. Document #PO-3397.
[87] Cited in news report by British Broadcasting Company (BBC). April 3, 2000.
[88] Cited in news report by British Broadcasting Company (BBC). April 3, 2000.
[89] Office of Public Affairs, United States Treasury Department. "Treasury Department Statement on the Designation of Wa'el Hamza Julidan." September 6, 2002. Document #PO-3397.
[90] "IIRO – Welcome." http://www.arab.net/iiro.
[91] Moneyclips, "Counter anti-Islam propaganda, says MWL sec-general," May 6, 1995.
[92] Moneyclips, "IIRO saves forty thousand Bosnians from starvation" July 4, 1993.
[93] Moneyclips, "IIRO saves forty thousand Bosnians from starvation" July 4, 1993.
[94] *Vecernje Novosti* (Belgrade), "Bombs in the Name of the Almighty: Part II," September 27, 2001.
[95] www.truthinmedia.org/images/muja82-3.jpg, accessed April 2002.

Gama`at Al-Islamiyya terrorist leader Abu Talal al-Qasimy (AKA Talaat Fouad Qassem).[96]

As reported by the BBC, **following the 1998 U.S. Embassy bombings in East Africa, IIRO's chapter in Nairobi was deregistered by the government of Kenya for its alleged connection to the terrorists responsible for the devastating blasts.**[97] IIRO's Nairobi office was reregistered in August 1998 by order of Kenya's Supreme Court.[98]

After American forces retaliated for the terror bombings, Indian police arrested a number of suspects attempting to counterstrike on the US consulates in Madras and Calcutta.[99]

- The **cell was led by Sayed Abu Nasir,**[100] **a Bangladeshi national, and receiving orders from Shaykh Ahmed Al-Gamdin, director of IIRO operations in Asia, among others.** After graduating from college in Dhaka, Bangladesh, **Abu Nasir was employed by IIRO**, which eventually transferred him from Thailand to Lahore, Pakistan in 1994.[101]
- **Abu Nasir was informed by his superiors that approximately 40 to 50 percent of IIRO's charitable funds were being diverted to finance terrorist training camps in Afghanistan and Kashmir**. As part of his duties, **Abu Nasir was to visit the training camps, assess what funding was needed, and make a formal report back at headquarters. Nasir himself was eventually instructed by Shaykh Al-Gamdin to undergo military training at one of the camps, where he met Osama bin Laden.**[102]

The **southern Philippines IIRO office** was established in 1992 and was **under the direct control and guidance of Mohammad Jamal Khalifa, the 37-year-old brother-in-law of Osama bin Laden.**[103] **According to the Philippine military's southern command, the IIRO local office in Zamboanga City is the prime coordinating center for the Abu Sayyaf organization**, a coalition of secessionist Islamic militants in the southern region of the country.[104]

- **American law enforcement officials detained Khalifa on December 16,** 1994 as he attempted to return from San Francisco to the Philippines.[105] **Travelling**

[96] Compass Newswire. November 1, 1995.
[97] BBC, Kenya: NGO Council Official Condemns Deregistration of Islamic NGOs," September 9, 1998.
[98] Agence France Presse, "Kenya Lifts Ban on Saudi-based Islamic NGOs," December 17, 1998.
[99] New York Times, "Pakistan Denies Role in Plotting Bombings in India," January 22, 1999.
[100] New York Times, "Pakistan Denies Role in Plotting Bombings in India," January 22, 1999.
[101] New York Times, "Anti-U.S. Plot in India Is Foiled; Militant Islamist Intended to Bomb 2 Consulates, Police Say," January 21, 1999.
[102] New York Times, "Anti-U.S. Plot in India Is Foiled; Militant Islamist Intended to Bomb 2 Consulates, Police Say," January 21, 1999.
[103] Sworn affidavit of FBI Special Agent Robert Walker. United States of America v. Benevolence International Foundation, Inc. April 29, 2002. District of Illinois, Eastern Division. Case number: 02CR0414.
[104] Sworn affidavit of FBI Special Agent Robert Walker. United States of America v. Benevolence International Foundation, Inc. April 29, 2002. District of Illinois, Eastern Division. Case number: 02CR0414.
[105] Sworn affidavit of FBI Special Agent Robert Walker. United States of America v. Benevolence International Foundation, Inc. April 29, 2002. District of Illinois, Eastern Division. Case number: 02CR0414.

with Khalifa on this occasion was Mohamed Loay Bayazid (AKA Abu Rida al-Suri), one of the founders and key international operatives of *Al-Qaeda*.[106]

- Khalifa's electronic organizer and personal address book contained entries for intimate associates of **Ramzi Yousef, the convicted bombmaker in the February 1993 World Trade Center attack.**[107] Investigators also discovered **documents on Khalifa "referring to the assassination of bishops and bombings of churches (at a time when evidence gathered in the investigation indicates that...others were planning to kill the Pope during a planned January 1995 visit to the Philippines and after churches had already been bombed in the Philippines in the preceding year)."**[108] Four days later, **a State Department cable to the American Embassy in Khartoum, Sudan referred to Khalifa as a "known financier of terrorist operations."**[109]

The Canadian government has stated that IIRO "secretly fund[s] terrorism."[110] According to Canadian court documents, Mahmoud Jaballah is a suspected member of Egyptian *Al-Jihad* and he has been jailed in Canada.[111] **Jaballah is accused of having contact with *Al-Qaeda* operatives and spent three years working for the IIRO in Pakistan.**[112] The Canadian Security and Intelligence Service (CSIS) "believes that Jaballah continues to actively support [Al-Jihad's] terrorist agenda."[113] CSIS concluded that "the degree of Jaballah's dedication to the cause is such that Jaballah would resort to violence and would direct others to resort to violence if he was ordered to do so by leaders such as Osama Bin Laden or Dr. Ayman Al-Zawaheri."[114] **Jaballah was suspected of cooperating with senior Canadian *Al-Qaeda* lieutenant Ahmad Saeed Khadr (AKA Abdel Rahman Al-Kanadi),** considered an influential figure in the international terrorist financing network.[115]

---

[106] Sworn affidavit of FBI Special Agent Robert Walker. United States of America v. Benevolence International Foundation, Inc. April 29, 2002. District of Illinois, Eastern Division. Case number: 02CR0414.
[107] Sworn affidavit of FBI Special Agent Robert Walker. United States of America v. Benevolence International Foundation, Inc. April 29, 2002. District of Illinois, Eastern Division. Case number: 02CR0414.
[108] Sworn affidavit of FBI Special Agent Robert Walker. United States of America v. Benevolence International Foundation, Inc. April 29, 2002. District of Illinois, Eastern Division. Case number: 02CR0414.
[109] Sworn affidavit of FBI Special Agent Robert Walker. United States of America v. Benevolence International Foundation, Inc. April 29, 2002. District of Illinois, Eastern Division. Case number: 02CR0414.
[110] Evidence introduced by the Canadian government in the Trial of Mahmoud Es-sayy Jaballah
[111] Respondent's (Moving Party) Motion Record." The Minister of Citizenship and Immigration and Mahmoud Jaballah. Docket: DES-6-99. June 2, 1999. *Pages 61-62.*
[112] Respondent's (Moving Party) Motion Record." The Minister of Citizenship and Immigration and Mahmoud Jaballah. Docket: DES-6-99. June 2, 1999. *Pages 61-62.*
[113] Respondent's (Moving Party) Motion Record." The Minister of Citizenship and Immigration and Mahmoud Jaballah. Docket: DES-6-99. June 2, 1999. *Pages 61-62.*
[114] Respondent's (Moving Party) Motion Record." The Minister of Citizenship and Immigration and Mahmoud Jaballah. Docket: DES-6-99. June 2, 1999. *Pages 61-62.*
[115] Respondent's (Moving Party) Motion Record." The Minister of Citizenship and Immigration and Mahmoud Jaballah. Docket: DES-6-99. June 2, 1999. *Page 10.*

During Jaballah's immigration trial, Mr. Arafat El-Asahi, the director of IIRO in Canada and a full-time employee of the Muslim World League, testified on Jaballah's behalf.[116] El-Asahi **admitted that Jaballah had "worked as a Principle of one of our organizations in Pakistan"** and that he had been recommended by IIRO's administrators in Pakistan for having "excellent character and good behaviour."[117] El-Asahi also offered the following sworn testimony:

> **Q: During those eight years that you have been with the IIRO here in Canada, have you ever heard anything to the effect that the Canadian government has any concern whatsoever with respect to your office?**
>
> A: Let me tell you one thing. **The Muslim World League, which is the mother of IIRO, is a fully government funded organization. In other words, I work for the Government of Saudi Arabia. I am an employee of that government.** Second, the IIRO is the relief branch of that organization which means that **we are controlled in all our activities and plans by the Government of Saudi Arabia.** Keep that in mind, please...I am paid by **my organization which is funded by the [Saudi] government...The [IIRO] office, like any other office in the world, here or in the Muslim World League, has to abide by the policy of the Government of Saudi Arabia. If anybody deviates from that, he would be fired; he would not work at all with IIRO or with the Muslim World League.**[118]

- One of the most influential members of IIRO's board of directors is Tariq Binladin, a close family relation of Osama bin Laden.
- Mohammed al-Zawahiri, leader of the Egyptian Islamic Jihad's military wing and the brother of Dr. Ayman al-Zawahiri (Bin Laden's personal physician and top advisor), worked and traveled around the world on behalf of IIRO.[119]
- Western intelligence sources have traced IIRO money transfers to bank accounts in London, England and Amman, Jordan.[120] That money was subsequently channeled through front groups to Hamas-affiliated organizations in Gaza and the West Bank.[121]
- **When leaving home, Fayez Ahmed Alshehri, one of the September 11 airline hijackers, told his father he was going to go work for the IIRO.**[122]

Saudi government officials have shown great commitment in their efforts to raise money for IIRO operations. In 1987 IIRO established an office in Saudi Arabia to invest and grow IIRO's charitable operations. That branch is known as *Sanabel Al-Kheer* (Seeds of Charity). IIRO sought to raise SR100 million annually for 10 years, and therefore create

---

[116] Reasons for Order." The Minister of Citizenship and Immigration and Mahmoud Jaballah. Docket: DES-6-99. Federal Court of Canada. November 2, 1999. Pages 81-88.
[117] Reasons for Order." The Minister of Citizenship and Immigration and Mahmoud Jaballah. Docket: DES-6-99. Federal Court of Canada. November 2, 1999. Page 85.
[118] Reasons for Order." The Minister of Citizenship and Immigration and Mahmoud Jaballah. Docket: DES-6-99. Federal Court of Canada. November 2, 1999. Pages 81-88.
[119] *Al-Hayat*, "Official sources deny reports on UAE's extradition of Islamist," June 7, 2000.
[120] New York Daily News, "It's More Then Just Who Plants The Explosive," July 31, 1996.
[121] New York Daily News, "It's More Then Just Who Plants The Explosive," July 31, 1996.
[122] Middle East Newsfile, "Another Saudi ' hijacker' turns up in Tunis," September 18, 2001.

a base capital investment for *Sanabel Al-Kheer* of 1 billion Saudi riyals ($267 million). IIRO further hoped to generate sufficient profits to cover the costs of IIRO's international operations and make it a self-sufficient entity.[123] **Ghazi Mahfooz Felemban**, IIRO Assistant Secretary-General for Finance and Investment, was responsible for fiscal oversight of *Sanabel* and IIRO.[124]

Sanabel Al-Kheer and IIRO hold annual fundraisers. A July 1992 fundraiser for the Muslims of Bosnia in Jeddah **was inaugurated by Prince Saud ibn Abdul Mohsen, acting governor of Makkah**, and **acting chairman of *Sanabel Al-Kheer*.** The event raised more than SR19 million in one day. **Abdul Mohsen Al-Kayal, chairman of the higher court in Jeddah, told the audience that "donating for a worthy cause is a kind of jihad and Muslims should generously help the Bosnian Muslims."** The largest single donors reportedly included **Prince Saud ibn Abdul Mohsen and Bakr bin Laden. Dr. Abdullah Omar Naseef (Secretary-General of the Muslim World League)** was also at the function.[125]

At a December 1993 fundraising drive to support Bosnian Muslims, IIRO collected SR15 million in less than two hours. **Prince Saud ibn Abdul Mohsen spoke as an honorary trustee and noted "the continuous support and encouragement of the Custodian of the Two Holy Mosques King Fahd" in promoting IIRO operations.**[126]

At a February 1994 conference IIRO and *Sanabel Al-Kheer* raised SR3.7 million. During his opening speech, **Prince Salman Bin Abdul Aziz, Governor of Riyadh,** told of how he had **personally solicited "donations from a number of benevolent Saudi people" for Sanabel and IIRO totalling SR6,979,462.**[127] Responding years later to allegations that Saudi charities were involved in bankrolling terrorism, **Prince Salman admitted, "I have...chaired several (charity) groups and I know that (the funds) are used in good deeds, and it is not the responsibility of the kingdom if there were people who turn those good deeds into evil ones."**[128] **Shaykh Abdulaziz bin Baz, Mufti of Saudi Arabia, also attended the 1994 IIRO conference.**[129]

The 1995 annual fundraiser in Riyadh raised SR8 million ($2.13 million) in the first day, including **SR1 million from Prince Salman bin Abdel Aziz and SR1 million from Prince Al-Waleed bin Talal bin Abdel Aziz.**[130]

By 1995, *Sanabel Al-Kheer* had collected an estimated total of SR297 million ($79.2 million) in total charitable funds since its foundation and had reported SR77.5 in investment revenue from "safe business propositions."[131] According to Dr. Ahmad Muhammad Ali, the **then-Secretary General of MWL, "much of [IIRO and Sanabel's] funding has been made possible by financial assistance from the Saudi government including King Fahd Bin Abdul Aziz, Deputy Prime Minister and**

---

[123] Arab News, "Islamic relief organization sets up income-bearing scheme," March 8, 1992.
[124] The Saudi Gazette, "Personality Profile: A born volunteer and friend of the poor," August 18, 1996.
[125] Arab News., "Bosnia committee receives SR19m," July 6, 1992.
[126] Arab News, "IIRO raises SR15m in-funds," December 22, 1993.
[127] The Saudi Gazette, "Saudis back fund-raising for Bosnian Muslims," February 26, 1994.
[128] The Associated Press, "Saudi Tycoon Defends Muslim Charity," November 2, 2002.
[129] Arab News, "Riyadh Governor Prince Salman donates SR1m to IIRO," February 23, 1994.
[130] Arab News, "SR8m raised on first day of Sanabel Al Khair," February 23, 1995.
[131] Arab News, "SR8m raised on first day of Sanabel Al Khair," February 23, 1995.

Commander of the National Guard Crown Prince Abdullah Bin Abdul Aziz and Chairman of the Board of Trustees of the Saudi Benevolent Society, [and] Second Deputy Prime Minister and Minister of Defense and Aviation Prince Sultan Bin Abdul Aziz."[132]

The IIRO/*Sanabel Al-Kheer* fundraiser in February 1996 raised more than SR6 million in three hours time. Donations included **SR1 million from Prince Salman Bin Abdul Aziz, SR1 million from Prince Sattam Bin Abdul (deputy governor of Riyadh), and SR10,000 from Shaykh Abdulaziz Bin Baz.** Princes Salman and Sattam were warmly greeted by **Dr. Abdullah Saleh Al-Obaid, the new Secretary General of MWL and chairman of IIRO's "founding council."**[133]

The tenth annual fundraising drive in 1997 collected over SR17 million[134] and the 12th annual *Sanabel Al-Kheer*/IIRO charity drive in 1998 netted over SR6 million in less then two hours, including **SR5 million from Prince Sultan bin Abdelaziz bin Saud (Second Deputy Premier and Saudi Defense Minister), SR1 million from Riyadh Governor Prince Salman, and SR10,000 from Shaykh Abdulaziz bin Baz.**[135]

IIRO, Sana-Bell & MWL in the United States

In the late 1980's and early 1990s, IIRO, SAna-Bell and the Muslim World League set up branch offices in the greater Washington, DC area.[136] The Muslim World League's U.S. offices were first organized at 555 Grove Street in Herndon, Virginia by Yaqub Mirza.[137] As closely related organizations, Sana-Bell, IIRO and MWL had overlapping mission statements, offices and executives.

In 2002, law enforcement and intelligence officials raided an *Al-Qaeda* safe house in Bosnia-Herzegovina. Among documents recovered was the coveted *Golden Chain* list, containing the original *Al-Qaeda* financiers from the late 1980s.[138] Former *Al-Qaeda* operatives have explained how *Golden Chain* financiers would donate funds earmarked for bin Laden by way of the Muslim World League.[139] **Included on the *Golden Chain* list are the names Salih Kamel and Ibrahim Afandi, two founding Trustees of Sana-**

---

[132] Info-Prod Research (Middle East) Ltd. – Middle East News Items, "Prince Salman Opens Fundraising Campaign for IIRO," February 28, 1995.
[133] The Saudi Gazette, "SR6m Raised in Three Hours at Sanabel Al-Khair Drive," February 6, 1996.
[134] The Saudi Gazette, "IIRO Bags SR17m in One Night for Sanabel Al-Khair," January 23, 1997.
[135] Arab News, "SR6m collected at Sanabel Al-Khair," December 24, 1998.
[136] Articles of Incorporation International Relief Organization, Inc. Commonwealth of Virginia, State Corporation Commission, July 17, 1991. Articles of Incorporation Sana-Bell, Inc. Government of the District of Columbia, Department of Consumer and Regulatory Affairs, July 28, 1989.
[137] Articles of Incorporation Muslim World League Foundation. Commonwealth of Virginia, State Corporation Commission.
[138] Wall Street Journal, "Al-Qaeda List Points to Saudi Elite," March 18, 2003.
[139] Wall Street Journal, "Al-Qaeda List Points to Saudi Elite," March 18, 2003.

Bell in Washington DC,[140] which was organized around the same time the Golden Chain was created.

Dr. Yaqub Mirza, the subject of a federal investigation in the Eastern District of Virginia was also on Sana-Bell's founding Board of Trustees.[141]

In the United States, Sana-Bell operated out of Falls Church and Herndon, Virginia, and was headed by Sulaiman Al-Ali, a former MWL fund-raiser.[142] From 1990 to 1997, Al-Ali, Sana-Bell and IIRO invested millions of dollars with BMI, Inc., an Islamic investment bank based in Secaucus, New Jersey.[143] According to FBI Agent Robert Wright, the **founders of BMI include SDGTs Musa abu Marzook (Hamas leader) and Yasin al-Qadi (*Al-Qaeda* financier)**, and two bin Laden brothers.[144] In a civil lawsuit, a BMI official later explained how al-Ali would invest in BMI land deals, and subsequently withdraw substantial sums in cash.[145] At one point, **a second BMI official confided to an FBI agent that he feared money he transferred overseas helped finance the East Africa Embassy bombings.**[146]

Section VI of **Sana-Bell's Articles of Incorporation indicates that upon dissolution, the assets of the organization shall be distributed to several Islamic organizations, including SAFA Trust, Inc.**[147] In the early 1990's, **SAFA Trust, along with its sister organization International Institute of Islamic Thought, were the primary financial backers of indicted terrorist leader and University of South Florida Professor, Sami al-Arian.**[148]

Another recipient of IIRO millions was a start-up chemical company out of Chicago, Illinois.[149] In a 1997 **federal investigation resulting in fraud convictions and jail sentences, Global Chemical was shut down amidst allegations of money laundering and terrorism support.**[150]

Saudi officials have tried to distance themselves from the activities of U.S. branches of MWL, Sana-Bell and IIRO. At his June 12, 2003 press conference, Adel Al-Jubeir stated that:

---

[140] Articles of Incorporation Sana-Bell, Inc. Government of the District of Columbia, Department of Consumer and Regulatory Affairs, July 28, 1989.

[141] Articles of Incorporation Sana-Bell, Inc. Government of the District of Columbia, Department of Consumer and Regulatory Affairs, July 28, 1989.

[142] Articles of Incorporation Sana-Bell, Inc. Government of the District of Columbia, Department of Consumer and Regulatory Affairs, July 28, 1989.

[143] IRS Form 990s filed by IIRO from 1990-1997 AND Sana-Bell, Inc. v BMI Real Estate, et al., US District Court, District Maryland (Greenbelt), December 23, 1998.

[144] Sworn Statement, FBI Special Agent Robert G. Wright, Jr. Chicago, Illinois. March 21, 2000.

[145] Deposition of Soliman Bihieri in Sana-Bell, Inc. v BMI Real Estate, et al., US District Court, District Maryland (Greenbelt), December 23, 1998.

[146] Sworn Statement, FBI Special Agent Robert G. Wright, Jr. Chicago, Illinois. March 21, 2000.

[147] Articles of Incorporation Sana-Bell, Inc. Government of the District of Columbia, Department of Consumer and Regulatory Affairs, July 28, 1989.

[148] Letter from Ramadan Abdullah to Dr. Mark Orr, December 11, 1991.

[149] IRS Form 990 filed by International Relief Organization for fiscal year 1995.

[150] Affidavit of FBI Special Agent Valerie Donahue, submitted in connection with USA v Mohammed Mabrook, United States Distrcit Court, Northern District of Illinois, Docket no. 98-CR-271.

> I want to also remind you that there are **a lot of charities that claim to be subsidiaries of charities based in Saudi Arabia that in fact are not. You have the Islamic Relief Organization here in America.** The parent company disassociated itself from them years ago, and did so publicly.
>
> And until today, I see reports that people say "a branch of a Saudi charity." It's not. **It's an American charity based in America that raises money in America.**[151]

In a similar attempt to clarify the Saudi connection to US activities, IIRO Secretary General Dr Adnan Basha proffered in an October 2002 press release that IIRO had no connection or links with the International Relief Organization.[152] However, documents filed in Washington DC and Virginia indicate that IIRO in the U.S. is indeed a branch of the Saudi organization.

The U.S. branch of IIRO was first organized as a Virginia corporation in July of 1991 by Sulaiman Al-Ali under the name *International Relief Organization, Inc.*[153] Less than one year later, Al-Ali incorporated the *International Islamic Relief Organization* in Washington DC.[154] The DC and Virginia organizations shared officers Tareq Al-Swaidan and Abdullah Al-Mahdi. On March 8, 1993, Al-Ali filed an assumed name certificate in Virginia for International Relief Organization in the name of *International Islamic Relief Organization.*[155]

International Relief Organization's Application for Recognition of Exemption under Section 501(c)(3) explains,

> We are very fortunate to have as our Executive Director Mr. Suliman Al-Ali. Since 1985 he has been involved in fund raising activities for the needy of the world. Mr. Al-Ali has worked for several non-profit organizations over the past 6 years successfully raising funds for the needy and poor. **Mr. Al-Ali's most recent pledge program for International Islamic Relief Organization (IIRO) netted about $500,000.**[156]

Al-Ali's biography explains that,

---

[151] News Conference, Saudi Embassy, June 12, 2003

[152] Saudi Arabian Information Resource. *IIRO has no link with International Relief Organization.* October 21, 2002.

[153] Articles of Incorporation International Relief Organization, Inc. Commonwealth of Virginia, State Corporation Commission, July 17, 1991.

[154] Articles of Incorporation International Islamic Relief Organization, Inc. Government of the District of Columbia, Department of Consumer and Regulatory Affairs, February 18, 1992.

[155] Assumed Name Certificate. International Relief Organization. Commonwealth of Virginia, State Corporation Commission, March 8 1993.

[156] Application for Recognition of Exemption under Section 501(c)(3) of Internal Revenue Code. International Relief Organization, Inc. October 25, 1991.

> [Al-Ali] became a fulltime fundraiser for the I.I.R.O., June 1990. From June 1990 until July 1991, the pledge programs he directed netted about half a million dollars a month. This relief program, which coordinates multi-million dollar relief programs in Africa, is supported in part by the Saudi government and people.[157]

A description of the founding capital for IRO, the application reveals that an $11,000 loan was provided by Sana-Bell USA. founder Farid Qurashi.[158]

According to the deposition of BMI executive Soliman Biheiri and corresponding court exhibits, when an investment dispute arose between Sana-Bell and BMI, Biheiri received a letter on IIRO Saudi Arabia letterhead from the **Secretary of the Investment Committee of IIRO in Saudi Arabia** with the following instructions:

> I request you to stop any transactions concerning the accounts managed by your firme under the name of (Sana-Bell, America), and to cancel the validity of Dr. Solaiman Al-Ali's signature in regard of all our accounts with your firm.
>
> **You will receive, later, a direct confirmation of these instructions from the Secretary General of the "Muslim World League", the Chairman of the Board of IIRO and Chairman of the Investments Committee.** He will, also, let you know how our accounts with your firm will be handled in the future.[159]

International Relief Organzation's 1992 Return of Organization Exempt from Income Tax discloses a payment to Bosnia & Somalia Relief Funds for over $275,000. The address listed for the Bosnia & Somalia Relief Funds, P.O. Box 14843, Jeddah 21434, is the address for IIRO's Saudi Arabian offices.[160] IRO's Tax Return for 1996 lists a $3.9 million disbursement for "Emergency relief supplies (medical supplies) to International Islamic Relief in Bosnia."[161]

The *Al-Haramain* Foundation

The *Al-Haramain* Charitable Foundation is a Saudi non-profit evangelical charity that engages in relief work around the world. It has more than 40 international branches, and

---

[157] Application for Recognition of Exemption under Section 501(c)(3) of Internal Revenue Code. International Relief Organization, Inc. October 25, 1991.

[158] Application for Recognition of Exemption under Section 501(c)(3) of Internal Revenue Code. International Relief Organization, Inc. October 25, 1991.

[159] Deposition of Soliman S. Biheiri. *In the Matter of The Sana-Bell, Inc. v. BMI Real Estate Development, Inc. et al*. October 27, 1999. Exhibit Mirza #16, 10/25/1999.

[160] Return of Organization Exempt From Income Tax. International Relief Organization. 1992.

[161] Return of Organization Exempt From Income Tax. International Relief Organization. 1996.

in 1999 spent more than $61 million on various projects worldwide.[162] *Al-Haramain* also maintains local offices in the continental United States, primarily in Missouri and Oregon.[163]

Since the mid-1990s, *Al-Haramain* has come under investigation by intelligence and law enforcement bodies across the globe. In January 1995, the Committee for the Defense of Legitimate Rights (CDLR), a Saudi dissident group aligned with Osama bin Laden, reported that Saudi authorities were scrutinizing the activities of *Al-Haramain*. According to CDLR, "[a]ttacks on voluntary work still continue after the closure of many voluntary organisations. [King] Fahd has now turned his beady attention to the *Al-Haramain* institution."[164]

When Italian counterterrorism police raided a suspected *Al-Gama`at Al-Islamiyya* terrorist guesthouse and headquarters in Milan in 1995, they discovered a confidential letter sent to **wanted Egyptian terrorist Shaykh Anwar Shaaban** from Albania **detailing efforts to distribute *Al-Gama`at's* official magazine, *Al-Murabitoun*, amongst the personnel working at the *Al-Haramain*** charitable organization in the Balkans.[165] Subsequently, **three members of the *Al-Qaeda*-linked Egyptian *Al-Jihad* were deported from Albania in June 1998.[166] All three were also connected to the "*Al-Haramain* Islamic Organization" and a search of their apartments revealed official government stamps used for producing false documents.**[167] In April 1999 a **report from a member of the *Al-Haramain* delegation in Albania** described scenes of Kosovar refugees and concluded, **"We ask Allah the Almighty and Majestic to repel the evil designs of the [infidels] back onto their own necks."**[168]

***Al-Haramain* was officially banned in Kenya shortly after the devastating U.S. Embassy bombings in August 1998 because the charity was believed to have been involved in the attack.**[169] At the time, John Etemesi, **chairman of the Kenyan Non-Governmental Coordinating Board, explained that *Al-Haramain* "had been found to be working against the interests of Kenyans in terms of security...Our investigations reveal that the operations of these organizations are inconsistent with the reasons for which they were registered."**[170]

---

[162] Agence France Presse, "Saudi Arabia's top Islamic charity denies any of its assets frozen," March 13, 2002.
[163] IRS 990 Form fiscal year 2000 for the "*Al-Haramain* Foundation."
[164] HEADLINE: CDLR MONITOR: No.30 ; Fri 13 JAN 1995 YOUR RIGHT TO KNOW
[165] DIGOS (Italy) Anti-Terrorism Report. "Searches at the Islamic Cultural Center, Viale Jenner 50, Milano, 6/26/1995." Dated September 15, 1997.
[166] "State Summarizing pursuant to section 40.1(1) of the Immigration Act." In relation to Mahmoud Jaballah. The Federal Court of Canada.
[167] "State Summarizing pursuant to section 40.1(1) of the Immigration Act." In relation to Mahmoud Jaballah. The Federal Court of Canada.
[168] "REPORT NO: 1 - Report On Kosovan Refugees." Report from the *Al-Haramain* Foundation; Tirana, Albania. April 2, 1999. http://kosova.hypermart.net/harameen.html.
[169] Associated Press, "U.S. blocks assets of Islamic charity's operations in Bosnia and Somalia," March 11, 2002.
[170] Associated Press, "Kenya bans six Islamic aid agencies after U.S. Embassy bombing," September 9, 1998.

Wadih el-Hage, Osama bin Laden's personal secretary, was a principle convicted conspirator in the 1998 embassy bombings. **El-Hage's book of business cards exhibited at the federal trials in New York contained a card for "Mansour A. Al-Kadi" as the "Deputy General Director and Head of Africa-Committee of *Al-Haramain* Islamic Foundation."**[171] **"Mansuor [sic] Al-Kadi" is also listed as the Vice President of *Al-Haramain*'s Ashland, Oregon office on IRS 990 Forms from fiscal year 2000.**[172] ***Al-Haramain*'s English-language website further identifies Al-Kadi as a member of its global Board of Trustees.**[173]

- Regarding the U.S. presence in the Muslim world, two months after the 1998 East Africa Embassy bombings the ***Al-Haramain*** **English-language newsletter** read:

> **The war of the Christian Crusaders is today at its most intense**...The Muslim whose mind has not been corrupted cannot bear to see the unbelievers wielding authority, and ordering and prohibiting in his own country. **Therefore such a Muslim strives his utmost to expel and distance them - even if he has to sacrifice his own life**, or his most cherished possession, for this cause.[174]

- *Al-Haramain's* website regularly covered the "The Jihaad In Chechnya," posting reports from its representative in Chechnya, Abdul-Lateef Ad-Diraan.[175] The **Russian FSB security service accused the *Al-Haramain* Foundation of transferring $1 million to Chechen Muslim rebels in 1999** and **arranging the purchase on their behalf of 500 "heavy weapons" from the Taliban in Afghanistan.**[176] According to the Washington Post, the FSB memo alleged written exchanges between Arab-Afghan military commanders in Chechnya and *Al-Haramain*'s "director" back in the Saudi Kingdom:

> **Today, *Al-Haramain* has $50 million for the needs of the *mujaheddin* ['holy warriors']...The reason *Al-Haramain* provides assistance a little bit at a time is because it is afraid of the accusations it is assisting the jihad.**[177]

- In the February 2000 *Al-Haramain* newsletter, a columnist wrote, "**Jihad is a religious obligation in Islaam. Its aim is to fight oppression and injustice and to remove obstacleswhich prevent the spread of Islaam. This is accomplish[ed] either by weakening or destroying the disbelieving prevalent**

---

[171] U.S. v. Usama bin Laden, et al. United States District Court for the Southern District of New York. 116 F. Supp. 2d 489; 2000 U.S. Dist. LEXIS 14507. October 5, 2000, Decided. October 5, 2000, Filed. Government exhibits GX-207 to GX-364.
[172] IRS 990 Form fiscal year 2000 for the "*Al-Haramain* Foundation."
[173] http://www.alharamain.org/alharamain/eng/inner.asp?order=1&num=1.
[174] Shaykh Abdul-Aziz Ibn Baz. "The Ideological Attack." *Al-Haramain* Newsletter. Vol. 2; No. 10. October 1998.
[175] http://www.alharamain.org/alharamain/chechniya/chech_eng01.html. See also: http://www.alharamain.org/alharamain/chechniya/chech_eng04.html.
[176] The Washington Post, "How Jihad Made Its Way to Chechnya Secular Separatist Movement Transformed by Militant Vanguard," April 26, 2003.
[177] The Washington Post, "How Jihad Made Its Way to Chechnya Secular Separatist Movement Transformed by Militant Vanguard," April 26, 2003.

political powers so that Muslims can prevent anyone from persecuting their brother Muslims wherever they may be."[178]

- German authorities detained and interrogated six men tied to the Al-Nur mosque in Berlin in March 2003.[179] One of the men, Tunisian-born Ihsan Garnoaui, was arrested after **a poison handbook, bomb-making ingredients, a loaded handgun, and a stolen passport were found in his belongings.**[180] **Masjid Al-Nur had come under scrutiny for its links to Mohammad J. Fakihi, Director of the Islamic Affairs Department at the Saudi Embassy in Berlin, who has been tied to *Al-Qaeda* and alleged September 11 conspirators active in Germany.**[181]
    - Reports indicate German investigators were examining the role of the ***Al-Haramain*** **Foundation in funding and sponsorship of the Al-Nur mosque. Shaykh 'Aqeel Ibn 'Abdul-'Aziz Al-'Aqeel, the "general director" of *Al-Haramain,* is listed as a co-owner of the land the mosque sits on, which was purchased only months after the arrival of Fakihi at the Saudi Embassy in Berlin.**[182]

Al-Haramain **is closely controlled and funded by members of the Saudi government, religious hierarchy, and royal family.** Most notably, according to *Al-Haramain*'s website www.alharamain.org, **the "superintendent of all Foundation activities" is Shaykh Saleh Ibn Abdul-'Azeez Aali Shaykh, the Saudi Minister of Islamic Affairs, Endowments, Call and Guidance. Shaykh Abdul-`Azeez Aali formally serves as "the chairman of the administrative board" of *Al Haramain.***[183]

The Bin Baz Foundation is headed by **Prince Salman bin Abdulaziz, the governor of Riyadh region, and Prince Abdulaziz bin Fahad bin Abdulaziz, the Saudi State Minister and Head of Council of Ministers Chamber.**[184] **The "General Director" of *Al-Haramain*, Shaykh 'Aqeel Ibn 'Abdul-'Aziz Al-'Aqeel, is a member of the Board of Trustees of the influential Saudi Bin Baz Foundation.**[185] Shaykh Al-'Aqeel has stated on several occasions that *Al-Haramain* operates only with the explicit permission and the Islamic mandate of the Kingdom of Saudi Arabia. Interviewed in the Washington Post, Al-'Aqeel explained, **"We do not have any relationship with any terrorist activities...We work under the supervision of the Saudi government."**[186] In other interviews, **Aqeel has indicated that the activities of *Al-Haramain* are "under**

---

[178] *Al-Haramain* Newsletter. Vol. 4; No. 3. February 2000.
[179] The Wall Street Journal, "Germans Investigate Saudi Official," April 22, 2003.
[180] The Wall Street Journal, "Germans Investigate Saudi Official," April 22, 2003.
[181] The Wall Street Journal, "Germans Investigate Saudi Official," April 22, 2003.
[182] The Wall Street Journal, "Germans Investigate Saudi Official," April 22, 2003.
[183] http://www.alharamain.org/alharamain/eng/inner.asp?order=1&num=1. See also: http://www.alharamain.org/english/ourobjectives.htm. January 27, 2002.
[184] http://binbazfoundation.org/english/leadership.html. See also: http://www.alharamain.org/alharamain/eng/inner.asp?order=1&num=1.
[185] http://binbazfoundation.org/english/leadership.html, accessed July 30, 2003.
[186] The Washington Post, "How Jihad Made Its Way to Chechnya Secular Separatist Movement Transformed by Militant Vanguard," April 26, 2003.

tight administrative and financial control"[187] and that over 95% of his group's funding comes directly from Saudi Arabia.[188]

Al-Haramain has posted endorsements from prominent Saudi officials on its English-language website. Among these, an "attestation" written by the former supreme religious authority in Saudi Arabia, Shaykh Abdulaziz Bin Baz, dated April 15, 1999:

> **I attach for you a check in the amount of 10,000 Riyals to assist the [*Al-Haramain*] Foundation in its charitable work. May Allah accept your efforts, multiply your reward and bless you in your work for indeed He is Most Generous and Most Kind.[189]**

Shaykh Mohammed Al-Uthaimeen, a lecturer at the Imam Muhammad bin Saud Islamic University and a member of the **Council of Senior Scholars of the Kingdom of Saudi Arabia** wrote in an endorsement dated October 22, 1998:

> ...I was very pleased with what the Foundation has done both domestically and internationally just as I was pleased with the opening of the breasts of the brothers who accepted Islam. I ask Allah (SWT) to make all of them firm and to provide us with sincerity and correct action.[190]

On May 1, 1999, Abdul-Lateef Saleh wrote on the letterhead of the Saudi embassy in Albania to *Al-Haramain* "superintendent" and Minister of Islamic Affairs Shaykh Saleh Ibn Abdul-'Azeez Aali Shaykh to "express my appreciation and praise for the efforts of *Al-Haramain* Foundation in the Albanian Republic... **We thank you for the cooperation of the Foundation in Albania with the Embassy of the Custodian of the Two Holy Mosques, King Fahd Ibn Abdul-Aziz**—may Allah preserve him. **If anything, this indicates the deep ties among Saudi society both governmentally and with its people."**[191] Six months later, Abdul-Lateef was expelled from Albania on suspicion of membership in "the radical Islamic Jihad group"[192] and was alleged to be linked directly to Osama Bin Laden.[193]

Support for the *Al-Haramain* Foundation runs to the most senior levels of the Al-Saud family. On **November 12, 2002, a charitable event in Riyadh co-sponsored by the *Al-Haramain* Foundation, IIRO, and the World Assembly for Muslim Youth (WAMY) was attended by, among others: Governor of the Riyadh region, Prince Salman bin Abdul Aziz; Grand Mufti of Saudi Arabia, Shaykh Abdulaziz bin Abdullah Al Al-Shaykh; Minister of Islamic Affairs, Shaykh Saleh Ibn Abdul-'Azeez Aali Shaykh;** and, *Al-Haramain* director Shaykh 'Aqeel Ibn 'Abdul-'Aziz Al-'Aqeel.[194]

---

[187] Agence France Presse, "Noose tightens around Islamic charities in Gulf," October 3, 2001.
[188] *Al-Sharq al-Awsat* (London), "Interview with Aqil al-Aqil, general manager of the charitable Al-Haramayn Foundation," March 16, 2002.
[189] http://www.alharamain.org/english/ourobjectives.htm. January 27, 2002.
[190] http://www.alharamain.org/english/ourobjectives.htm. January 27, 2002.
[191] "REPORT NO: 12 - A Letter of Commendation." Report from the *Al-Haramain* Foundation; Tirana, Albania. May 1, 1999. http://kosova.hypermart.net/harameen.html.
[192] AP, 11/14/99 (Citing to Gazeta Shqiptare and Koha Jone 'that we should get translated') (Independently confirmed by government official who spoke on condition of anonymity.)
[193] Deutshe Presse-Agentur, "Albanian Police Said to Have Handed Suspected Terrorist to CIA, November 14, 1999.
[194] Saudi Press Agency, "Prince Salman patronizes charity ceremony," November 12, 2002.

Less than two weeks later, **Prince Abdul Majeed Ibn Abdul Aziz, Governor of the Mecca Region, pledged a personal contribution of approximately $40,000 during a joint ceremony organized by *Al-Haramain* and WAMY.**[195] Elsewhere, **Prince Mohammed bin Fahd bin Abdul Aziz, Governor of the Eastern region of Saudi Arabia, was a featured guest at yet another joint charitable function organized in November 2002 by IIRO, WAMY, and *Al-Haramain*.**[196] After **pledging a donation of over $250,000, Prince Mohammed bin Abdul Aziz delivered a speech to attendees congratulating the assistance "given by the government of the Kingdom of Saudi Arabia under the leadership of...King Fahd Ibn Abdul Aziz, Crown Prince Abdullah Ibn Abdul Aziz and Prince Sultan Ibn Abdul Aziz, Second Deputy Prime Minister and Commander of the National Guard to charities and charitable deeds."**[197]

On March 11, 2002, the U.S. Treasury froze the assets of the *Al-Haramain* branches in Somalia and Bosnia.[198] *Al-Haramain* spent roughly $26.7 million total in Somalia, and over $260,000 per year in Bosnia in the last ten years.[199] **Investigators suggested that *Al-Haramain*'s Bosnia office had been linked to the terrorist group *Al-Gama`at Al-Islamiyya*, and that Wa'il Jalaidan was authorized to withdraw money from its local bank account.**[200]

Shaykh 'Aqeel Al-'Aqeel has flatly denied that any *Al-Haramain* branch office could be operating independently of the Saudi central headquarters. When asked in Arab news interviews whether *Al-Haramain* retains "tight control" over its affiliates, Al-'Aqeel responded:

> Yes, of course. **The offices' directors are employees who follow the directions of the main office with regards to hiring workers at the offices and making any decisions on cooperation with any party. In the main office, there are 19 auditors. Each of the foundation's specialized committees has an auditor. There are monthly, quarterly, and yearly reports on the foundation's revenue and expenditure.**[201]

Shaykh Al-'Aqeel has dismissed U.S. government action against *Al-Haramain*'s regional offices. **He insists, "we have a large number of offices all over the world. We still can do the work in Bosnia and Somalia even if our offices there were closed. We can run the work through preachers. They can close the offices but they cannot arrest all the preachers."**[202] According to Al-'Aqeel, ***Al-Haramain* has opened three more**

---

[195] Ain Al-Yaqeen, November 29, 2002, http://www.ain-al-yaqeen.com/issues/20021129/feat7en.htm.
[196] Ain Al-Yaqeen, November 29, 2002, http://www.ain-al-yaqeen.com/issues/20021129/feat7en.htm.
[197] Ain Al-Yaqeen, November 29, 2002, http://www.ain-al-yaqeen.com/issues/20021129/feat7en.htm.
[198] Executive Order 13224 Blocking Terrorist Property and a Summary of The Terrorism Sanctions Regulation, US Department of the Treasury Office of Foreign Assets Control.
[199] Agence France Presse, "Saudi Arabia's top Islamic charity denies any of its assets frozen," March 13, 2002.
[200] *Dani* (Sarajevo), "Blockading Young Muslims' Way—Misuse of Humanitarian Funds To Support Terrorism," November 22, 2002.
[201] *Al-Sharq al-Awsat*, "Interview with Aqil al-Aqil, general manager of the charitable Al-Haramayn Foundation," March 16, 2002.
[202] *Al-Sharq al-Awsat*, "Interview with Aqil al-Aqil, general manager of the charitable Al-Haramayn Foundation," March 16, 2002.

affiliate offices since 9/11 and has garnered greater government recognition; "Our (relief and fund-raising) activities have not been affected at all by the September 11 attacks…In fact, we have expanded our activities."[203] 'Al-Aqeel cites a 3 percent rise in revenues (about $1.9 million) since September 11;[204] he has said, **"We are like heroes in the Islamic world because America is against us."**[205]

The Saudi royal spokesman has routinely claimed there is no evidence linking *Al-Haramain* to Islamic radicalism and terrorism. In recent days, though, the Saudis have admitted that *Al-Haramain* was engaged in activities that were not in accordance with its stated mission. In a June 12 news conference, Adel Al-Jubair announced that *Al-Haramain* "would be shutting down all of its foreign offices"[206] after Saudi investigators "discovered that in many cases the financial controls were not up to par. The individuals working in those offices, the vast majority of them were non-Saudis, about whose background the head organization knew very little. And so we worked with the organization, and they came to the conclusion that the best thing they can do is shut down those offices."[207] Despite these assertions, **there is no available evidence indicating that the *Al-Haramain* Foundation has ceased its operations**.

World Assembly of Muslim Youth

The World Assembly of Muslim Youth (WAMY) is the world's largest Muslim youth organization. According to a letter signed by WAMY Assistant Secretary General Dr. Hameed al Shaygi, WAMY has offices in London, Washington DC, Kuala Lampur, Auckland, Dhaka, Nairobi, Dakar, Moscow, Cordoba (Argentina), and headquarters in Riyadh. WAMY's US website, www.wamyusa.org, says "WAMY has 66 regional, local offices and representatives in the five continents."[208] WAMY's US office was incorporated in Falls Church, Virginia in 1992 by Osama bin Laden's brother, Abdullah bin Laden.[209] Abdullah continued to be listed on WAMY's IRS forms 990 through at least 1998.[210] WAMY's goal, according to its pamphlet *Islam at a Glance* is to "arm the Muslim youth with full confidence in the supremacy of the Islamic system over other systems."

There is ample evidence that WAMY is primarily a Saudi organization, if funded by government officials, and is at least indirectly involved in terrorism.

---

[203] Arab News, "Saudi societies fight back America's uncharitable charges a year on," September 9, 2002.
[204] *Al-Sharq al-Awsat*, "Interview with Aqil al-Aqil, general manager of the charitable Al-Haramayn Foundation," March 16, 2002.
[205] Reuters, "Saudi Charity Denies U.S. Charges of Terror Links," July 1, 2003.
[206] News Conference with Adel Al-Jubeir, Adviser to the Saudi Crown Prince. http://www.saudiembassy.net/press_release/statements/03-ST-Adel-embassy-0612-transcript.htm. June 12, 2003.
[207] News Conference with Adel Al-Jubeir, Adviser to the Saudi Crown Prince. http://www.saudiembassy.net/press_release/statements/03-ST-Adel-embassy-0612-transcript.htm. June 12, 2003.
[208] http://www.wamyusa.org/about.about%20wamy.htm, as of December 11, 2002.
[209] WAMY IRS Form 1023 Application for Recognition of Exemption, filed November 9, 1992.
[210] IRS Form 990 filed by WAMY International, April 30, 1999.

In an interview with Middle East Newsfile, Dr Abdul Wahab Noorwali, Assistant Secretary General of WAMY, said, "**Saudi Arabia's support has been enormous since the establishment of WAMY in 1963**. The Kingdom provides us with a supportive environment that allows us to work openly within the society to collect funds and spread activities. **It also provides us with protection abroad through Saudi embassies and consulates, in addition to financial support.**"[211]

WAMY's leadership is also prominent in the Saudi Government establishment:

- At a November 2001 joint fundraiser for WAMY, the International Islamic Relief Organization (IIRO) and *Al-Haramain* Charitable Organization, "Riyadh governor Prince Salman contributed SR 1.5 million, while his deputy Prince Sattam donated SR1 million."[212]
    - Prince Salman also donated SR1.5 million to a 1999 fund-raiser conducted by the same three organizations.[213]
- WAMY is headed by Saudi minister of Islamic affairs Saleh al-Alshaikh.[214] "His Royal Highness" Prince Ghazi addressed the Eighth International Conference of the World Assembly of Muslim Youth in October 1998.[215] The following year, Crown Prince Abdallah bin Abd-al-Aziz, Deputy Premier and Commander of the National Guard, "received guests of the ninth international conference of the World Assembly of Muslim Youth and its officials who came to greet him on the occasion of the end of the conference, which was held here under the auspices of the crown prince."[216] The Prince told his visitors, "Not only Saudi Arabia, Iraq, the Sudan or any other country... But rather Islam is the target."[217]
- Maneh ibn Hammad Al-Johani was Secretary-General of WAMY when he died in August 2002. He was a **member of the Shura Council**, and an "**active member of the 120-member consultative body.**"[218] In an interview after al-Johani's death, WAMY's assistant Secretary-General Saleh Al-Wohaibi said he was "to **brief Prince Abdullah on the organization's activities**. He was going to update the regent on WAMY's upcoming ninth international..."[219]
- King Fahd bin Abdul Aziz is funding this year's WAMY Hajj drive.[220]
- Prince Abdul Majeed Bin Abdul Aziz, Governor of the Makkah Region of Saudi Arabia, "graced Monday evening the charity function held by the International Islamic Relief Organization (IIRO) in association with the World Assembly of

---

211 Middle East Newsfile, "WAMY Team in Afghanistan Risks Life to Deliver Aid," November 20, 2001.
212 MiddleEast Newsfile, "Fund Raising Event Generates SR6.5 million," November 29, 2001.
213 MiddleEast Newsfile, "Salman donates SR1.5m in a Major Fund-Raising Event," December 16, 2001.
214 http://www.saudiinstitute.org/hate.htm, accessed July 27, 2003.
215 Amman Jordan Times, "Jordan's Prince Ghazi Addresses Muslim Youth Conference," October 21, 1998.
216 BBS, "Saudi Crown Prince Receives Dignitaries, says Islam Targeted," November 2, 2002.
217 BBS, "Saudi Crown Prince Receives Dignitaries, says Islam Targeted," November 2, 2002.
218 ArabNews, "WAMY chief Johani dies in car crash," August 5, 2002.
219 ArabNews, "WAMY chief Johani dies in car crash," August 5, 2002.
220 http://www.saudinf.com/main/y5346.htm, accessed July 27, 2003.

Muslim Youth (WAMY) and the Haramain Charitable Organization (HCO) here."[221]

- According to the Saudi Arabian Information Resource web page, "Custodian of the Two Holy Mosques King Fahd bin Abdul Aziz has issued directives to provide some of the governmental authorities and Saudi embassies and a number of Islamic organizations inside and outside the Kingdom of Saudi Arabia with 1.6 million copies of the Holy Quran and its meanings in various languages, published by the Madinah-based Custodian of the Two Holy Mosques King Fahd Complex for Printing the Holy Quran." The article continues, "The Minister of Islamic Affairs, Endowments, Call and Guidance, Sheikh Salih Al-Al-Sheikh, announced this in a statement to SPA. He noted that in line with monarch's directives...the World Assembly for Muslim Youth...will be provided with copies of the Holy Quran and its translations."[222]

- "There is growing evidence of Wahhabi activities in Iraq. Last month's issue of The Future of Islam, **a monthly [WAMY publication]...carried a cover interview with Saudi cleric Ayed al-Qarni. Al-Qarni, an adviser to Prince Abdel-Aziz bin Fahd, youngest son of Saudi Arabia's King Fahd, stated that he prays for the destruction of America several times a day. He also urged Saudi subjects to go and fight in Iraq or contribute money.**"[223]

- The Wall Street Journal has simply referred to WAMY as "a Saudi government-backed group."[224]

- In November 1999, the Institute of Islamic and Arabic Sciences in America (IIASA) held a Symposium on "One Hundred Years of the Kingdom of Saudi Arabia."[225] In the invitation to that event, **Abdullah Naseef, Vice Chairman of the *Majlis as-Shura* of the Saudi Arabian Government, Vice Chairman of WAMY and former Secretary-General of the Muslim World League,** said "Praise is due to Allah SWT and then to the kings of of [sic] Saudi Arabia who supported this pioneering organization and other non-governmental bodies such as the Muslim World League in Makkah in 1962 and the World Assembly of Muslim Youth in Riyadh in 1973."[226]

The Saudi government also provides material support for WAMY. *Islamic Views* is an Arabic language book written by WAMY and printed by the **Saudi Government's *Armed Forces Printing Press*.** Under the heading "The Prophet asks for Jihad," Islamic Views says, "The Prophet Mohammad fought against the infidels and the Jews till he triumphed over them and conducted himself about twenty invasions and he sent tens of

---

[221] MiddleEast Newsfile, "Abdul Majeed launches IIRO charity drive; Emir donates SR300,000 to Three Organizations," November 20, 2002.
[222] http://www.saudinf.com/main/y2320.htm, accessed July 27, 2003.
[223] Scotsman Publication, "Terror Alliance Targets US Forces in Iraq," June 15, 2003.
[224] Wall Street Journal, "Reports Link Charity to an *Al-Qaeda* Front," September 20, 2003.
[225] http://www.iiasa.org/researchcenter/symposium.htm, accessed July 27, 2003.
[226] http://www.iiasa.org/researchcenter/symposium.htm, accessed July 27, 2003.

regiments led by his companions for *Jihad*...**Damn from Allah to the Jews** who made graves of their prophets as Masjid."[227]

Later, *Islamic Views* says **Islam "is a religion of *Jihad*"** and that *Jihad* "was an answer for the Jews, the liars."

> **[T]each our children to love taking revenge on the Jews and the oppressors**, and teach them that our youngsters will liberate Palestine and al-Quds when they go back to Islam and make *Jihad* for the sake of Allah.[228]

Islamic Views exhorts Muslims to wage "*Jihad* against the Satan,"[229] and that "You should not back the Jews and the Christians and the Communists against the Muslims; the Communists, the Infidels, the Jews, and the Christians, those who do not believe in Mohammed. You should say they are infidels."[230]

WAMY also directly supports terrorist attacks. WAMY invited Khaled Mishal, Political Head[231] of Hamas to their "Muslim Youth and Globalization" conference on October 29, 2002.[232] According to Agence France Presse, "[Mishal] was hugged and kissed by hundreds of participants."[233]

The Arab News of April 12, 2002 reported, "The World Assembly of Muslim Youth (WAMY) has decided to raise its monthly contribution to Palestinian Intifada from SR3 million [$800,000] to SR10 million [$2.7 million]..."[234] The increase in monthly aid to the Intifada was "in addition to the over $70 million they had collected from donations through WAMY offices abroad and on special occasions."[235]

WAMY has been particularly active in Pakistan, both in support of Afghan warlords and Kashmiri terrorists. According to a Pakistani Government website,[236] WAMY is located at PO Box 1055 in Peshawar.[237] The Office of Foreign Assets Control (OFAC) lists PO Box 1055, Peshawar, Pakistan as an address of the Specially Designated Global Terrorist Organization, Benevolence International Foundation (BIF).[238]

The Associated Press and CBS News report that WAMY's Peshawar office was raided in November 2001 in a joint FBI-Pakistani intelligence operation.[239] A **WAMY employee**

---

[227] Islamic Views, Saudi Armed Forces Printing Press.
[228] Islamic Views, Saudi Armed Forces Printing Press.
[229] Islamic Views, Saudi Armed Forces Printing Press.
[230] Islamic Views, Saudi Armed Forces Printing Press.
[231] Christian Science Monitor, "King Charts New Mideast Course," September 24, 1999.
[232] Agence France Presse, "Muslim Youth Urged to Embrace 'Moderate Islam' at Riyadh Conference," October 29, 2002.
[233] Agence France Presse, "Muslim Youth Urged to Embrace 'Moderate Islam' at Riyadh Conference," October 29, 2002.
[234] Arab News, "WAMY to raise monthly contributions to Palestinian Intifada to SR10 million," April 12, 2002.
[235] Arab News, "WAMY to raise monthly contributions to Palestinian Intifada to SR10 million," April 12, 2002.
[236] www.epb.gov.pk/epb/jsp/ngo.jsp, as of December 12, 2002
[237] www.epb.gov.pk/epb/jsp/ngo.jsp, as of December 12, 2002.
[238] http://www.treas.gov/offices/enforcement/ofac/sanctions/terrorism.html, as of December 12, 2002.
[239] AP, "Pakistan Questions Sudan Man About Tape," December 9, 2002.

was subsequently questioned for hand delivering a recorded message from Osama bin Laden to local media.[240] In that tape, bin Laden praised various terrorist attacks, including the Bali nightclub bombing that killed over 200 people, and the Chechen takeover of a theatre in Moscow that led to over 150 deaths.[241]

Nazir Qureshi is assistant Secretary-General of WAMY. He has been accused by the Indian government of supplying money to Kashmiri terrorist groups headed by Syed Ali Shah Geelani.[242] The Pakistani paper The News reported on March 25, 2001 that the Pakistani youth organization *Jamiat Taleba Arabia* is the only Pakistan-based member organization of WAMY. The article continued, "**WAMY is also involved in religious and *Jehadi* training** for its member organizations."[243] According to The News, *Jamiat Taleba Arabia*, the WAMY member-organization, was:

> involved in Afghanistan from the very beginning. It joined the *Jehad* in Kashmir as soon as the Kashmiris started their armed struggle in 1990 and was fully involved by 1993. The members of the *Jamiat Taleba Arabia* fought under the umbrella of Gulbadin Hakmatyar's *Hizbe Islami* in Afghanistan and, in Occupied Kashmir, under the discipline of the *hizbul Mujahideen*[244]...Jehad has become the focus of the *Jamiat's* activities in the last two decades.[245]

According to the Indian magazine *Frontline*, Mohammed Ayyub Thukar, President of the World Kashmir Freedom Movement,[246] was a financier of *Hizbul Mujahideen*, a Kashmiri terror organization.[247] During his exile in Saudi Arabia, Thukar was affiliated with MWL, WAMY, and the Muslim Brotherhood.[248]

Sardar Ija Afzal Khan, Amir of *Jamaat-e-Islami* since early June, 2002,[249] "highlighted [the] freedom struggle of the Kashmiris at the forums of World Assembly of Muslim Youth..."[250]

The Indian government contends that "90 percent of the funding [for Kashmir militants] is from other countries and Islamic organizations like the World Association of Muslim Youth..."[251]

Beyond the Middle East and India, WAMY works to immerse its students in its hateful ideology. For example, Philippine resident Zam Amputan told the Christian Science

---

[240] AP, "Pakistan Questions Sudan Man About Tape," December 9, 2002.
[241] AP, "Pakistan Questions Sudan Man About Tape," December 9, 2002.
[242] The Press Trust of India, "Two Detained for Passing on Fund to Geelani," June 12, 2002.
[243] The News, "By the Book, for the Book," March 25, 2001.
[244] The News, "By the Book, for the Book," March 25, 2001.
[245] The News, "By the Book, for the Book," March 25, 2001.
[246] http://www.flonnet.com/fl1913/19131120.htm, as of December 11, 2002.
[247] http://www.flonnet.com/fl1913/19131120.htm, as of December 11, 2002.
[248] Ethnic Newswatch, "India Zooms in on Kashmir Militancy's Chief Financier," July 5, 2002.
[249] Pakistan Newswire, "Sardar Ijaz Afzar elected as Amir JI, AJK," June 6, 2002.
[250] Pakistan Newswire, "Sardar Ijaz Afzar elected as Amir JI, AJK," June 6, 2002.
[251] http://www.hvk.org/articles/0402/133.html, as of December 11, 2002.

Monitor that WAMY paid for him to attend a *madrassah* in Peshawar in 1987. According to the Monitor, "There he was exposed to the Wahhabi ideology." Amputan told the Monitor he returned to the Philippines "**thinking of ways to create a separate Islamic state in the Southern Philippines.**"[252] The Washington Quarterly reports that "**IIRO is not the only charitable organization in the Philippines suspected of financing terrorism. Manila is investigating five other Muslim charities active in the Philippines...[including] the World Alliance of Muslim Youth...**"[253]

Similarly, according to Professor S.V. Seshagiri Rao, the organization *Deendar Anjuman* "was involved in militant activity in Bosnia, Kosovo and Chechnya through the **World Association of Muslim Youth (WAMY), a Saudi Arabia based fundamentalist outfit.**"[254] *Deendar Anjuman* is banned by the Indian government.[255]

WAMY may also be tied to the 1993 World Trade Center bombing. When Ahmed Ajaj was arrested in 1992[256] investigators confiscated his belongings. Among them was an official WAMY envelope printed with the organization's return address in Saudi Arabia.[257] After serving a six-month prison term for attempting to enter the U.S. with a false passport, Ajaj was released.[258] Ajaj was rearrested and convicted in connection to the 1993 World Trade Center bombing on March 4, 1994. He was sentenced to 240 years in prison on May 24, 1994.[259]

The envelope marked "WAMY" contained a manual titled "Military Lessons in the *Jihad* Against the Tyrants that detailed how to establish and maintain clandestine cells."[260] The same manual, with several added sections, was found in the London apartment of African Embassy bomber Khalid al-Fawwaz in 1998.[261] Fawwaz has since been indicted, and the United States is seeking his extradition from England.[262]

The Ajaj manual refers repeatedly to the role and importance of the "youth" in carrying out *Jihad* and re-establishing Muslim rule.[263] The manual's "dedication" says, "what [the apostate regimes] know is the dialogue of bullets, the ideals of assassination, explosion and destruction, and the politics of the machine gun."[264] It continues:

> An Islamic state has not and will not be formed through peaceful solutions or through the Assemblies of Polytheism. It will be

---

[252] Christian Science Monitor, "The Tenets of Terror," October 18, 2001.
[253] Washington Quarterly, "Forging an Indirect Strategy in Southeast Asia," Spring 2002.
[254] http://groups.google.com/groups?q=wamy+bosnia&hl=en&lr=&ie=UTF-8&oe=UTF-8&selm=8le2ql%24cei%241%40nnrp1.deja.com&rnum=7.
[255] Times of India, "2 Deendar Activists held," May 11, 2002. See also: http://www.hinduonnet.com/thehindu/2001/05/04/stories/01040007.htm.
[256] Newsday, "New Suspect Charged in WTC Blast," May 7, 1993.
[257] United States of America v. Usama Bin Laden, el al, S5 93 CR 180, Government Exhibit 2800-A.
[258] Washington Post, 'Retracing the Steps of a Terror Suspect; Accused Bomb Builder Tied to Many Plots," June 5, 1995.
[259] Chicago Sun-Times, "Trade Center Bombers Sentenced to 240 yrs," May 24, 1994.
[260] New York Times, "A Sixth Suspect Charged in Blast," May 7, 1993.
[261] Guardian Unlimited, "Crackdown on British Cell," September 23, 2001 AND United States of America v. Usama Bin Laden, el al, S5 93 CR 180, Government Exhibit 2800-A.
[262] Sunday Telegraph, "We Have Made a Paradise for Terrorists in Our Own Backyard," May 4, 2003.
[263] United States of America v. Usama Bin Laden, el al, S5 93 CR 180, Government Exhibit 2800-A.
[264] United States of America v. Usama Bin Laden, el al, S5 93 CR 180, Government Exhibit 2800-A.

> formed as it did through the written words and the gun, through the word and the bullet.

The manual instructs that "the principal mission for the military organization is to overthrow the atheist regimes and replace them with Islamic ones," and lists strategies such as kidnapping enemy soldiers, assassinating personnel and foreign tourists, spreading rumors, and blowing up, destroying, and sabotaging places of entertainment as secondary duties of the military organization. The ultimate goal, repeated over and over, is "get[ting] rid of people who stand in the way of the Islamic Call," and "establishing an Islamic State."[265]

The manual goes on to provide in-depth instructions for obtaining and storing false documents, finding housing, obtaining and storing weapons, conducting reconnaissance, planning attacks, carrying out attacks, avoiding detection, and using other tactics.[266]

When asked about accusations that WAMY is a funding front for terrorists, Secretary-General Dr. Saleh al-Wohaibi "blamed the Zionist-controlled media and anti-Islamic organizations in the US…"[267]

<u>WAMY in the United States</u>

WAMY has provided financial support to the US-based Council on American-Islamic Relations (CAIR), a civil rights organization which received some of its initial seed money from the Holy Land Foundation for Relief and Development (HLFRD). On December 4, 2001, the Treasury Department listed HLF as a Specially Designated Terrorist. According to Treasury Department, HLF "raises millions of dollars annually that is used by HAMAS."

CAIR's founders Nihad Awad and Omar Ahmed came from leadership positions of the Islamic Association for Palestine (IAP).

An August 2002 court decision against the Holy Land Foundation states "the Islamic Association for Palestine has acted in support of Hamas."[268]

According to Steven Pomerantz, a retired FBI Assistant Director who also served as Chief of the FBI Counterterrorism section in the mid to late 1980's:

> "…CAIR has defended individuals involved in terrorist violence, including Hamas leader Musa Abu Marzouk, and he has embraced people who have engaged in promoting violence or hateful and bigoted rhetoric. The modus operendi has been to falsely tar as 'anti-Muslim' the U.S. government, counter-terrorist officials, writers, journalists and others who have investigated or exposed the threat of Middle East based terrorism…"[269]

---

[265] <u>United States of America v. Usama Bin Laden, el al,</u> S5 93 CR 180, Government Exhibit 2800-A.
[266] <u>United States of America v. Usama Bin Laden, el al,</u> S5 93 CR 180, Government Exhibit 2800-A.
[267] <u>Arab News,</u> "WAMY Keen to Boost its Activities Despite Smear Campaign: Wohaibi," August 27, 2002.
[268] Holy Land Foundation for Relief and Development vs. John Ashcroft in his official capacity as Attorney General of the United States. Civil Action # 02-422 (GK)
[269] Spring 1998 *Journal of Counterterrorism & Security International.*

Despite CAIR's statement in November 2001 that they "...do not support directly or indirectly, or receive support from, any overseas group or government,"[270] it appears that the Saudi-based WAMY has funded CAIR both before and after this proclamation.

According to a December 23, 1999 *Arab News* article, Dr. Hamid Shaygi, assistantSecretary General of WAMY announced at a Riyadh press conference, with Nihad Awad in attendance, that WAMY "was extending both moral and financial support to CAIR in its effort to construct headquarters at a cost of $3.5 million in Washington, DC." The article continued saying WAMY would also "introduce CAIR to Saudi philanthropists and recommend their financial support for the headquarters project."[271]

In 1998, the *Saudi Gazette* reports that CAIR's Executive Director Nihad Awad addressed a press conference at the WAMY headquarters in Riyadh, Saudi Arabia. According to the report, "He [Awad] said CAIR needed funds to fight discrimination against Muslims, to promote the true image of Islam and to combat the anti-Islamic propaganda."[272]

In 2002, the *Muslim World* reported that WAMY was extending its support to CAIR for its media campaign in the US.[273]

CAIR has also received funds in part by the International Islamic Relief Organization (IIRO). The 1997 tax form 990 for the International Relief Organization (IRO) lists a grant to CAIR for $10,000. The 1995 tax form 990 for the IRO lists a grant to CAIR for $2,172.

QATAR CHARITABLE SOCIETY (QCS)

Another humanitarian organization actively financing *Al-Qaeda* and other designated international terror groups is the **Qatar Charitable Society (QCS)**, the oldest and largest such group in Qatar.[274] **QCS is a part of the Islamic Coordination Council (ICC)**, a coordinating body of Muslim charitable groups established in 1985 in Peshawar, Pakistan to maximize the financial assistance reaching Afghanistan.[275] **Shaykh Abdullah Azzam was a member of the ICC leadership prior to his assassination in Peshawar in 1989.[276] Other ICC members include the IIRO, the SRC, and WAMY.[277]**

Much like the various Saudi charities that have funded *Al-Qaeda* over the past decade, QCS draws much of its funding primarily from official sources, including the Qatari

---

[270] Press Release from CAIR National, *Islamaphobe Smear Campaign Goes Public,* November 8, 2001.
[271] "WAMY spends SR12m on new mosques," Arab News, December 23, 1999
[272] "Nike Violating agreement on Offensive Logo says CAIR, *Saudi Gazette*, July 3, 1998
[273] *The Muslim World*, page 1, "WAMY supports CAIR campaign against US anti-Islamic sentiment," November 29, 2002
[274] "Voluntary and Charitable Organizations." http://www.dohaislamicsummit.org/qatar/english/islamic-e.htm. March 1, 2003.
[275] http://www.yellowpages.liwal.net/asistance/icc.htm. March 1, 2003.
[276] Middle East Policy, "The new global threat: transnational Salafis and Jihad," December 1, 2001.
[277] http://www.yellowpages.liwal.net/asistance/icc.htm. March 1, 2003.

government itself. In October 2002, the Emir of Qatar, Shaykh Hamad bin Khalifa Al Thani, and the Qatari Foreign Minister, Shaykh Hamad bin Jassem bin Jabr Al Thani, invited the President of QCS, Shaykh Abdul Aziz bin Abdulrahman Al Thani, to join them in high-level meetings with the visiting United Nations High Commissioner for Relief, Ruud Lubbers.[278] An advertisement for QCS relief activities in Kosovo refers to a collaborative partnership with the state-supported Qatar Red Crescent Society.[279] Moreover, until recently, a WHOIS[280] lookup of the Qatar Charitable Society's website (www.qsociety.org) listed Hashem Hussein as both the Administrative and Billing Contact for the site. His corresponding e-mail address, "hashim@MMAA.GOV.QA," indicates that Mr. Hussein was an employee of the Qatari Ministry of Municipal Affairs and Agriculture.

More recently, a VIP social event was organized by QCS in Bosnia to inaugurate a new relief project ordered by a "Decree of His Excellency the Emir [of Qatar]." The party was attended by, among others, Ambassadors from Egypt, Saudi Arabia, Libya, and Iran.[281]

According to its website, the Qatar Charity Society "aims to offer relief and help to orphans, victims of war and disasters by supporting them financially, socially and culturally up to the age of eighteen. QCS aids widows to meet living expenses, particularly those who lost all relatives and friends."[282] By 1995, QCS claimed to have initiated over 250 projects worldwide in thirty-five countries including India, Pakistan, Bangladesh, Afghanistan, Somalia, Sudan, Bosnia, Palestine, Yemen, and the Philippines.[283] In **one fiscal quarter of 1997 alone, QCS was reportedly engaged in worldwide projects estimated at a total value of over 3 million Qatari Riyals.**[284] QCS advertised twenty numbered bank accounts in the Qatar Islamic Bank and the Qatar International Islamic Bank ready to receive wired donations from at home and abroad.[285]

QCS' charitable mission acted as a cover for its material support to terrorists. In trial proceedings surrounding the prosecution of individuals associated with the African Embassy bombings, **QCS was named as a major financial conduit for *Al-Qaeda*.** Former *Al-Qaeda* member and star government witness **Jamal Al-Fadl testified how he had worked closely with QCS in 1993.**[286] Al-Fadl was asked to discuss **Dr. Abdullah Mohamed Yousef, a fundamentalist veterinarian and director of QCS.** He explained:

> The guy [Yousef], he runs a group, **he is one of our membership, one of the *Al-Qaeda* group membership, and also he is [Sudanese] Islamic National Front membership,**

---

[278] "UNHCR briefing notes: Liberia, Côte d'Ivoire, Rwanda." http://www.reliefweb.int. Dated October 12, 2002.
[279] "Urgent Relief for the Muslems of Kosovo." http://www.qcharity.org/qenglish/images/kosovo/new_page_2.htm. March 1, 2003.
[280] www.register.com.
[281] "Qatar Relief Organization Builds 112 Houses for the Bosnian Returnees." *Al-Rayah*. August 31, 2002.
[282] http://www.qcharity.org/qenglish/index.html. March 1, 2003.
[283] Riyadh Daily, "Qatar organization carry out welfare projects," January 13, 1995.
[284] Middle East News Items, "Projects carried out by Qatar Charitable Society," September 8, 1997.
[285] http://www.qcharity.org/qenglish/banks.htm. March 1, 2003.
[286] United States of America v. Usama Bin Laden, el al. February 6, 2001. Testimony Transcript; Page 329.

> **and he was in Afghanistan.** So he helped our people for the travel, documents, and also if some money come from the Gulf area to the organization, he gives the group some money from that money.[287]

In the Sudan, QCS actively aided radical quasi-official militias associated with the National Islamic Front (NIF) in fighting the Christian and animist groups of the South. In a fundraising brochure for the Sudan distributed by QCS in Qatar, **the Society appealed to its donors to help protect "our brotherly Sudan" from "wild savage invaders,"** who were accused of "destroying the Sudanese territorial integrity, security, stability, and unity." The brochure further noted, "Every tiny support is great and important especially in this holy month, Ramadan. It is the month of Allah [sic] blessings…and the month of 'Jihad' in one's person, one's wealth, and one's dwellings. Support for those brave heroes who are sacrificing their persons will be of great mercy, forgiveness and freeing from the Hell fire."[288] During one short period of 1999 alone, the chairman of the QCS reported the transfer of 1 million Qatari Riyals in the form of "emergency aid" to the Sudan.[289]

In 1995, **Osama bin Laden reportedly confirmed to Jamal Al-Fadl that $20,000 supplied by Dr. Abdullah Yousef through QCS was used by *Al-Qaeda* to bankroll the attempted assassination plot that year against Egyptian President Hosni Mubarak in Addis Ababa, Ethiopia.** At the time, **bin Laden sternly rebuked the financiers of the abortive terror plot for their carelessness in concealing the true source of the funds,** and expressed serious concerns that **"*Al-Qaeda*'s abilities to use charities to fund operations might be compromised as a result."**[290]

During the mid-1990s, Dr. Yousef used the Qatar Charitable Society's resources to serve the financial needs of the Eritrean Islamic Jihad Movement (EIJM).[291] At the time, **EIJM recruits, seeking to overthrow their own government and replace it with an Islamic regime, were receiving military training from senior *Al-Qaeda* lieutenants in the Sudan** after having been recruited to follow Osama bin Laden's international agenda. Several years later, the **Deputy Emir of EIJM, Abul Bara' Hassan Salman, confirmed in an interview, "As for the latest Christian onslaught which is being led by America…I say to the Muslim people everywhere: supporting Jihad and the *Mujahideen* is the way to remove the nightmare** of degradation and humiliation which has rested on the chests of our community in its various forms."[292]

---

287 United States of America v. Usama Bin Laden, el al. February 6, 2001. Testimony Transcript; Page 330.

288 http://www.qcharity.org/qenglish/helpsuda.htm. Dated December 27, 1997.

289 *Al-Rayah*. August 16, 1999.

290 "Government's Evidentiary Proffer Supporting the Admissibility of Co-Conspirator Statements." United States of America v. Enaam M. Arnaout. United States District Court Northern District of Illinois, Eastern Division. Case #: 02 CR 892. January 31, 2003. *Page 103*.

291 United States of America v. Usama Bin Laden, el al. February 6, 2001. Testimony Transcript; Page 330.

292 "'The Governing Regime is a Terrorist Regime Which Acts With Enmity Against the Eritrean People': An Interview with the Deputy Amir of the Eritrean Islamic Jihad Movement – Abul Bara' Hassan Salman." *Nida'ul Islam*. Issue 22; February-March 1998.

Outside of Africa, the Qatar Charitable Society was also extremely active in the Balkans and the turbulent Muslim republics of the Caucasus. In **November 1994, one Egyptian QCS "aid worker" was killed and another badly burned in a mysterious "gas explosion" in Sarajevo.**[293] QCS also helped distribute a collection of fundamentalist articles titled "Obstacles to the Islamic Resurgence" edited by former Bosnian President Alija Izetbegovic.[294] In the wake of September 11, Izetbegovic stepped down amid controversy that his administration had provided safe haven and travel documents to hundreds of Muslim militants loyal to *Al-Qaeda*.[295]

In October 2001, **the Azerbaijan Ministry of Justice forcibly closed down its own local QCS office for, "under the disguise of charity," conducting "damaging activities that violate our national interests, as well as [cooperating] with terrorist structures and [distributing] propaganda inciting radical sectarianism, religious hatred and fanaticism."**[296] In 1995, a QCS office founded in neighboring Daghestan (adjacent to Chechnya) dispensed 3 million Qatari Riyals in less than two years.[297] Russian intelligence became suspicious when they discovered that the QCS branch was being run by an Egyptian citizen named Yasir Ibrahim. **Daghestani state tax police initiated an inquiry into the organization, and uncovered forged documents and invoices detailing hundreds of thousands of dollars of illicit financial transactions. From the evidence they collected, investigators estimated that QCS had given perhaps as much as $1 million to unspecified "Chechen extremists."** The Russians found, **"most of the 'charitable contributions'...were not recorded anywhere. The same goes for how the money was distributed."**[298]

By liquidating charity bank accounts into untraceable cash withdrawals in war-torn states (often with no reliable banking systems), QCS was able to make this money simply disappear. Journalists confronted Qatari Foreign Minister Hamad Bin Jasim Bin Jabr Al-Thani with Russian allegations that QCS was openly and actively supporting "certain Arab individuals…fighting with the Chechen fighters." With little reflection, Al-Thani flatly admitted that, indeed, this might be the case:

> [W]e as a government cannot control the aid going abroad, some of which may go for humanitarian goals, and some may start as humanitarian but end up in another way. However, **there is no monitoring because people are sympathizing...We as a government may be able to control our sympathy, although in the end we are only human beings and**

---

[293] Agence France Presse, "Egyptian aid worker, injured in gas explosion, due for evacuation," November 26, 1994.
[294] http://www.qcharity.org/qenglish/book_1.jpg. March 1, 2003.
[295] http://www.aimpress.org/dyn/trae/archive/data/200110/11030-002-trae-sar.htm, accessed July 30, 2003. See also: SRNA News Agency, "Muslim leader denies there are Bin-Ladin's supporters in Bosnia," Broadcast in Serbo-Croat language in Bijeljina, October 9, 2001.
[296] Interfax News Agency, "Azerbaijan closes offices of Arab relief organizations due to illegal activity," April 10, 2002. See also: Turan News Agency (Baku), "Azerbaijan shuts down Kuwaiti, Qatar charity organizations," Broadcast in Russian language, April 9, 2002.
[297] *Al-Rayah*, "Charity denies Russian charges of assisting Dagestan rebels," September 20, 1999.
[298] *Segodnya* (Moscow). November 16, 1999.

> **Muslims**...[t]herefore we cannot restrain the people's feelings in this regard.[299]

Even after the September 11 suicide hijackings, the Qatari regime has resisted to US efforts to curtail *Al-Qaeda* fundraising through religious charities, including the Qatar Charitable Society.[300] **In September 2001 QCS' official newsletter carried an article titled "Jihad is the Solution!"** The author urged faithful Muslims:

> The **only way to liberate Palestine is the holy Jihad** which mobilizes all potentialities in the Arab and Islamic countries, and in which all Muslims stand as one behind the *Mujahideen* and support them in their Jihad...**The time has come for Muslims to follow in the footsteps of Salahudeen and to restore Jerusalem and Palestine to the Arabs and the Muslims**. For Jerusalem is in your hands, Oh, Muslims. There is no solution to the matter save Jihad. 'You shall readily mobilize, light or heavy, and strive with your money and your lives in the cause of GOD. This is better for you, if you only knew.' (Quran 9:41)[301]

Conclusion

Due to the release of the Joint Inquiry Report, the Saudi government's role in funding and supporting terrorism has taken center stage in the U.S. war on terror. Notwithstanding the decision to redact an embarrassing 28 pages from the report, the Saudis remain firmly under the microscope as prime engineers of Islamic radicalism throughout the globe. Since the 9/11 attacks, the U.S. has enjoyed some success in shutting down Saudi charities, such as the Benevolence International Foundation, that raised money for the violent terrorist group Hamas and Al-Qaeda, among others.

Yet there needs to be a more comprehensive government investigation into Saudi conduits for terrorism and Islamic extremism, as evidenced by the evidence showing ties between WAMY, the Saudi Red Crescent, the *Al-Haramain* Foundation and a host of other Saudi-funded entities. Even greater scrutiny needs to be focused on these and all Saudi charities and organizations operating within the United States, regardless of their stated humanitarian goals.

The U.S. must demand the Saudis display the maximum amount of cooperation in rooting out and containing the terrorist threat. This means the immediate cessation of funding to any charitable group or organization that the U.S. deems a terrorist sponsor or front. The Saudis themselves must also do a much more efficient job of locating and apprehending *jihadists* within Saudi Arabia in order to prevent future attacks similar to 9/11.

---

[299] *Al-Jazeera* Television, Bin Qinnah, Khadijah. "Minister denies Russian report on funding for Chechen militants," Broadcast in Arabic language, November 22, 1999.
[300] Agence France Presse, "Noose tightens around Islamic charities in Gulf," October 3, 2001.
[301] Qatar Charitable Society Magazine, "Oh Muslims, Jerusalem is calling you! Jihad is the Solution!" September 2001.

If the United States is to prevent another 9/11 from happening again, our government must let evidence of Saudi fingerprints to terrorism be acted upon by law enforcement without any special treatment or exemptions from prosecution or investigations. If Saudi foundations or conduits are operating in the United States with evidence tying them to terrorist groups, then the principles of equal treatment under the law should apply. The Department of Justice, Treasury, and FBI ought to be fully empowered to investigate and prosecute suspected terrorist conduits and just as much as it prosecutes indigenous Americans who violate the law. Being outside the United States is no longer grounds for immunity from prosecution for terrorism; and being of foreign wealth should long ago have ended corrupt deals in which wealthy foreigners escape the reach of American justice.

The security of the American people should always come before any relationship governed by the accumulation of petrodollars. The anti-Western, anti-Semitic vitriol found in state-sponsored Saudi textbooks and preached by high-ranking Saudi clerics is an indicator of just how far apart U.S. and radical Saudi interests presently lie. In the end, the very integrity of the Saudi regime is at stake as was demonstrated by the recent series of suicide bombings in Riyadh.

If Saudi money has been funneled to Al Qaeda and Hamas, and continues to fund much of the worldwide terror network, this information should be made available for public consumption. A candid reassessment of the U.S. relationship with Saudi Arabia, sorely needed in light of the Joint Inquiry Report, is impossible unless the United States puts aside its old loyalties to protecting the Kingdom of Saudi Arabia and seriously confronts the nefarious influence posed by the flow of funds to terrorist conduits. Unless the terrorist connections are severed and unless Saudi institutions stop preaching and exporting the inflammatory Wahhabi Islamic doctrine, the war on terrorism will never be won; we will be permanently relegated to hopelessly trying to win a battle against smoke and mirrors where reality is inverted in a charade designed to protect special interests rather than unravel them. Two years after 9/11, the time has come to stop the charade.

In the name of God, the Compassionate, the Merciful

CAIR

Council on American-Islamic Relations

453 New Jersey Avenue, SE
Washington, DC 20003-2604
Tel: 202-488-8787
Fax: 202-488-0833

August 13, 2003

The Honorable Susan M. Collins
Senate Committee on Governmental Affairs
340 Dirksen Senate Office Building
United States Senate
Washington, DC 20510

Dear Chairwoman Collins:

On behalf of the American Muslim community, I ask you to please submit this statement for the record.

CAIR is North America's largest mainstream civil rights and advocacy group that serves the American Muslim community by protecting their rights to practice their faith, participate fully in our nation's civic life and live as contributing members of American society. We are a non-partisan, non-sectarian organization that does not promote anything other than mainstream and moderate Islamic beliefs and practices. We have consistently condemned terrorism in all its forms.

It is my unfortunate duty to express our deep concerns about an unbalanced panel, and particularly, the statement of Steven Emerson, who testified before the Senate Committee on Governmental Affairs on July 31, 2003. Mr. Emerson is a highly controversial figure, best known for his controversial 1994 PBS program "Jihad in America." Muslims say he has a long history of defamatory and inaccurate attacks on the Islamic community in this country. Mr. Emerson rashly claimed Muslims were behind the 1995 bombing in Oklahoma City, asserting the bombing showed a "Middle Eastern trait" because it "was done with the intent to inflict as many casualties as possible." Mr. Emerson wrongly attributed the 1996 downing of TWA Flight 800 to Muslims and once said Islam sanctions "genocide…as part of its religious doctrine." (CBS News, 4/19/95; Reuters, 7/31/96 and CNBC, *Rivera Live*, 8/23/96; *Jewish Monthly*, 3/95)

CAIR is an independent organization. We are not influenced by any foreign movement or government. We represent the interests of all Muslims in America, regardless of ethnicity or national origin. In light of this scrutiny on foreign Muslim organizations, it is important that CAIR, a domestic Muslim organization, be given the opportunity to represent itself and refute any false claims against it.

A large portion of Mr. Emerson's testimony deals with a possible connection between the World Assembly of Muslim Youth (WAMY) and terrorist groups. Mr. Emerson irresponsibly implies that CAIR has received financial support from WAMY to build our DC headquarters. This claim is unfounded. Notwithstanding our amicable relationship, CAIR did not receive financial support to build our DC headquarters from WAMY. In fact, it is well known that our DC headquarters were funded largely by a grant from the Islamic Development Bank (IDB), a multinational financial institution similar to the World Bank.

Mr. Emerson falsely claims that CAIR received some of its "initial seed money" from the Holy Land Foundation for Relief and Development (HLFRD). Our organization did not receive any seed money from HLFRD. CAIR raises its own funds and Mr. Emerson has not provided a shred of evidence to show otherwise.

We support all lawful and legitimate efforts to combat terrorism against our nation. CAIR has worked and continues to work with local and national law enforcement agencies on many security-related issues. Our cooperation with the FBI has included a joint news conference in Florida seeking the Muslim community's help in finding a terror suspect, as well as a number of workshops, town hall meetings and sensitivity training sessions across the country. In order to facilitate the needs of the Justice Department, CAIR has commissioned numerous publications including *A Correctional Institution's Guide to Islamic Religious Practices* and *Law Enforcement Official's Guide to the Muslim Community*.

CAIR is a widely-respected organization that seeks to ensure that Islam and the American Muslim community are portrayed accurately and objectively. We serve all Muslims regardless of affiliation or level of practice.

We applaud the timeliness of the committee hearing on terrorism financing, but we are very much concerned that a biased and unbalanced panel will not serve the best purpose of the hearing. Indeed, it is in the interest of all Americans, including Muslims, to disrupt funds that are dispersed to terrorist groups. We urge you to closely scrutinize the inflammatory and unsubstantiated statements made by Mr. Emerson, which mislead the committee. We urge you to completely disregard any such statements.

We humbly request a meeting with you to address these issues and are willing to provide answers to any concerns you may have.

Thank you for your prompt attention to this matter.

Sincerely,

Nihad Awad
Executive Director

From FAIR (Fairness and Accuracy In Reporting)
http://www.fair.org/extra/9901/emerson.html

As Emerson's fame mounted, so did criticism. Emerson's book, *The Fall of Pan Am 103*, was chastised by the **Columbia Journalism Review**, which noted in July 1990 that passages "bear a striking resemblance, in both substance and style" to reports in the **Post-Standard** of Syracuse, N.Y. Reporters from the Syracuse newspaper told this writer that they cornered Emerson at an Investigative Reporters and Editors conference and forced an apology.

A **New York Times** review (5/19/91) of his 1991 book *Terrorist* chided that it was "marred by factual errors…and by a pervasive anti-Arab and anti-Palestinian bias." His 1994 **PBS** video, *Jihad in America* (11/94), was faulted for bigotry and misrepresentations--veteran reporter Robert Friedman (**The Nation**, 5/15/95) accused Emerson of "creating mass hysteria against American Arabs."

Emerson was wrong when he initially pointed to Yugoslavians as suspects in the World Trade Center bombing (**CNN**, 3/2/93). He was wrong when he said on **CNBC** (8/23/96) that "it was a bomb that brought down TWA Flight 800."

Emerson's most notorious gaffe was his claim that the 1995 Oklahoma City bombing showed "a Middle Eastern trait" because it "was done with the intent to inflict as many casualties as possible." (**CBS News**, 4/19/95) Afterward, news organizations appeared less interested in Emerson's pronouncements. A **CBS** contract expired and wasn't renewed. Emerson had been a regular source and occasional writer for the **Washington Post**; his name doesn't turn up once in **Post** archives after Jan. 1, 1996. **USA Today** mentioned Emerson a dozen times before September 1996, none after.

"He's poison," says investigative author Seymour Hersh, when asked about how Emerson is perceived by fellow journalists.

Dubious document

Yet Emerson seems irrepressible. In 1997, for example, an **Associated Press** editor became convinced that Emerson was the "mother lode of terrorism information," according to a reporter who worked on a series that looked at American Muslim groups.

As a consultant on the series, Emerson presented **AP** reporters with what were "supposed to be FBI documents" describing mainstream American Muslim groups with alleged terrorist sympathies, according to the project's lead writer, Richard Cole. One of the reporters uncovered an earlier, almost identical document authored by Emerson. The purported FBI dossier "was really his," Cole says. "He had edited out all phrases, taken out anything that made it look like his."

Another **AP** reporter, Fred Bayles, recalls that Emerson "could never back up what he said. We couldn't believe that document was from the FBI files."

Emerson's contribution was largely stripped from the series, and he retaliated with a "multi-page rant," according to Cole. **AP** Executive Editor Bill Ahearn does not dispute that the incident happened, but refuses to comment or to release documents because the episode was deemed an "internal matter." A ranking **AP** editor in Washington says: "We would be very, very, very, very leery of using Steve Emerson."

Also during Emerson's lean years, he scored a November 1996 hit in the **Pittsburgh Tribune-Review** (11/3/96)--owned by right-wing Clinton-basher Richard Mellon Scaife, who also partially funded *Jihad in America*. Considering Scaife's patronage, it is not surprising that Emerson declared that Muslim terrorist sympathizers were hanging out at the White House. Emerson had a similar commentary piece printed three months earlier in the **Wall Street Journal** (8/5/96), one of the writer's few consistent major outlets.

Responses of John S. Pistole
Acting Assistant Director
Counterterrorism Division, Federal Bureau of Investigation
Based Upon July 31, 2003 Testimony
Before the Senate Committee on Governmental Affairs

<u>Question Posed by Senator Lautenberg</u>

1. Are the multilateral initiatives intended to curtail terrorist financing working? How successful are the anti-money laundering programs run by the UN Counter-Terrorism Committee, the International Monetary Fund, the World Bank, and the Financial Action Task Force? Is the G-7 a good forum for international counter-terrorism endeavors?

<u>Response</u>:

Multilateral initiatives intended to encourage governments to take action to curtail terrorist financing are definitely working. A principal international forum in which the United States participates is the Financial Action Task Force (FATF) of the Organization for Economic Cooperation and Development (OECD). The FATF is involved in various anti-money laundering initiatives. In particular, it has issued 40 recommendations to combat money laundering; it has developed a list of non-cooperating countries in money laundering; and, with respect to terrorist financing, FATF has made eight special recommendations. These recommendations are the international standards for effective and efficient anti-money laundering and anti-terrorist financing efforts. FATF encourages its member states and other countries to adopt its recommendations and implement them in domestic laws, and this has led to the adoption of anti-money laundering legislation in many countries. FATF has proven to be a highly effective forum for the development of anti-money laundering techniques and, since 9/11, has been particularly effective in addressing terrorist financing. The Departments of the Treasury and Justice, through the Asset Forfeiture and Money Laundering Section, regularly participate in negotiations and discussions at the FATF. Representatives of the FBI's Counterterrorism Division and the Criminal Division's Counterterrorism Section have made periodic presentations at the FATF.

The Department of Justice, with the indirect assistance of the FBI, has also actively supported the multi-lateral anti-money laundering and anti-terrorist financing efforts of the Organization of American States (OAS) through its anti-narcotics subcommittee (CICAD) and its anti-terrorism committee (CICTE).

In addition to the multilateral initiatives at the FATF and the OAS, the FBI's Terrorist Financing Operations Section (TFOS) and Training Division have participated with the Department of Justice, the IRS, and the State Department in raising an awareness of terrorist financing issues in target countries. These bilateral and multilateral training initiatives, which address both money laundering and the use of powerful asset forfeiture statutes to disrupt and dismantle criminal and terrorist organizations, have enhanced interagency awareness and promoted greater cooperation with foreign counterparts in the criminal, intelligence and financial sectors. This training is scheduled to expand in 2004.

The role of the G-7 and G-8 (G-7 plus Russia) to encourage governments to adopt laws curtailing money laundering cannot be overemphasized. The international monetary flow includes the proceeds of transnational crime and provides a conduit for the financing of terror. The G-7/G-8, with its working group on terrorist financing, can exercise substantial influence in shaping monetary policy and encouraging other countries to enact anti-money laundering laws. It is important that the G-7/G-8 approach the problem with a unified strategy and, like FATF, set standards which other countries can use as a model to develop and measure effective anti-money laundering laws.

Questions Posed by Senator Akaka

1. You responded in the affirmative to my question as to whether there was adequate funding for personnel and training. Given that most federal agencies are expecting a huge wave of retirements within the next few years, what is the FBI's Counterterrorism Division doing to fill this expected void in an area as critical to our nation's security?

Response:

The following reflects the number of separations within the FBI over the past three years and for FY 2003, effective through 8/31/03, broken down by Special Agent (SA) and support. The total number of separations includes individuals leaving due to mandatory, disability, and voluntary retirement.

FBI Separations						
FY	Total SAs in FBI at end of each FY	Total SA Separations (including resignations, removals, deaths)	Percentage of the SA Population	Total Support in FBI at end of each FY	Total Support Separations (including resignations, removals, deaths)	Percentage of the Support Population
2000	11,399	575	5.0%	16,218	744	4.5%
2001	11,122	530	4.8%	15,715	642	4.0%
2002	11,507	570	4.9%	15,612	708	4.5%
2003	11,723	486	4.1%	15,991	616	3.8%

The following reflects the number of SAs who will become eligible for retirement in FYs 2004 and 2005. This does not include the 1,227 SAs who are currently eligible for retirement but choose to remain on the rolls. Based on the trend for the past three to four FYs, it is anticipated that between 400 - 500 SAs may retire during each of the next two FYs.

- FY 2004: 434 (eligible)
- FY 2004: 135 (mandatory)

- FY 2005: 342 (eligible)
- FY 2005: 129 (mandatory)

The following reflects the number of support personnel who will become eligible for retirement in FYs 2004 and 2005. This does not include the 841 support employees who are currently eligible for retirement but choose to remain on the rolls. Based on the trend for the past three to four FYs, it is anticipated that between 300 - 400 support personnel may retire during each of the next two FYs.

- FY 2004: 379

- FY 2005: 385

The FBI's recruiting efforts have become increasingly aggressive over the past few years to enable us to fill newly budgeted vacancies and positions created through the FBI's reorganization to meet our expanding responsibilities. Future staffing goals will be established by factoring in newly authorized positions, current staffing levels, and anticipated short and medium term attrition. The FBI continues to streamline and enhance its application and hiring processes. Vacancies deemed critical to the top priorities of the FBI, including investigative analysts (such as Intelligence Research Specialists, Intelligence Operations Specialists, Investigative Analysts, and Financial Analysts) and Language Specialists, will receive priority processing. In addition, the FBI will continue to aggressively recruit highly qualified candidates to the Special Agent ranks. These efforts will assist the FBI in meeting its staffing goals and will help to minimize vacancies due to the separation of current employees.

2. The joint Congressional inquiry into the terrorist attacks of September 11, 2001 reported that "[t]he linguistic expertise needed to identify, analyze, and disseminate intelligence relating to the al-Qa'ida threat includes an understanding of colloquial expression in..."terrorist languages" and dialects... The majority of Intelligence Community language employees, however, do not have the skills necessary to understand terrorist communications." Do you agree with the joint inquiries, and what steps is the FBI taking to address any deficits in language skills?

Response:

The FBI disagrees with the statement that "[t]he majority of Intelligence Community language employees . . . do not have the skills necessary to understand terrorist communications" when that statement is applied to translators supporting the FBI's Foreign Language Program (FLP). More than 95% of all FBI translators are native speakers of the foreign language. Their native-level fluencies ensure not only a firm grasp of colloquial and idiomatic speech, but also of religious, cultural and historical references needed to effectively perform the wide array of services required of an FBI translator. Additionally, FBI translators typically work closely with agents and analysts involved in the cases they support, ensuring a coordinated exchange of information and ideas related to the case.

Prior to being hired or placed under contract by the FBI, all translators undergo a series of language examinations in order to ensure the required level of proficiency in the foreign language and English. Once on board, a translator's work assignments are routinely subject to review by a senior translator in accordance with the FBI's quality control program.

3. The written testimony of Steve Emerson, who testified on the second panel, concluded "...there needs to be a more comprehensive government investigation into Saudi conduits for terrorism and Islamic extremism." Do you agree with his assertion?

Response:

The FBI is investigating terrorists and terrorism plots and activities regardless of location. While the status and results of those investigations are classified, the FBI has increased resources to fight the global war on terrorism and has seen precedent-setting cooperation from the Saudis. Some of the FBI's new resources are:

The Terrorist Financing Operations Section

Prior to the events of September 11, 2001, the FBI had no dedicated mechanism to provide a centralized approach to terrorist financial matters. The Terrorist Financing Operations Section (initially called the Terrorism Financial Review Group) was created immediately following the events of September 2001 to examine the financial dealings of terrorists and terrorist organizations. The broad mission of the Terrorist Financing Operations Section (TFOS) is to investigate, prosecute, disrupt, and dismantle terrorist-related financial and fund-raising activities. "Following the money" plays a critical role in identifying those involved in criminal terrorist activity, establishing links among them, and developing evidence of their complicity. Financial trails can be exploited to identify previously unknown terrorist cells, uncover potential terrorist activity/planning, and prevent potential terrorist acts. In forming TFOS, the FBI built upon its traditional expertise in conducting criminal financial investigations and its long-established relationships with domestic and international financial services communities.

TFOS has engaged in extensive coordination with foreign governments, leading to joint terrorist financing investigative efforts throughout the world. These joint investigations have successfully targeted the financing of several overseas al-Qa'ida cells. The newest such venture, the Joint Saudi Financial Investigative Unit, has combined the investigative powers of the Mabahith, the FBI, and the Treasury Department. Furthermore, with the assistance of relationships established with the central banks of several strategic countries, successful disruptions of al-Qa'ida financing operations have been accomplished in several counties.

Creation of the Arabian Peninsula Unit

In late 2002, the FBI established a task force dedicated to the issue of Saudi Arabia. The task force was originally comprised of members representing the Counterintelligence Division (CD), the Counterterrorism Division (CTD), the Criminal Investigative Division (CID), and the Terrorist Financing Operations Section (TFOS), but has since been formalized into the Arabian Peninsula Unit, International Terrorism Operations Section, CTD. This Unit will seek information concerning threats to U.S. security originating in this region and define strategies to address this threat, recognizing that training, finances, recruiting, logistical support, pre-attack planning, and preparation are all required components of terrorist operations.

Post-Hearing Questions for the Record
Submitted to Richard Newcomb
From Senator Frank Lautenberg

"Terrorism Financing: Origination, Organization, and Prevention"

July 31, 2003

1. **Could you please describe to us the Administration's efforts since 9/11 to block the flow of funds through the underground hawala system from reaching al-Qaeda and other terrorist groups of global reach? I am particularly interested in your assessment of what efforts have worked, and which have been less successful. Can the hawala system be successfully integrated into international banking and financial systems?**

Informal value transfer systems exist in many cultures, of which the hawala system is but one type. Informal value transfer systems have a few salient features, a key point of which is their informality. In other words, informal value transfer systems depend at least as much on the relationship of trust amongst the operators of a particular system as they do on any formal contractual agreements. In many cases, these bonds of trust are based on kinship affiliations or similar strong familial relationships. Informal value transfer systems are but one type of a broader class of entities that are often collectively referred to as money transmitters, and the class as a whole includes, for example, businesses that provide electronic wire transfer services.

Informal value transfer systems are less likely to be dependent on more formal financial systems, which are markedly more dependent on formal agreements among all parties. However, money transmitters can be and are partners with members of the international banking and financial systems. The center of these systems, with respect to funds transfers, is the payment system, which contains depository institutions as its key members. Money transmitters may utilize this payment system, as customers of banks, in order to settle their transactions.

In addition, the United States, as well as other countries, has in effect strong regulatory controls to guard against money laundering and terrorist financing in all types of money transmitters, including informal value transfer systems. In respect to controls against money laundering and terrorist financing, informal value transfer systems, like all money transmitters, have in the United States been integrated or combined within a common set of financial services providers subject to such controls.

Of course, regulations are but one part of this effort, and challenges remain. Enforcement action against entities operating outside the law is vital. On November 7, 2001 the U.S. designated the al Taqwa and al Barakaat networks which included a total of sixty-two (62) individuals and entities being designated pursuant to E.O. 13224. As reported in the Department of the Treasury's press release, dated November 7, 2001, the al Barakaat network moved money and which at its core was a hawala conglomerate operating in 40 countries around the world. The international community joined the U.S. in freezing al Barakaat's assets and isolating its access to the world financial system.

2. Are you concerned that al-Qaeda has been financed in the past and continues to be financed by traditional, time-honored methods of rogue groups world-wide, such as bulk cash smuggling, diamond dealing, and global trade in gold and other commodities that are easily moveable and stored?

Terrorists and terrorist support networks use individuals, charities, businesses, banks, informal transfer systems – including trade in commodities – and human couriers to raise and move money throughout the world. Which system will be employed depends upon convenience and potential scrutiny faced by the transactor(s). If a method for raising funds or a conduit for moving money is foreclosed to a terrorist support network, the terrorist support network will shift to a more convenient method for raising money – licitly and illicitly – and seek new or additional conduits for moving money – both by the international banking system and through informal transfer systems.

Appendix D of the recently-issued *2003 National Money Laundering Strategy* provides a detailed discussion of commodities-based money laundering, as well as terrorist financing. A copy of the *2003 Strategy* is attached to these responses for your information.

3. Are the multilateral initiatives intended to curtail terrorist financing working? How successful are the anti-money laundering programs run by the UN Counter-Terrorism Committee, the International Monetary Fund, the World Bank, and the Financial Action Task Force? Is the G-7 a good forum for international counter-terrorism endeavors?

International cooperation is critical to addressing the threats of terrorist financing and anti-money laundering. To this end, we have a broad multilateral effort underway, as detailed in the *2003 Nation Money Laundering Strategy*, Goal 1. (As noted above, a full copy of the *Strategy* is being provided with these responses.) Our objectives are to deny terrorists access to the international financial system by blocking terrorist and illicit assets, establishing and promoting international anti-money laundering and terrorist financing standards, ensuring that countries implement these international standards, and focusing efforts on financing mechanisms suspected of being of particular use by terrorists. Internationally, we have implemented this comprehensive strategy on anti-money laundering and the combating of financing of terrorism (AML/CFT) in a number of international fora, with significant positive results.

Since September 11, 2001, both the G-7 and G-20 have been at the point of the international efforts to combat and stop the means and mechanisms of terrorism financing. At US urging, both bodies issued 'action plans' for countries to adopt appropriate measures both domestic and international necessary to curb terrorism at home and abroad. These efforts have been far-reaching, and have focused world attention on shortcomings and successes in the fight against terrorism financing. This work continues unabated, and the fight against terrorist financing and the alternative mechanisms of terrorist financing remains an important item on the G-7 and G20 agendas going forward.

We have found that the G-7 and G-20 frameworks have provided central points for discussion and review of policy, and it has allowed for quite rapid forging of consensus and then moving forward quickly. At Dubai in September 2003 at the time of the IMF/World Bank annual meeting, G-7 Ministers of Finance met with non-G7 countries to discuss cross-border flows of charitable funds and the flow of remittances through informal financial channels, with the ultimate goal to support the efforts of these non-G-7 countries to build financial systems that are transparent and accountable. A follow up technical meeting is scheduled for late February. These types of outreach meetings hold significant potential for positive developments in meeting the challenges ahead on a multilateral basis.

Working with the international financial institutions (IFIs), we have made major progress in institutionalizing the international framework for comprehensive, world-wide assessments of the international Financial Action Task Force (FATF) AML/CFT standard. These developments reflect the urging of the U.S. and the G-7. In the fall of 2001, the IMF and the World Bank recognized the FATF Recommendations as the appropriate standard for combating money laundering and terrorist financing, and that work should go forward to determine how the FATF 40 should be made operational to the IFIs' work. As of late 2003, a pilot program was concluded, with over 50 country/jurisdiction assessments conducted by the IFIs, the FATF and the FATF style regional bodies, all using a common AML/CFT methodology based on the FATF Recommendations (40 + 8). This work has progressed successfully. Our goal is that the IMF and World Bank make such AML/CFT assessments a permanent part of their surveillance and oversight of country financial sectors.

The FATF has taken numerous important steps in addition to collaborating with the IFIs. For example, the FATF has partnered with the G-8 Counter-Terrorism Action Group (CTAG) to identify the terrorist financing vulnerabilities in key jurisdictions so that technical assistance can be delivered. FATF has also developed Interpretive Notes and Best Practices for compliance with international terrorist financing standards, including those that cover the freezing and confiscating of assets, alternative remittance systems, wire transfers, and charities. These papers clarify the standards and offer guidance on implementation. FATF has also published guidance for financial institutions to aid them in detecting terrorist financing.

The work of the United Nations on combating the financing of terrorism, particularly by the UN Counter-Terrorism Committee (CTC) and 1267 Sanctions Committee (Al-Qaida/Taliban Committee) has been an important component of the international effort to stop terrorism. As with all our efforts, however, we always seek ways to strengthen and improve the efficiency of such undertakings. Looking at the UN effort broadly, the US has been by far the largest contributor of names to the list of terrorists and supporters maintained by UNSCR 1455, yet as a result of our international efforts, many others are taking their own actions, pursuant to their own investigations, to crack down on the individuals and entities that support those terrorist networks.

Additionally, the UN CTC is a vital link in the mechanism of international cooperation focused on stopping terrorist financing – joining the FATF, the IFIs and the G-8 CTAG as part of that process. This process fosters information sharing, enhances the coordination of existing or planned multilateral assessments of country performance, and avoids duplication and maximizes the use of resources and human capital. As part of the process for identifying and delivering priority technical assistance, the UN CTC and the CTAG will provide input on priority countries and associated criteria.

4. Do you think the Administration has made use of the powers given to the Secretary of the Treasury under the Patriot Act of 2001 to designate individual foreign jurisdictions or financial institutions as being of "primary money laundering" concern to the United States?

To date, Section 311 has been used sparingly, though with great effect. The Secretary of the Treasury has designated three jurisdictions as "primary money laundering concerns" under Section 311 – Ukraine, Nauru, and Burma. Each of these designations was in conjunction with global multilateral action taken by the Financial Action Task Force to protect the international financial system from jurisdictions that are non-cooperative in the international fight against money laundering. And each of these actions was highly effective, resulting in almost immediate action – including the enactment of significant legislation – by the targeted countries in efforts to have the designations lifted. Moreover, in numerous instances the mere threat of the imposition of a Section 311 designation was sufficient to secure remedial action by targeted countries.

In addition to jurisdictional designations, the Secretary has recently designated two Burmese banks – Myanmar Mayflower Bank and Asia Wealth Bank – as "primary money laundering concerns" due to their links with narcotics trafficking organizations. This represents the first time Treasury has used its authority under Section 311 to target foreign financial institutions. The results have already been encouraging, as Burma has announced publicly that it is launching investigations into the two institutions. Treasury will continue to monitor financial institutions throughout the world and take action judiciously and strategically under Section 311.

Post-Hearing Questions for the Record
Submitted to Richard Newcomb
From Senator Daniel Akaka

"Terrorism Financing: Origination, Organization, and Prevention"

July 31, 2003

1. **The written testimony of Steve Emerson, who testified on the second panel, concluded "...there needs to be a more comprehensive government investigation into Saudi conduits for terrorism and Islamic extremism." Do you agree with his assertion?**

The Department of the Treasury agrees that it is important to continue to target all conduits for terrorism and Islamic extremism, including Saudi conduits. The United States, often working with the Saudi government, has actively pursued Saudi-based sources of financing for terror, many of which have been designated in the UN. For example, in March 2002, following a trip by then Secretary O'Neill, the U.S. and Saudi Arabia jointly designated the Al-Haramain Islamic Foundation branch offices in Bosnia-Herzegovina and Somalia. Six months later in September 2002, the U.S. and Saudi Arabia jointly designated and submitted for inclusion on the UN 1267 list Wa'el Hamza Julaidan, a known al Qaida associate. Most recently, on December 22, 2003, the Saudi and U.S. governments joined again to designate the reformulated Al-Haramain branch in Bosnia, which was renamed and operating as Vazir. These public, joint actions are important steps that the Saudi and U.S. governments have taken to stem the flow of terrorist funding out of Saudi Arabia.

The U.S. is also working with the Saudi government to improve its investigative and enforcement capacity and to develop joint investigative strategies. Improving Saudi investigation and implementation in these areas and institutionalizing joint efforts with Saudi authorities should significantly improve our collective ability to trace financial flows from Saudi Arabia. The recent establishment of the joint U.S.-Saudi terrorist financing task force is an important step in further coordinating and targeting terrorist financing emanating from the Kingdom of Saudi Arabia.

Examples of ongoing joint Saudi-U.S. initiatives involving OFAC include plans to provide training to appropriate Saudi Arabian officials in sanctions implementation. Training would focus both on the analytic process of identifying targets for possible designation and the follow-up activities required to maintain the effectiveness of a sanctions program. For example, OFAC would assist Saudi Arabia with setting up a compliance program to supplement existing Saudi Arabian Monetary Authority procedures for publicly notifying designations and assisting entities and individuals in complying with sanctions which prohibit dealings with designees. Training would also emphasize the need for fostering international cooperation and coordination to maximize the effectiveness of sanctions. The goal of this plan is to assist the Saudi Arabian government with establishing the necessary administrative and regulatory regimes in order for it to meet its U.N. obligations, as well as have the ability to designate on a regional or bilateral basis and to share information with other governments to support sanctions enforcement in foreign jurisdictions.

Post-Hearing Questions and Responses for the Record
Submitted to Dore Gold
From Senator Frank Lautenberg

"Terrorism Financing: Origination, Organization, and Prevention"

July 31, 2003

Q. Do you believe that the new Palestinian finance minister, Salaam Fayyad, who has brought a degree of transparency and accountability to the Palestinian Authority, will allow continued Saudi financing for Hamas? Does his finance ministry have any control over the funds channeled to the Popular Committee for Assisting Palestinian Mujahideen and the support committee for the al-Quds Intifadah, and the al-Aqsa fund?

A. During August 2003, Saudi funding of Hamas continued, largely by direct aid from Saudi-base charities, like WAMY and IIRO, directly to Hamas front charities. Salaam Fayyad, the new Palestinian Finance Minister, cannot deal with the problem of Saudi funding of Hamas alone. He is already confronting many interest groups as he has sought to increase the transparency of the Palestinian Authority. Other Palestinian ministries are also involved in the use of Saudi-supplied aid to extremist groups (see paragraph 3) . Fayyad requires the backing of his most important political allies, Prime Minister Mahmoud Abbas and Muhammad Dahlan. In many respects, Fayyad's ability to confront this issue is dependent on the political status of both Abbas and Dahlan Still there have been some recent notible developments. On August 28, 2003, the Palestinian Authority froze the bank accounts of 12 Hamas front charities, many of which receive aid directly from Saudi Arabia. This was a move in the right direction, however it was not complete. The Palestinian Authority did not go after the personal accounts of the Hamas leadership nor did it actually close down these charity groups. Had the Palestinian Authority actually proposed alternative funding mechanisms for those who received Hamas aid in the past, then the initiative would have looked more permanent. At present, under pressure from the Palestinian street, the Palestinian Authority could un-freeze these bank accounts as easily as it froze them.

Funds from the al-Aqsa fund, intended for the families of suicide bombers and Palestinian prisoners continue to flow, in any case. This is handled by other ministries and not just the office of Sallam Fayyad. Yasser Arafat's office is involved, for moneys to these families can buy Arafat influence with Hamas and Islamic Jihad. There is also a social affairs ministry in the Palestinian Authority that can claim jurisdiction in this issue.

Q. How closely linked are the financiers of al-Qaeda with those of Hamas and other Palestinian rejectionist groups? Do you foresee, based on your vast political experience representing Israel, a convergence in the tactics and objectives of al-Qaeda and the Palestinian groups?

A. The overlapping conduits of funding for al-Qaeda and Hamas have been well documented over the last few years. There is the case of the Saudi businessman, Yassin al-Qadi, who is suspected of having funded both. Certain banking institutions have also been associated with terrorist funding for both Hamas and al-Qaeda: Bank al-Taqwa and institutions belonging to al-Rajhi Banking and Investment Corporation. Apparently, Benevolence International, which helped al-Qaeda, and the Holy Land Foundation, associated with Hamas, also had a relationship.

It is important to remember that al-Qaeda is a network of terrorist groups that have cooperated in the past. Thus al-Qaeda has drawn resources from the Groupe Islamique Arme of Algeria, Chechen and Kashmiri groups, and Jemmah Islamiyya in Southeast Asia. Hamas-al-Qaeda cooperation until now has been minimal. Hamas dispatched some of its terrorists for training in Afghanistan.

Still it is important to remember that Hamas is cut from the same ideological cloth as al-Qaeda; both emerged from the Muslim Brotherhood, although al-Qaeda was more reliant on the input of militant forms of Saudi Wahhabism, as well. Both groups rely on the same Saudi clerics to justify their killing of innocent civilians by suicide bombers. But each group has had a very different focus; while al-Qaeda has been concerned with the global jihad against the West, Hamas is focusing on its own jihad to destroy Israel. Lately, Hamas has been taking a more global view. It used Pakistani-British Muslims in a suicide attack on the Israeli night-club, "Mike's Place" in Tel Aviv.

At present. Hamas has not joined al-Qaeda's global jihad, but it would be a mistake to rule out such a development occurring in the future.

Response of Jonathan M. Winer August 18, 2003
To Hearing Questions for the Record
Submitted from Senator Frank Lautenberg July 31, 2003

Question: You have referred, both in your testimony and in the Council on Foreign Relations Report, to the importance of the Saudi government "going public" or taking public action against terror financing. What exactly does the Saudi government need to tell its people? Does it need to take responsibility for past financing? Do the Saudis need to publicly discredit al-Qaeda's mission, as we finally saw them do in May of this year, after the attacks on the western compound in Riyadh? Will publicly condemning those who finance terrorism affect the public opinion of the Saudi people?

Response: The Saudi government routinely makes public statements regarding its efforts to counter terrorism, naming alleged terrorist criminals in press releases. For example, on August 5, 2003, the Saudi Ministry of Interior issued a release listing the names of persons who had sheltered wanted terrorists, as well as the names of terrorists who had themselves been arrested. The statement declared that security personnel are continuing to follow up on wanted individuals and warned all those who harbor, shield, or sympathize with wanted terrorists that they too face punishment. Similarly, the Saudi embassy in Washington frequently issues public statements about its efforts against terrorism. These too identify particular terrorists who have been the subject of governmental action. For example, a mid-July press release states that due to Saudi government action, Yousif Salih Fahad Al-Ayeeri, a.k.a. Swift Sword, a major Al-Qaeda operational planner and fundraiser, was killed on May 31 while fleeing from a security patrol; that Ali Abdulrahman Said Alfagsi Al-Ghamdi a.k.a. Abu Bakr Al-Azdi, considered one of the top Al-Qaeda operatives in Saudi Arabia and suspected of being one of the masterminds of the May 12 bombings in Riyadh, had been arrested by Saudi authorities, and that Turki Nasser Mishaal Aldandany, another top Al-Qaeda operative and mastermind of the May 12 bombings, was killed along with three other suspects in a gun battle with security forces that had them surrounded.

While the audiences for such statements surely include public opinion in the US and the world, public opinion within the Kingdom is inevitably also affected by such statements. The process of naming alleged terrorists provides a warning to others that planning terrorist attacks is a risky business in which the planner risks both prison and execution.

Notably, the Saudi government has not chosen to undertake similarly public statements about terrorist financiers. (Swift Sword was an al Qaeda logistics manager, as well as a funds-mover, and hence is in a very different category from the wealthy Saudis whose resources were abused by Al Qaeda and then managed by persons such as Swift Sword.) The failure of the Saudi government to issue such statements raises the question of whether the Saudis actually are taking action against terrorist financiers, thus undermining whatever deterrent action that may arise as a result of the Saudi government's actions against terrorists themselves.

It does not currently appear that the Saudi government or senior government officials have intentionally funded al Qaeda terrorism of the kind that took place in the September 11 attacks, although Saudi support for Hamas may well have contributed to the facilitation of suicide bombings in Israel. Rather, a portion of the funds provided by wealthy Saudis, including some members of the royal family, to charities, appear to have been used to facilitate some terrorist recruitment and logistics. The Saudis need to acknowledge truth as sunlight is indeed the best disinfectant and to date, Saudi refusals to acknowledge such truths invite skepticism and suggest cover-up.

Accordingly, what the Saudi government needs to tell its people is the following:

1) We will not tolerate any financial support for terrorists, including any terrorists associated with Hamas, Hezbollah, Muslim Brotherhood, Islamic Jihad or any movement that seeks political change through attacks on civilians. (It is critical that Saudi statements specify such groups by name.)
2) We have identified several individuals in Saudi Arabia who have engaged in such actions in the past. These include (and here the Saudi government needs to identify individuals, such as Saudi businessman and U.S. designated terrorist financier Yasin Al-Qadi, who funded terrorist organizations).
3) We have seized accounts and properties from the following individuals, in the following amounts, including real property in the following locations. (To date, such announcements have been limited to aggregate reports.)
4) Anyone in Saudi Arabia who does business with these people or companies will themselves have their assets seized.
5) Terrorist finance violates Shari'a and will be punished under the laws of Shari'a. The following individuals will receive the following punishments as a result of their engaging in terrorist finance: (list individuals by name). The following charities will be closed as a result of their engaging in terrorist finance: (list charities by name). The following businesses will be seized by the government of Saudi Arabia as a result of their forfeiture to the government due to their owner having engaged in terrorist finance.
6) Terrorist financiers will be subject to the same punishments as terrorists, which under Shari'a as interpreted in Saudi Arabia may include public execution or amputation. We anticipate exacting such punishments against money launderers shortly.

Such public statements would underscore to the Saudi public that the Saudi government is serious in its efforts to combat terrorist finance, and is not merely engaging in blame shifting or cover-up. Such statements could also discourage wealthy Saudis from putting themselves and their assets at risk with charitable donations to charities in the absence of strict scrutiny of the activities of the recipients. Greater scrutiny of such recipients could over time have a profound impact in reducing the threat of terrorist abuses of the charities.

Finally, to win Saudi public opinion, the Saudis will need to take action to reduce the sense of grievance too many Saudis feel against the Saudi government, the Israelis, the United States, and others. Reducing grievances will require action by the Saudi government to strengthen domestic economic and political opportunity, participatory democracy, freedom of the press, and to combat corruption among Saudi's elites. Winning public opinion may also require greater Saudi economic support for social services in Gaza and the West Bank to displaced Palestinians through vehicles other than Hamas. Using Saudi money to visibly improve the lives of other Muslims through mechanisms that avoid militant and terrorist groups could constitute simultaneously both good public policy and good public relations for the Saudis.

Post-Hearing Question and Response for the Record
Submitted to Steve Emerson
From Senator Frank Lautenberg

"Terrorism Financing: Origination, Organization, and Prevention"

July 31, 2003

Q. You have written extensively about the socio-cultural values of Wahabiism and how they are affecting the youth of Saudi Arabia. Do you believe that since 9/11 - - with the heightened attention globally to what is going on inside the Kingdom - - the Saudis are beginning to recognize that they have to change some of their educational materials, such as curriculum and textbooks? Do you think that the Saudi government has recognized that it is crucial for its own sustainability to make changes to the way Saudi youth are taught about foreigners, westerners, and non-Muslims?

A. I believe that since 9/11, there have been some efforts to reign in the radical Islamic exhortations and incitement within Saudi Arabia. Unfortunately, the efforts have been episodic and sporadic at best—and they have usually been undermined or neutralized by other key decisions by Saudi officials to continue financing Islamic terrorist groups and the incendiary incitement promoted by Saudi clerics, Saudi broadcasts, and Saudi schools. The problem within Saudi Arabia is that no one speaks or acts in one voice: essentially the regime survives by allowing competing forces of power and finance to do their own thing. Therefore, those that are against incitement are only able to exercise influence to a point; that point is when they start to interfere with the agenda of other forces. In order to survive as an entity, Saudi Arabia has devolved into different centers of religious and political gravity. Each center of gravity is allowed to control things in its respective orbit as the price by which everyone shares in Saudi riches. So while there are some Saudi officials who truly recognize the dangers to their own existence by Islamic militant incitement, there are others who thrive on this incitement and are allowed to promote it without encountering any obstacles. Regarding changes in curricula and textbooks, there are Saudi text books published today that continue to promote hatred. Still, there are new textbooks promoted by more enlightened forces that promote tolerance and pluralism.

○